Spanish American Saints

and the
Rhetoric of Identity

Spanish American Saints

and the
Rhetoric of Identity
1600–1810

Ronald J. Morgan

THE UNIVERSITY OF ARIZONA PRESS
Tucson

The University of Arizona Press
© 2002 The Arizona Board of Regents
First printing
All rights reserved
∞ This book is printed on acid-free, archival-quality paper.
Manufactured in the United States of America
Jacket and text design by Chelsea Cloeter
07   06   05   04   03   02   6   5   4   3   2   1

Library of Congress Cataloging-in-Publication Data
Morgan, Ronald J. (Ronald Jay), 1958–
    Spanish American saints and the rhetoric of identity, 1600–1810 / Ronald J.
Morgan.
        p.   cm.
    ISBN 0-8165-2140-9 (alk. paper)
    1. Christian saints—South America—Biography.   I. Title.
BX4659.L3 M67 2002
282'.092'28—dc21
                                        2001005284

British Library Cataloguing-in-Publication Data
A catalogue record for this book is available from the British Library.

For
Janine, Daniela, and Lara

Contents

Figures

Acknowledgments

This book is the fruit of seven years of research, writing, and refinement. During those years, numerous mentors and colleagues have contributed academic feedback and personal encouragement essential to its completion. Those individuals, as well as the entities that provided financial support, deserve words of appreciation.

The Department of History at the University of California at Santa Barbara provided a very collegial environment in which to grow as a scholar and teacher. I wish to thank Professors Sarah L. Cline, Francis Dutra, and Jeffrey Burton Russell for reading and commenting on the earlier drafts of this manuscript, as well as for imparting their expertise around the seminar table. Other members of the UCSB history faculty who aided my intellectual development through formal or informal means included Randy Bergstrom, Sharon Farmer, Abraham Friesen, Carol Lansing, David Rock, and the late C. Warren Hollister. Fellow graduate students Robert Carpenter, Christie McCann, Monica Orozco, and Brian Wilson also provided valuable feedback at various stages of this project. At Biola University, where I have taught since 1998, Professor Dietrich Buss and Dean David Dunbar graciously reduced my teaching load in fall 2000 so that I might complete the manuscript. Since 1995, colleagues with scholarly expertise in colonial Spanish American religion and literature have read and critiqued my work, as well as directed me toward helpful resources. My special thanks go to Jodi Bilinkoff, Asuncion Lavrin, Kathleen Myers, Stafford Poole, Antonio Rubial García, and John F. Schwaller, who gave unselfishly of their time and knowledge to aid a fellow scholar.

Historical research can go only as far as one's access to historical sources. Thanks are in order to the research and inter-library loan staffs at the UCSB Davidson Library and the Biola University Library, as well as to the research staffs of the following special collections: Sutro Library (San Francisco State University), Nettie Lee Benson Latin American Collection (University of Texas at Austin), Bancroft Library (University of California at Berkeley), and John Hay Library (Brown University).

The University of California provided me with the Regents Special Fellowship through my first four years of graduate studies at UCSB. Thereafter, the Department of History awarded me with a Dissertation Fellowship and the Philip Wayne Powell Award for 1997. At Biola University, the Faculty Research Committee generously provided me with a Faculty Research Grant for 2001, thus enabling me to complete the final revisions.

Finally, I wish to thank my parents, Page and Joyce Morgan, for instilling in me a love for history and a spirit of self-discipline that has enabled me to remain focused during the course of these seven years. Most of all, I express my heartfelt love and admiration to Janine, Daniela, and Lara, the three angels in my life, who enrich my heart, soul, and mind each day through their gifts of love, faith, and laughter, as well as their appreciation of good literature.

Spanish American Saints

and the
Rhetoric of Identity

Introduction

For nearly two millennia, Christians have memorialized the lives of their spiritual heroes, the saints, in written form.[1] During the first Christian centuries, they produced pious literature, or hagiography,[2] that ranged in form from the funeral eulogy to the collection of hermit's sayings to the single entry in a Christian book of martyrs. By the thirteenth century, however, the predominant form was the saint's Life, a self-contained narrative of "hagiography proper" that recounted the saint's life, virtues, miracles, and exemplary death.[3] The saint's Life was not simply a religious text; it was for centuries a vehicle through which towns, religious communities, or ecclesiastical factions formulated community identities and articulated group interests. Religious communities, towns, lay confraternities, and individual spiritual directors often appropriated the spiritual prestige of the would-be saint in order to enhance their own spiritual status. In other words, the creation of a pious tradition, including the elaboration of the life of the saint through religious biography, was an exercise in the formulation of community identity.[4] Accordingly, one scholar has described the saint's Life as "the literary crystallization of the perceptions of a collective conscience."[5]

This book examines this collective function of the saint's Life in the New World Spanish colonies from the dawn of the seventeenth century until the end of the colonial era. My reading of the Spanish American Life privileges both its primary function—that of proving the protagonist's sanctity and moving the faithful to veneration and imitation—and its secondary role, namely the articulation and rein-forcement of group solidarity and pride. By highlighting the conver-gence of religious and sociopolitical discourse, I attempt to shed light on group identity formation in general, but especially on the broader historical process that historians of colonial Spanish America refer to as "criollo identity formation."[6] I am not suggesting that a direct link exists between colonial-era sacred biography and the Spanish American nationalism of a later period. I am arguing, however, that *criollos*—descendants of Spanish immigrants who considered the New World, not Spain, to be their home—used the saint's Life and related media, both consciously and unconsciously, to exalt criollo achievement, defend criollo character, and define criollo identities.

From the earliest stages of New World settlement to the nine-teenth-century wars for national independence and beyond, Spanish *conquistadores* and their criollo descendants produced a unique literary tradition—letters, chronicles, polemical treatises, verse—that celebrat-ed, among other things, their own sense of honor and merit. The saint's Life (Spanish, *vida de santo*) was an important element of this criollo literary tradition. For criollos, "the exaltation of autochthonous persons [as saints] became an exercise in self-affirmation." For one thing, the presence of saints in the criollos' New World homelands gave eloquent testimony to God's favor toward the *americano* church. Furthermore, American-born hagiographers in regions such as New Spain and Peru recognized that to memorialize a fellow criollo as a saint was to celebrate the virtues and achievements of the criollo com-munity in general. This writing became even more meaningful during the seventeenth and eighteenth centuries, a time of heightened rivalries between American-born and Iberian-born Spaniards. For increasingly self-conscious criollos, "the canonization of [their own] saints . . . proved their equality to the Europeans."[7]

The concept that religious symbols and discourse were central to americano self-awareness during the colonial period is not a new one. Almost thirty years ago, Jacques Lafaye, in *Quetzalcoatl and Guadalupe,* demonstrated the historical importance of Our Lady of Guadalupe as a cultural and political symbol in colonial New Spain (later Mexico); Stafford Poole's more recent contribution reflects the continuing importance of that theme in Mexican historiography.[8] On the other hand, scholarly research on New World saints and their cults has been comparatively slower to develop, especially when one considers the influence printed hagiographic texts had in their day, their abundance and accessibility for the modern scholar, and their value as historical sources. Indeed, it is surprising how little scholarly attention was given before the 1990s to hagiography as a window to corporate self-consciousness—regional, ethnic, or proto-national—in Spain's colonies. For decades, while Roman Catholic intellectuals and churchmen diligently prepared modern editions of the now-rare colonial texts and used them to write their respective national ecclesiastical histories, professional historians and literary scholars were content to ignore hagiography as tendentious history or inferior literature.[9]

Since about 1990, however, Latin American historians and literary scholars interested in questions of cultural and ethnic identity have begun dusting off the once-neglected hagiographies. They were encouraged in this direction by new trends in cultural history, which legitimated narrative as historical source and pointed to "the strength and meaning of ritual, symbol, and custom as ways of binding a community together."[10] An important milestone for the historiography of Latin America was the 1991 publication of D. A. Brading's *The First America,* a remarkable synthesis of the intellectual and ideological history of the Spanish American colonies and early republics. In that work Brading explained that because "the Catholic monarchy exercised a rigorous censorship and attracted a quasi-religious veneration, patriotic sentiment [in the colonies] could only find expression in historical or religious myths or symbols." Although Brading devoted minimal attention to the emergence of New World saints, he did briefly acknowledge the symbolic importance of homegrown saints Rosa de Lima (d. 1617) and Martín de Porres (d. 1639) to the criollo class of colonial Lima.[11]

Since the publication of *The First America,* scholars whose interests range from the evangelization efforts of the mendicant orders to the social and cultural life of female convents have produced a burgeoning literature that privileges saints, pious traditions, and hagiographies from the colonial Spanish American period.[12] Much of this literature, especially that published in Mexico and Peru, examines the growth of saints' cults and hagiographic traditions as a window to emerging social identities, especially among urbanized criollo elites.[13]

One scholar whose work has significantly influenced my own is

Mexican historian Antonio Rubial García, whose *La santidad controver-tida* (1999) showcases the careers and posthumous reputations of five colonial Mexican holy persons who were unsuccessful candidates for beatification.[14] Like Rubial García, I highlight the cases of five holy persons, eschewing the biographical reconstruction of their lives in order to focus on how their personae were interpreted and transformed in the service of "a didactic, moralizing and 'nationalistic' function."[15] However, whereas Rubial García devotes significant attention to the politics of the canonization processes, I emphasize hagiographic discourse. And while he limits his attention to New Spain, I consider both *novohispano* and Peruvian cases.

Evolution of New World Spanish Society

Criollo patriotism appeared in the early seventeenth century.[16] By mid-century, notes Anthony Pagden, "the native-born (criollo) elite in Mexico and Peru . . . had already acquired a clear sense of belonging to a culture that in many, if not yet all, respects was independent of the 'mother country'." This tendency of criollos to perceive and define themselves as a distinct social group grew out of direct social and economic competition with the Iberian-born Spaniard, or *peninsular*. The conflicts of interest grew so strong during the latter half of the eighteenth century that by the time Napoleon's 1808 invasion of Spain precipitated a political crisis and insurrection in her American colonies, many criollos "were [already] conscious that they . . . were no longer Spanish."[17]

From the sixteenth to the nineteenth centuries, American-born Spaniards based their claims to privileged social and economic status in the New World on two crucial pillars of personal and community identity; namely, place of birth and family lineage. The former set criollos apart from Iberian-born newcomers *(advenizos)*, who enjoyed the highest administrative offices and commercial privileges in the colonies. The second pillar of criollo identity, purity of blood *(limpieza de sangre)*, gave them distinct social advantages over nonwhite ethnic types or *castas*.[18] The fact that American-born Spaniards were inconsistent in their self-characterizations—sometimes emphasizing their prerogatives as New World natives, at other times accentuating their European origins, loyalties, and bloodlines—suggests that the construction of a criollo identity was a delicate balancing act. This preoccupation with social origins, which criollo society inherited from its Iberian ancestors and adapted to the diverse social settings of the Indies, finds subtle and not-so-subtle expression in criollo hagiographies. In the paragraphs that follow, I examine the criollo adaptation of these two pillars of social identity to the americano context.

The criollo sense of group interest and identity had its roots in the experiences of the earliest Spanish immigrants, the self-styled conquistadores. For decades following their military successes against the indigenous empires in Mesoamerica and the Andes, Spanish conquistadores and their descendants petitioned the Spanish crown for special privileges—for example, preferential access to the labor and tribute payments of indigenous peoples—on the basis of seniority *(antigüedad)* and merit.[19] Faced with competition from new arrivals from Spain, the conquistadores argued, "We came here first, long before these Spaniards 'who arrived yesterday.'"[20] Returning continually to the theme of risks taken and services rendered, the conquistadores boasted, "We won this land for Your Majesty." By the middle decades of the sixteenth century, such claims of special status were being made not only by the first-generation adventurers, but also by their offspring, the so-called *hijos de conquistadores* (children of the conquerors). These first-generation criollos based their petitions for special privileges on the achievements of their fathers. For example, when royal officials attempted around mid-century to curtail private ownership of *encomiendas,* criollos argued that as hijos de conquistadores, they continued to deserve the perquisites their fathers had earned.[21] In the written apologia of these conquistadores and their offspring—petitions, letters, histories—we see the birth of a criollo literary tradition. This segment of the Spanish population in the New World had begun to defend its group interests, identifying itself in terms of seniority and heroic services in the Americas.

However, the hijos de conquistadores were thwarted in their attempts to maintain certain socioeconomic privileges, such as encomienda, in perpetuity. In addition, immigrants continued to flock from Spain to the New World in ever-increasing numbers. As a result, the articulation of the criollo identity underwent changes around 1600. Writing in 1604, for example, Balthasar Dorantes de Carranza defended the interests of "those who were born and reared here, the descendants of the conquerors and first settlers, [and] those who, with the passage of years, . . . have come and been naturalized here, marrying and setting down roots, and spreading their lineages, families, and descendants through the breadth of such far-flung provinces."[22] As this statement suggests, a time had arrived when "place of birth, not conquest, . . . conferred membership in the [criollo] community."[23] This shift transformed the social rivalry from one of conquerors versus newcomers to one of New World–born Spaniards versus Iberian-born immigrants and crown officials. Something else had changed as well. The new rivalry entailed more than rights to land and encomiendas; the control of institutions was now at stake. For example, the rivalry between criollos and peninsulares that preoccupied the various mendicant orders in Spanish America led the crown to implement a system of rotating leadership known as the *alternativa*.[24] Similar power struggles took place in the female convents that were being established by 1600. Moreover, the royal practice of limiting criollo access to the higher civil and ecclesiastical offices exacerbated these tensions, heightening the americano sense of group solidarity.[25] The latter source of resentment was reinforced by the Bourbon Reforms of the late eighteenth century, which would foster criollo sentiment for political separation from Spain in the years leading up to 1808.

Whereas criollos consistently promoted their individual and group interests on the basis of New World birth, their peninsular competitors often used this argument against them, questioning the character and political loyalty of criollos. Consider, for example, a 1567 letter in which provisional Governor Lope García de Castro warned the crown about political conditions in the viceroyalty of Peru, a region that had been racked by civil strife since the 1530s. In his letter, García de Castro warned about the threat to royal sovereignty of a potential coalition of non-Iberian groups. "It is certain," wrote the governor, "that if Your Majesty does not act in time, these [mulattoes and mestizos] may join together with the sons of the conquistadores and . . . disturb this land." A few months later, García de Castro attributed the ongoing sociopolitical instability in Peru to the fact that "this land is full of criollos, which are those who have been born here, as well as mestizos and mulattoes."[26]

For some Iberian-born observers, the difference between criollo and peninsular was not a simple matter of birthplace and allegiance; it also implied qualitative differences. As early as the 1560s and 1570s,

Iberian-born missionary-ethnographer Bernardino de Sahagún and geographer Juan López de Velasco suggested that New World climate and astral conditions transformed the Spaniard's body type, skin tone, and personality. This was especially true, observed Sahagún, for those born in New Spain.[27]

Such theories grew more prevalent throughout the colonial era, becoming a sort of conventional wisdom by the eighteenth century, to the delight no doubt of Bourbon reformers who sought to wrest administrative and economic control of the colonies from the hands of criollo elites. Iberian critics of criollo capabilities did not stop at alleging the ill effects of the stars and climate, however. In their franker moments, they questioned the purity of criollo blood. This sentiment is discernible in the text of a 1784 letter from an Iberian-born royal administrator, Francisco de Viedma, to his superiors in Spain: "How can we possibly appoint to . . . office people who do not even know who their fathers are?"[28] Viedma and other peninsular royal officials found that raising questions about the americanos' morality and Spanish lineage provided a useful justification for anti-criollo policy. It is no wonder, notes Anthony Pagden, that "the criollos' identity, their pride in all that separated them from the Old World Spaniard, the *gachupín,* was in part a necessary response to the persistent hostility and undisguised contempt on the part of metropolitan authorities."[29]

In response to criticism like that leveled by Viedma, criollo "sons of the land" had to fall back on the second pillar of origin, namely, lineage. Herein lies one of the contradictions that characterized criollo consciousness; while the struggle for access to wealth and office sometimes motivated American-born Spaniards to emphasize their New World origins, at other times they downplayed differences between themselves and Iberians in order to undermine allegations of tainted blood or moral inferiority.

Criollo preoccupation with limpieza de sangre had its roots both in the social history of late-medieval Spain and in the unique conditions of New World society. The population of medieval Iberia included Jews, Arab and Berber Muslims, and Roman Catholics of diverse ethnic origins. During the reign of Queen Isabel of Castile (r. 1469–1504), church and crown implemented policies aimed at forcing religious conformity on Castile's non-Catholics. In Castile (1492) as well as Portugal (1498), Jews were forced to convert to Catholicism or emigrate.

Those Jews who remained in Castile as *conversos* (literally, converts) faced continued discrimination. By the late sixteenth century in Spain, postulants to male religious orders and female convents, as well as aspirants to civil and ecclesiastical office, had to prove not only their religious orthodoxy but their unbroken Christian lineage as well.[30] The resulting social and legal distinctions between the "New Christians" and the so-called "Old Christians" discriminated against members of the former group based not on the individual's actual religious beliefs and practices, but rather on the religious and ethnic identity of his or her ancestors. Thus, what had begun in late-medieval Iberia as religious discrimination took on the character of racial policy, reflecting a concern not simply with religious unity, but also with social and ethnic origins.

An awareness of these developments in Spain is crucial for a proper understanding of the racial rules and mentalities that would come to permeate colonial society in the New World. The treatment of New Christians in Spain, note James Lockhart and Stuart B. Schwartz, "represented an important precedent for the treatment of non-Europeans in the New World."[31] In fact, social conditions in Spain's American colonies were such that obsession with purity of blood was almost certain to increase. In the New World, Spaniards interacted socially and sexually with persons of Amerindian and African descent, resulting in new social types, the *mestizo* and the *mulato*. At a time when lineage-based discrimination against New Christians was growing in Spain, the Spanish builders of colonial society in New Spain and Peru institutionalized a similar system. Limpieza de sangre requirements restricted access to religious institutions, royal appointments, and membership in merchant or trade guilds. In such a social climate, to be called mestizo was to suffer insult.[32] It would seem natural, then, that in their politically charged interactions with the Spanish civil-religious hierarchy and European-born Spaniards in general, criollo elites would defend the purity of their own blood by demonstrating the racial and cultural gulf that separated them from the castas.

Criollos resented Iberian misconceptions about the New World and found particularly galling the tendency of peninsulares to confuse American-born Spaniards with other New World racial types. Around 1800, Mexican patriot Fray Servando Teresa de Mier lamented how consistently he encountered such notions in Spain:

In a royal office in Madrid that I happened to go into, when I
stated that I was an American they were amazed. "But you aren't
black," they said to me. "A countryman of yours came by just
now," the friars at the monastery of San Francisco in Madrid said
to me, and when I asked how they knew that, they answered that
he was black. In the Cortes [Spanish parliament] the deputy from
Cádiz, a Philippine priest, asked me whether we Americans were
white and professed the Catholic religion. . . . When I arrived in
Las Caldas, the mountain folk "came to see the Indian."[33]

A similar complaint can be found in Juan Meléndez's late-seventeenth-century *Tesoros verdaderos,* a history of the Dominican order in
Peru. The Lima-born criollo laments the apparent unwillingness of
European Spaniards to acknowledge the differences between Amerindians and American-born whites. Having passed through Spain around
1680 en route to Italy, Meléndez later reflected on his experience:

[If] a son of an *español* and an *española* comes to Spain, bringing an indio as his servant, the [peninsular] Spaniards prefer to
confuse the origins of each one, calling both of them "indios."
What greater incongruency *(desconformidad)* can there be than
to want to call by a single term these two [groups] who are as
different from one another in their natures as they are in their
origins? Even so, we [American-born Spaniards] would be willing for them to call us by the same term [that they use for Indi-
ans] if they did not also want to attribute to both groups the
same nature.[34]

Meléndez attributes the confusion in part to a misuse and misun-
derstanding of ethnic labels. As a remedy, he proposes that criollo
Spaniards should refer to themselves by the unambiguous epithet *hijos
de españoles* rather than another common term, *indiano,* noting that the
latter term is too easily confused with *indio.*

This identity bind—pride in their status as New World natives but
reluctance to be confused with non-Spanish groups—is implicit in the
contemporary uses and connotations of the word criollo. While historians and linguists differ on the term's origin, they generally agree that
in the colonial-era Spanish Indies, to be criollo was to have local origins. "Criollo" described New World cultural forms, climate, or cui-
sine, as well as individuals and social groups. José de Acosta suggested
in his famous *Historia natural y moral de Indias* (1590) that the label "crio-

llo" designated "those born to Spaniards in the Indies."[35] Famed mestizo writer Garcilaso de la Vega (d. 1616), who had suffered exclusion
from the criollo group because of an Indian mother, narrowed Acosta's definition to reflect his personal experience: "The children of
Spaniards by *Spanish women* born [in the Indies] are called criollo or
criolla."[36] According to Garcilaso's usage, a criollo belonged to a rather
elite club. Yet for American-born Spaniards zealous to have their exclusive status as Spaniards of pure blood be recognized, the "criollo" label
presented problems, for the term was often applied to Indians and black
slaves.[37] Thus, while the label "criollo" could empower American-born
Spaniards in their ideological struggles against peninsular rivals by
asserting their special rights in the New World, it could also blur the
line between themselves and nonwhites, a fact that peninsulares would
use against them.

This evolution of Spanish colonial society, with its social rivalries
and resulting ethnic definitions and ideologies, provides an important
backdrop for an informed reading of the contemporary vida de santo.
Criollo hagiographers were not exempt from these prejudices and concerns. Their literary products, which focus primarily on devotional and
theological themes, reveal the strong imprint of criollo consciousness
and social rivalry. Indeed, in light of the fact that sociopolitical discourse was usually secondary to religious concerns, it could be argued
that the consistency with which criollo hagiographers touch on matters
of social origin and ethnic identity reveals how deeply those issues
affected them.

This book centers around five core chapters in which I examine the
sacred biographies of five New World holy persons: Blessed Sebastián
de Aparicio, St. Rosa de Lima, St. Mariana de Jesús, Catarina de San
Juan, and St. Felipe de Jesús. My emphasis on identity rhetoric has
guided my choice of objects for analysis. Rather than select five holy
persons—perhaps the most widely venerated, the most prototypically
criollo, or the most representative in terms of social type or saint-
type—I highlight five sets of hagiographic texts that consistently and
compellingly express themes of group origin and identity.[38] Furthermore, my attention to discourse has shaped my reading of these colo-

nial vidas. Rather than read each saint's Life for its commonalities with the broader hagiographic genre, I prefer Roger Chartier's emphasis on "particularity over preconceived generalization in the consideration of textual and typographical genres."[39] For although the hagiographer imitated the standard motifs and language of his literary genre, he also tended to "interpret their meaning in such a way as to give them an entirely new content." As a result, "similar miracles, similar phrases, similar gestures could mean different things in different contexts."[40]

By preferring microhistory (the individual Life) over macrohistory (the genre), I am not overlooking the fact that the seventeenth-century saint's Life belonged to a literary genre that was conventional in form, style, and content. Indeed, during the course of my readings in medieval and early-modern hagiographies I have frequently experienced a sensation of déjà vu. There can be no doubt that the modern reader who wishes to understand the individual vida must be familiar with the genre's conventions. At the same time, a reading of this literature must be informed by a recognition that biography, religious or otherwise, reveals as much about the authors and their intended readership as it does about the biographical subjects.[41] Thus, although I am attentive to the rules and requirements of the genre, I avoid the pursuit of "tradition, the norm, the representative example,"[42] preferring to call attention to how each religious biographer maneuvers within the genre.[43] This allows me to treat each saint's Life as an act of self-definition performed by an individual author on behalf of the community or communities to which he belongs.

In chapter 2, I consider the transference of the hagiographic genre to the New World in the sixteenth century. There I treat such matters as authorship, purpose and function of hagiographic texts, and dissemination. Chapters 3 through 7 comprise the aforementioned case studies. In chapter 3, I consider the hagiographic traditions surrounding Fray Sebastián de Aparicio (d. 1600), an Iberian-born Franciscan lay brother who lived most of his life in and around the city of Puebla, New Spain. The case of Fray Aparicio illustrates the transference of European persons and cultural traditions to the New World. In Aparicio's vidas, I discover a high degree of continuity between Old World and New, particularly in the way his hagiographers portray him as a near-perfect replica of St. Francis of Assisi. But I find discontinuity as well, for while Aparicio imitates St. Francis—practicing heroic virtue, performing miracles and receiving divine favors—he does so in the evolving sociocultural setting of New Spain. Perhaps of greatest significance given my interest in the criollo obsession with origins, it is notable that although Aparicio spent many more years in New Spain than in his native Galicia, he would forever remain a *gallego* in the minds of his most loyal devotees. His reputation for sanctity was rooted in the soil of New Spain, but his glory belonged primarily to his native Galicia. The criollos of Puebla might embrace the Iberian-born holy man as an object of local pride and veneration, but they could not ultimately claim him as their own.

Chapter 4 concerns the pious traditions surrounding St. Rosa de Lima (1586–1617), a Dominican tertiary whose meteoric elevation to the altar in 1672 was preceded by a papal bull granting her special status as "principal patroness of the Americas, Philippines, and Indies" (1671). The earliest Lives of Rosa de Lima are notable more for their similarities to Raymond of Capua's fourteenth-century Life of St. Catherine of Siena than for any New World innovations. Indeed, I find very little hint in these hagiographic narratives of Rosa's New World identity; readers might easily mistake her for a holy woman of Spain or Italy. Even so, when I examine these vidas alongside an epic poem and the iconography that honored her, I find evidence of two historic tensions that pressured Peruvian criollos to identify themselves closely with peninsular Spaniards. The first was the maritime threat posed to Roman Catholic Lima by English and Dutch corsairs. In a period of heightened struggle between Spain and its Protestant competitors, piracy represented a challenge that was at once military, economic, and religious. During the course of the seventeenth century, *limeños* came to venerate Rosa as protectress of their port, coastal towns, and silver shipments (see figure 1.1). A second major source of concern for the Peruvian criollo sector was the immense Amerindian population that inhabited the Andean highlands. On the one hand, the Spanish elites of Peru depended on native labor for the extraction and processing of silver, metallic lifeblood of the colonial economy. Like the Protestant pirates, these native peoples posed a military threat, as the frequency of their uprisings would suggest. In addition, the persistence of their prehispanic religious practices presented a spiritual challenge to Roman Catholic institutions and goals. In the minds of her white devotees, Rosa's intercession protected them from such challenges to their eco-

FIGURE I.I. Devotional image of St. Rosa de Lima dressed as Our Lady of the Rosary, to whom she was greatly devoted during her lifetime. St. Rosa holds an anchor on whose flukes rest the city of Lima, reflecting her importance as patroness and preserver of Peru's viceregal capital (see chapter 4). Anonymous, eighteenth century. Property of the Monastery of Santa Rosa de Santa María, Lima. From José Flores Araoz et al. *Santa Rosa de Lima y su tiempo* (Lima, 1995), 256. (From the Colección Arte y Tesoros del Péru; courtesy of the Banco de Crédito del Perú)

nomic and religious goals by converting indigenous pagans or defeating their uprisings with her prayers. Because of both major threats—Protestant pirates and pagan Incas—Peruvian criollos maintained close alliances with peninsular Spaniards, tending to emphasize their shared identities.

The canonization of Rosa de Lima as the first American-born saint empowered criollos from New Spain to the Rio de la Plata. It also opened the way for a new hagiographic paradigm, for uncloistered criollo women could now imitate the exemplary life of an americana compatriot. In chapter 5, I demonstrate how a Jesuit hagiographer from the region of Quito compares his local holy woman, Mariana de Jesús (d. 1645), with the Rose of Lima, emphasizing their shared sanctity as spiritual products of American soil. But as my analysis will show, criollo identity—or better, identities—were multifaceted and complex. Criollismo was not simply the exuberant expression of americano pride in the face of peninsular discrimination and disdain. Rather, American-born Spaniards viewed themselves as members of many social entities, including family, religious order, trade guild, Catholic confraternity, city, and province. Accordingly, the promotion of New World saints in religious art, sermons, hagiographies, and verse allowed criollo devotees to articulate these multiple identities and loyalties, including love of the *patria chica* (literally, small homeland). When the hagiographer of Mariana de Jesús juxtaposes his "Lily of Quito" with the "Rose of Lima," he is also proudly comparing his home province of Quito with the more famous viceregal capital.

In chapter 6, I consider the intriguing case of Catarina de San Juan (d. 1688), an Asian-born holy woman who lived most of her life in Puebla. Following the establishment of a Spanish colony in the Philippine Islands around 1570, there emerged a profitable maritime trade between Asia and Spanish America. People and goods, including silk and porcelain, came and went each year between Manila and the novohispano port of Acapulco. Thus did young Catarina, a victim of kidnapping for the purpose of sale, arrive in New Spain around 1617. By the time she died some seven decades later, this illiterate domestic servant had gained a reputation for sanctity based on the mystical visions she claimed to experience. In order to validate her claims and assuage the concerns of ecclesiastical censors, Catarina's Jesuit hagiographer, Alonso Ramos, attempted to improve upon her obscure and troublesome origins by describing her childhood as a light-skinned descendent of India's ruling Mughal dynasty. This attempt to narrow the social and racial gap between Catarina and the elite poblano laypersons who would potentially venerate her and patronize her cause speaks volumes about the Spanish obsession with ethnic origin.

Chapter 7 examines the literary promotion of Felipe de Jesús of Mexico City, whose reputation for sanctity resulted from his death as a Christian martyr in Japan in 1597. His cult, which developed contemporaneously with the patriotic tradition of Our Lady of Guadalupe, was quite popular in mid-colonial New Spain. However, whereas the criollo faithful of Lima had an officially recognized homegrown saint by 1672, Felipe's novohispano devotees would petition Rome in vain for similar consideration until 1862. Frustrated pro-Felipe preachers and hagiographers grew more combative in tone after 1750 as they responded to rumors that questioned their saint's origins and moral character. Resentful of European intellectual theories that denied their capabilities, as well as of Spanish imperial policy that excluded them from the highest colonial offices, these criollo apologists began to blame such rumors on a broader anti-criollo conspiracy. One devotee in particular spent years in search of definitive proof that his beloved "santo criollo" was indeed a fruit of Mexican soil.

This study presupposes not only that the printed Lives of New World saints reflect identity values, but also that they helped to disseminate those values. Because this assumption begs the question of authorship and readership, I now turn my attention to the writing of the colonial-era vida in order to understand its content, purpose, and influence.

2

A New World of Piety

Writing the Saint's Life in Spanish America

In 1536 a Franciscan friar named Francisco Jiménez wrote one of the first religious biographies in Spanish America, a Life of Fray Martín de Valencia, the recently deceased leader of the famous Franciscan "Twelve Apostles." In the opening lines of his biographical narrative, Jiménez expressed the hope that his literary endeavor might bring "much profit to the souls of Spanish clergymen and laymen born in this land [New Spain], as well as to those from our old Spain."[1] Although his manuscript was lost within a few decades and only rediscovered some four centuries later, Jiménez had helped to initiate what would become a rich tradition of religious writing in the New World. For centuries thereafter, Roman Catholics throughout the Americas (including the French regions of North America) composed hagiographies and religious biographies of their exemplary heroes.[2]

This chapter examines the rise and function of the hagiographic genre in Spanish America, as well as some of the forces that shaped the hagiographic process. I consider, for example, which social types became subjects or authors of sacred biographies, and explore the dynamic that existed between hagiographers and their subjects. My discussion of hagiographic motivations and purposes casts light on the economic, bureaucratic, and ideological factors, as well as the more strictly religious concerns, that affected the timing, form, and content of the typical vida. Finally, I turn to the matter of dissemination and influence, arguing that the saint's Life exerted a broader influence than one might expect, especially in light of the high cost of publishing and distributing these texts. Through other media—sermons, religious chronicles, *novenas*,[3] and sacred art—broader sectors of society, especially pious urban elites, became acquainted with these holy persons and their stories.

Archbishop Juan de Zumárraga established the first colonial printing press in Mexico City in 1539.[4] Even so, Francisco Jiménez's Life of Martín de Valencia remained unpublished. Indeed, religious writers and publishers in New Spain directed their sixteenth-century literary production toward the conversion of indigenous peoples. In an era of limited human and financial resources, priority was given to the writing and publication of grammars and dictionaries of the region's native languages, as well as bilingual confessionals and catechisms. Consequently, only about a third of all editions printed in Mexico City between 1539 and 1600 were works in Castilian.[5]

For this reason, a study of Spanish American hagiography must focus on a later period, beginning around 1600, when a "hispanization" of the printing press occurred in New Spain (and soon thereafter in Peru). By this time, a broader historical process was underway in the New World regions of heaviest Spanish penetration; namely, the development of a colonial Spanish culture. The growing American-born Spanish population, together with the increasing stream of Iberian immigrants, contributed to a rapid urbanization. New Spanish cities emerged in places like Puebla, Lima, and Santiago de Chile where none had existed, while preconquest indigenous urban centers like Quito, Cusco, and Tenochtitlán (Mexico) drew large Spanish populations. Lucrative agricultural and mining industries allowed prosperous criollos and peninsulares to channel surplus wealth toward the construction of cathedrals, the foundation of male and female convents, the establishment of institutions of higher learning, and the endowment of pious works *(obras pías)*. More and more, Roman Catholic ecclesiastical personnel turned their attentions from the spiritual needs of Indians in *doctrinas* and *congregaciones* to the religious concerns of urban-dwelling Spaniards. The nature of their literary production shifted accordingly, with texts in Castilian comprising five-sixths of works printed in seventeenth-century Mexico City.[6] The vida de santo was an important part of this mid-colonial literary production, exercising directly and indirectly a central role in the religious, intellectual, and socioeconomic life of the most hispanized sectors of colonial society. Whereas the earliest vidas had memorialized the faith and achievements of Iberian-born Spaniards such as Martín de Valencia and Francisco Solano, the seventeenth century witnessed a shift, as criollo subjects were more frequently commemorated in writing.[7]

In early modern Spanish America as elsewhere in the Roman Catholic world at that time, the protagonist of the hagiographic Life was, more often than not, a member or close associate of one of the major religious orders. Such had been the case in Europe since the thirteenth century, when members of the new mendicant orders became more frequent candidates for canonization than kings, queens, or cloistered monks and nuns.[8] In the New World of the sixteenth century, the first protagonists of Catholic hagiographies were male religious like Martín de Valencia who, as leaders in the effort to convert the native peoples to Christianity, had demonstrated extraordinary piety, virtue, and dedication to the evangelical mission. The cases of Franciscan Francisco Solano, Dominican Luis Beltrán, and Jesuit Pedro Claver are best known today as a result of their eventual canonization by Rome.[9] Although these cases are rare in terms of their canonical success, they are representative of the hundreds of mendicant preacher/evangelizers whose memories were preserved by hagiographers or chroniclers from their respective orders.

Missionaries were not the only hagiographic subjects in Spain's New World colonies. The general process of hispanization and urbanization provided a context for the emergence of other types of holy persons, including bishops, nuns, and lay men and women, including the occasional person of mixed race. In keeping with the reformist and centralizing priorities of the post-Tridentine church and the Spanish crown, bishops Pedro Moya de Contreras (Mexico City, 1573–91), Toribio Alfonso Mogrovejo (Lima, 1581–1606), and Juan de Palafox y Mendoza (Puebla, 1640–54) attained posthumous reputations for sanctity and became subjects of hagiographic works.[10] In addition to bishop-reformers, other male saint types of this period were the occasional martyr, the hermit, and the pious layman of humble social status, each of which had some affiliation with one of the mendicant orders.[11]

As the Spanish population in New Spain and Peru increased and "surplus" daughters were less compelled to marry, female convents began to proliferate. At the same time, male and female biographers began to write hagiographies and religious biographies of the founders and spiritual heroines of these religious houses. The city of Puebla, New Spain, witnessed a remarkable expansion of its female religious foundations and literary production during the seventeenth and eighteenth centuries, and saw several of its cloistered daughters memorialized by clerical hagiographers.[12]

Some of these cloistered women wrote spiritual biographies of their fellow nuns, as well as spiritual autobiographies. The writings of these women, who spent their lives in the convents of such diverse regions as New Spain, Chile, and Nueva Granada, reflect the spiritual and literary influences of the famed Spanish Carmelite reformer, St. Teresa of Avila (canonized 1622).[13] Like St. Teresa, Spanish American nuns chronicled the foundations and early histories of their convents, examined the life of interior piety (mysticism), and edified their fellow nuns with letters and short biographies. Their religious biographies, rarely published prior to the twentieth century, were distinct in nature from hagiography proper, however; once a woman gained a reputation for sanctity, male clerics took over the hagiographic process.[14] For this reason, the body of texts I have chosen for analysis includes no works by women writers. Readers interested in female literary production in early modern Spain and Spanish America may consult a burgeoning scholarly literature.[15]

However, most urban women of deep spiritual sensibility did not have the option of taking the veil and pursuing their religious vocation within the cloister. Poverty, family pressures to marry, or conventual racial restrictions rendered such a path unlikely, if not impossible, for most Spanish and casta women who might otherwise aspire to it. Such was the case for Rosa de Santa María, Mariana de Jesús, and Catarina de San Juan, three women whose vidas I examine in chapters 4, 5, and 6. Despite such restrictions, the uncloistered holy woman or *beata*[16] often maintained some sort of spiritual relationship with one or more religious communities, whose members then promoted her posthumous reputation for sanctity and wrote her hagiographies. Like her cloistered counterparts, the beata's reputation for sanctity was based upon her rigorous asceticism, her mystical experiences, and the efficacy of her works of intercession on behalf of the faithful. In comparison to cloistered nuns, however, the beata enjoyed a greater degree of social interaction with lay society. This allowed her to practice diverse types of charitable activity that endeared her to a broad range of social sectors. The beata's career and reputation for sanctity shared much with those of the holy lay brother, although he tended to maintain more formalized ties to the male religious orders, while she usually practiced a more internal mystical life.

Not surprisingly, members of the mendicant orders and the Jesuits were the most common authors of hagiographic texts.[17]There were, of course, exceptions to this general rule. For instance, members of the secular clergy—that is, bishops or parish priests—did write sacred biographies of fellow secular clerics.[18]

In rare cases, moreover, a layman might compose the holy person's vida. Such was the case in the 1620s when Licenciado Bartolomé Sánchez Parejo penned a life of Sebastián de Aparicio (see chapter 3). Even in such cases, however, the lay author would likely have had some affiliation with the deceased holy person's religious order, perhaps as a member of one of the order's lay confraternities. This may have been true in the case of Sánchez Parejo, who was clearly a loyal devotee of the Franciscan lay brother whose hagiography he wrote. Such cases were rare, however. Indeed, the Sánchez Parejo work was never published.

In the preceding paragraphs I have identified a general pattern regarding the writing of saints' Lives in Spanish America. With few exceptions, male members of the regular clergy wrote hagiographies of men or women associated with their respective religious orders. But what was the nature of the relationship between hagiographer and subject?

In some cases, the hagiographer composed the Life of a coworker or spiritual mentor whom he had known personally. For example, Francisco Losa, who had spent years as a companion and disciple of the hermit Gregorio López, published the latter's vida in 1613. Similarly, Mallorcan-born Francisco Palou memorialized Fray Junípero Serra, his senior partner in the eighteenth-century Franciscan campaign to evangelize the indigenous peoples of Upper California.[19] In the case of a saintly beata or nun, a male confessor with firsthand knowledge of her interior life was the most likely candidate for writing her vida. In New Spain, for example, Father José Eugenio Ponce de León, O.P., composed vidas of several nuns whose spiritual lives he had directed, as did the Franciscan Joseph Gómez for his spiritual protégé, Antonia de San Jacinto.[20] As we shall see in chapters 4 and 6, personal confessors of Rosa de Santa María (St. Rosa de Lima) and Catarina de San Juan wrote and published hagiographies very shortly after each woman's death.

Often, however, the hagiographer undertook his project many years after his protagonist's death. With no recourse to persons who had known the purported saint personally, the writer had to depend on earlier literary, legal, and oral sources. For matters of modern historical analysis, the second- or third-hand narrative—including most of the texts I examine in this book[21]—presents both advantages and disadvantages. Obviously, such an account does not convey the immediacy and intimacy of an eyewitness version. Yet such a narrative, more distant in time from the events it describes, is not necessarily less historically accurate than a firsthand account. For one thing, its author might be less subjective in his judgments than an eyewitness hagiographer whose life and career formed part of the story he sought to narrate. Moreover, in a case where ecclesiastical authorities had already authorized public investigations into the holy person's sanctity, the second- or third-generation hagiographer often enjoyed a key advantage over the firsthand narrator; namely, access to the written records *(procesos)* of those investigations, which recorded the testimonies of numerous eyewitnesses. Admittedly, however, the hagiographer who composed his vida decades after the fact was more likely to interpret his subject's life in historical and public terms, or to yield to the temptation to mythologize that life. But while that quality might diminish the value of the later-generation hagiography as a biographical account, it renders such a work even more valuable for a study such as mine, which seeks to elucidate sociopolitical discourse about group origins.

Historically, the writer of the saint's Life has aimed his literary project at the attainment of multiple, interconnected goals. Hence, in order to accurately interpret colonial Spanish hagiography, one must recognize the hagiographer's various aims. Like his contemporaries in Europe, the hagiographer in Spanish America pursued four primary goals: (1) to edify his readers with inspirational stories of the saint's virtue, faith, and miracles; (2) to bring fame and honor to the various communities—religious order, social corporation, ethnic group, town, or province—that would share in the saint's eventual glory; (3) to convince members of his target audience to venerate the potential saint as their own special patron or patroness, and to demonstrate that devotion by sponsoring the inchoate cult (including the beatification process); and (4) to convince church officials of the authenticity of his protagonist's sanctity. In order to accurately interpret colonial Spanish hagiography, one must recognize all of these goals and how they shaped the individual text.

One of the primary functions of the saint's Life was to edify the faithful. The hagiographer demonstrated how his protagonist had embodied such Christian virtues as humility, faith, chastity, and love for God and souls, as well as how God had shown his favor toward the saint by granting special experiences (visions, ecstasies, etc.) and by working miracles for and through him or her. In this way, the narrator not only proved the holy person's sanctity—for the Roman Catholic Church recognized sanctity primarily in terms of virtues and miracles—but also provided readers with a model of Christian living. The hagiographer invited devotees to take two types of action: to imitate actions and attitudes that were within their reach, and to marvel at those signs of sanctity—mystical experiences or miracles—that lay beyond their ken.

This edifying dimension of the saint's Life accounts for certain of its organizational and structural features. Richard Kieckhefer has traced the Christian hagiographic genre to two distinct literary traditions of antiquity. From the Christian Gospels, Christian hagiography borrowed its preference for dividing the holy person's life into discrete episodes. Christian hagiography borrowed its principal themes from the Gospels as well, portraying the holy person as imitator of Christ's virtues, miracles, and most importantly, his death.[22] This attention to episodes and stories, miracles and pious death, reinforced the didactic or edifying nature of the hagiographic text.

In addition to borrowing from the Gospels, Christian hagiographers imitated biographers of Greco-Roman antiquity, especially Suetonius, in their organization of the protagonist's life story. For example, Sulpicius Severus's Life of St. Martin of Tours followed Suetonius's practice of "giv[ing] a chronological survey of his subject's life up to the high point of that subject's career, then proceed[ing] to thematic discussion of his accomplishments and personality."[23] This organizational structure, together with a thematic emphasis on virtues, miracles, and pious death, ultimately shaped the typical division of the saint's Life into four major sections: early life; religious life and virtues; miracles; and death and posthumous reputation for sanctity. The emphasis on edification affected not only the shape of the vida, but its function and dissemination as well. The hagiographer of Mariana de Jesús (chapter 5) constructed her Life as a concatenation of sermonic texts in order to supply future preachers with hortatory material.

A second important motive for writing a holy person's Life was the desire to glorify the various communities to which the saint-protagonist had belonged. There is no denying that the saint's Life, while primarily a pious text, communicated a certain level of self-consciousness, indeed of self-interest, on the part of hagiographer and audience. As spokesman for a religious order and province, the writer presented the heroic virtue of one of its most saintly members as a representation of the spiritual attainments of that community. If he was a criollo and proud local son, he portrayed the sweet spiritual fruit of the soil of his patria as evidence of the type of spiritual plant that budded and bloomed there generally. Self-promotion was individualistic as well as corporate. For example, the confessor-hagiographer inevitably ventured into the arena of autobiography when he revealed the interior spiritual life of a female penitent whom he personally had directed. Furthermore, as scholar and writer, he had the opportunity to make a name for himself in the eventuality of the work's publication.

In order to promote the glory of his community or communities, the writer of sacred biography employed a number of strategies. He might, for example, digress from the saint's life story at various points in order to narrate local or institutional history—to describe, for example, the urban edifices and educational facilities whose funding reflected both the wealth and piety of local citizens.[24] He would often insert into the published work, as a preface to the hagiographic narrative itself, a letter of dedication *(dedicatoria)* that praised both the individual or corporate patron of the book and the larger community or audience whose honor he sought to promote. In addition, the title page, indeed the book title itself, could convey a message of community achievement and glory. Such was the case with the Jesuit-authored Life of Quito's Mariana de Jesús (see figure 2.1).

Closely connected to the hagiographer's goal of honoring the saint's community was a third major hagiographic aim, that of stimulating devotion and patronage. To support a saint's cult was an extremely

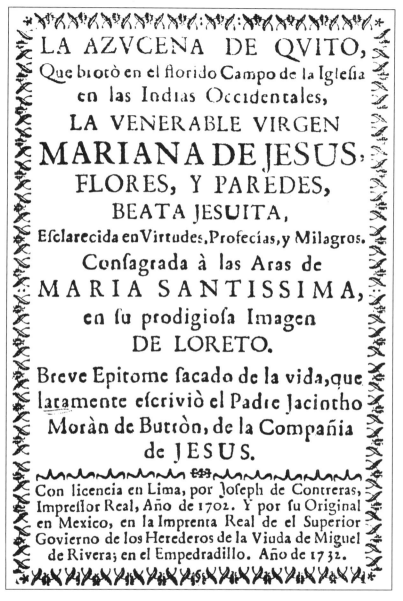

LA AZVCENA DE QVITO,
Que brotò en el florido Campo de la Iglesia
en las Indias Occidentales,
LA VENERABLE VIRGEN
MARIANA DE JESUS,
FLORES, Y PAREDES,
BEATA JESUITA,
Esclarecida en Virtudes, Profecías, y Milagros.
Consagrada à las Aras de
MARIA SANTISSIMA,
en su prodigiosa Imagen
DE LORETO.

Breve Epitome sacado de la vida, que
latamente escrivió el Padre Jacintho
Moràn de Butròn, de la Compañia
de JESUS.

Con licencia en Lima, por Joseph de Contreras,
Impressor Real, Año de 1702. Y por su Original
en Mexico, en la Imprenta Real de el Superior
Govierno de los Herederos de la Viuda de Miguel
de Rivera; en el Empedradillo. Año de 1732.

FIGURE 2.1. Title page from Jacinto Morán de Butrón's abbreviated and economical *La Azucena de Quito que brotó en el florido campo de la iglesia en las Indias* . . . (México: 1732), a reprint of Morán's original *Compendio* (Lima, 1702). The Jesuit author identifies Mariana de Jesús as the "Lily of Quito" and offers her life as evidence of the spiritual achievements of his religious order and homeland. (Courtesy of the Sutro Library, a branch of the California State Library)

expensive affair; there were churches to build, altars and altarpieces to design, and hagiographic texts to publish, not to mention bureaucratic and legal costs to bear. As a result, the clerical promoter of a saint's cult and reputation was by necessity a fundraiser. Armed with official licenses for collecting alms, he used hagiography as a means for attracting and motivating potential contributors. He was aware that his holy person's canonical future might well depend upon his ability to persuade persons and corporate entities of financial means to embrace the saint's cult and shoulder the expenses of its promotion.

Toward that end, the hagiographer-promoter sought to establish strong affective links between saint and community, which in the process affected both the form and content of the Life. For example, he employed the letter of dedication for that very purpose, usually recounting a history of affection and pious deeds linking the saint-protagonist to the book's individual or corporate patron. The hagiographer's need to demonstrate connections between his saint and wealthy patrons spilled over from the dedicatoria into the hagiographic narrative itself. First, by interweaving events from the saint's life with the history of the local community, the hagiographer showed readers that this was *their* saint. Second, by enumerating the ways in which the saint had already favored local people through miraculous works, he established a relationship of mutual obligation and mutual dependence between saint and devotees. Third, by suggesting that the saint's failure in the past to receive recognition by the church reflected poorly on the patria, family, or religious community, the hagiographer implied that more was at stake than the saint's reputation alone.

Finally, the colonial-era hagiographer's fourth major purpose arose from his role as promoter of the saint's beatification. The seventeenth- or eighteenth-century Roman Catholic hagiographer, regardless of where he lived in the world, was more conscious than Life writers from earlier generations of the need to convince church officials of the authenticity of his protagonist's sanctity. Changes in the saint-making process forced devotees of the would-be saint to comply with new, rigorous demands in the promotion of his or her cult. And although, as I stated in chapter 1, I will largely eschew the politics of canonization, it is nevertheless appropriate at this stage to consider the post-Tridentine reforms that so greatly altered canonization, for these changes affected the hagiographic process as well.

The proclamation of a holy person as a saint worthy of veneration by the faithful was a prerogative that had long since been taken from the local church. At the height of the medieval papal monarchy, Pope Gregory IX (1227–41) had made papal canonization the only legitimate means of establishing a saint's cult.[25] Roman control of saint-making increased significantly between the sixteenth and eighteenth centuries, in part as a response to criticism by Catholic humanists and Protestants, and in part due to the desire by Rome to assert its authority over local religion.

Roman Catholic bishops placed new restrictions on saints' cults at the Council of Trent (1545–63). While they defended such Catholic traditions as the mass, the doctrine of purgatory, and the veneration of saints, the bishops moved to regulate certain elements of popular piety including, as they put it, the "boisterous festivities and drunkenness" that often accompanied "the celebration of saints and the visitation of relics." Henceforth, the faithful were not to erect new images, accept new accounts of miracles, or recognize new relics without episcopal approval.[26] The local bishop, moreover, was to form his opinion regarding a reputed holy person in consultation with "theologians and other pious men" and, if doubts persisted, to submit the matter to Rome. The goal of such "counterlocal" measures, notes William Christian, was "to sanitize local religious custom, ensure that it was under diocesan control, and eliminate any conflicts with religion as ordained from Rome."[27]

Regulation of the canonization process did not end with the Council of Trent. Rather, Rome followed up on the Council's decrees by further centralizing and bureaucratizing the process. In 1588, Pope Sixtus V created the Sacred Congregation of Rites, a standing committee of cardinals whose purpose was to oversee a multistep process of investigation into the merit of all candidates for the altar. A few decades later, Pope Urban VIII (1623–45) added further restrictions, thereby making the process more lengthy, legalistic, and costly.[28] Through a series of reforms known collectively as *non cultu,* Urban VIII forbade public veneration of any reputed saint—including publication of books of the saint's miracles or revelations—pending a papal decree of beatification. Such measures, it was hoped, would ensure that claims about each new "saint" were both historically accurate and doctrinally sound, and would guarantee that the evaluation of such claims would be carried out by the proper ecclesiastical officials.

This post-Tridentine regulation of the saint-making process began to affect the work of would-be hagiographers throughout the Roman Catholic world in profound and concrete ways. In response to the public expressions of devotion that accompanied the death of a perceived saint, local officials petitioned papal and royal offices for permission to investigate the case. If adequately convinced, the Roman Sacred Congregation of Rites would approve the first stage of investigation into what would become, if successful, a multistage "cause of canonization" (hereafter, *causa*).[29] This initial *proceso diocesano,* as it was called, would generate a dossier of sworn testimony by local church officials, notaries, medical experts, and devoted laypersons. Ecclesiastical officials in Rome might subsequently approve the next stage of investigations, known as the *proceso apostólico*. Through such regulation, the causa became in the seventeenth century a highly bureaucratized affair, characterized by intermittent stages of local investigation and Roman evaluation, often with long lulls in between.

These developments in the canonization process influenced the timing of the hagiographic endeavor. Hagiographers—often fulfilling part of their obligation as procurator of their saint's causa—tended to compose their vidas in conjunction with a particular stage of the process. They developed their arguments and strategies with an eye to canonization legalities. This factor could not help but affect the structure, language, and tone of the vida.

It is instructive, for example, to consider the various prefatory documents—elements that together comprise what literary scholars refer to as the "paratext"[30]—which accompanied the printed Life by the seventeenth century. With brief statements that bore such titles as "Licencia," "Suma de privilegio," and "Tassa," civil and ecclesiastical bureaucrats licensed the work for publication, granted a maximum period of time for this to occur, and regulated the price at which each printed exemplar was to be sold. Of course, since both the papacy and the Spanish crown closely censured book publication, licensing required prior approval of a given text. Thus, in documents alternately entitled "Censura" (Censure), "Parecer" (Opinion), or "Aprobación" (Approval or Endorsement), qualified clergymen testified to having read the work and having found it both edifying and inoffensive. Their sworn statements tended to be very formulaic: "I (We) find nothing [in this work] that disagrees with our Faith nor with the purity of our customs."[31]

Another important prefatory document, the "Protesta del autor" (Authorial disclaimer), responded directly to papal rules of non cultu. Here the author would disclaim any pretension of knowing for certain whether his protagonist was a saint or not, and would subject all judgments regarding the virtues, miracles, and status of his protagonist to authorities in Rome. Finally, the author's "Carta al lector" (Letter to the reader) engaged more directly with the main text itself, pointing readers to major themes, and in some cases suggesting proper and improper ways of reading and understanding the text. This strategic use of the carta al lector was most common in the vida of the female visionary. There, the hagiographer or a colleague might admonish readers to admire the protagonist but not attempt to imitate her. By imposing in advance "an orthodoxy or prescribed reading on the text," authors and publishers hoped to protect themselves from accusations of impropriety.[32]

These various elements of the book paratext point to a convergence of bureaucratic regulation with authorial self-protection. Functionaries of the Spanish Holy Office (Inquisition) and the Roman Sacred Congregation of Rites used the system of review and licensing to control which texts could be published. They also banned from circulation books containing sensitive material that had slipped through the system and had been printed. At the same time, the author-hagiographer understood the rules and parameters. He was aware that by conforming to these rules, he was more likely to see his book in print and his purported saint raised to the altar. While he might venture into controversial discussions of such matters as interior piety, frequency of communion, or the status of souls in purgatory, he would do so with relative caution.[33]

It would be inaccurate to conclude, however, that all clerical hagiographers were purveyors of a top-down, official version of sanctity.[34] This notion, which in my view reflects modern scholars' tendency to view institutions and social relations almost exclusively in terms of dominance and resistance, rests on two erroneous assumptions. First, it attempts to distinguish between the "official saint" and the "popular saint," as if there were some objective, qualitative difference between the two. In point of fact, the only difference between official saint and popular saint is that one ultimately received papal recognition and the other did not.[35] The dividing line between saint and heretic was a thin one, as the career of St. Teresa of Avila illustrates.[36] It is simply unproductive to make an arbitrary distinction between the popular saint beloved by the frustrated masses and the official saint imposed on the faithful from above.

In the second place, the assertion that clerical hagiographers present nothing more than Rome's "party line" incorrectly views the clergy or the church as a monolithic entity of control.[37] If such were the case, why would so many high-ranking clergymen (bishops, members of cathedral chapters, officials in religious orders) have fomented the cults and causas of holy persons who did not measure up as official saints (i.e., who never received official ecclesiastical recognition)? Consider the five would-be saints examined by Antonio Rubial García. For generations, high-ranking lay and clerical devotees vigorously promoted these holy persons' causes for canonization, but to no avail. In each case, Rome found no compelling reason to beatify or canonize the candidate. Are we to conclude that the clerical elites who promoted these causas were renegade priests or somehow unable to distinguish between the popular and official saint?

Just as I avoid making a distinction between popular saint and official saint, I reject the notion that, with regard to the writing and publishing of pious texts, there existed distinct, competing factions consisting of scholar-writers on the one hand and bureaucrat-censors on the other. "Although it might be tempting," notes Magdalena Chocano Mena, "to characterize censorship as an external bureaucratic apparatus forced upon colonial scholars, such an approach misses the point that censorship in New Spain emerged from within the scholarly group itself." The scholarly group, she adds, "was not clearly differentiated from the bureaucratic sector."[38] In fact, the same individual who might on the one hand make a hagiographic case for his own saint's sanctity, could on the other hand fulfill his role as inquisitorial censor (calificador) by refusing to approve for publication a manuscript Life of some other holy person. In a similar way, a bishop or other prelate who fomented the cult of a non-canonized local holy person found himself obliged by post-Tridentine restrictions on the public veneration of unapproved holy persons to appear to be suppressing premature activity. Thus, as attractive as it may at first seem, the official saint/popular saint dichotomy obscures more than it enlightens.[39]

While the colonial-era hagiographer did his best to stay within the

boundaries of orthodoxy and established protocol, this did not necessarily mean that his literary product diverged from popular belief and
practice. In my view, it is more accurate to view him as a mediator
between devotees of the saint on the one hand and papal bureaucrats,
theologians, and Inquisition censors *(calificadores)* on the other. He put
forward the claims of the former group while attempting to conform to
the rules and norms set down by the latter group. Indeed, the fact that
inquisitors on occasion chose to ban from circulation printed vidas that
other censors had previously approved for publication suggests that not
only the individual hagiographers, but at times the book censors as
well, were not always in sync with the "official" point of view.

I argue in this book that these Lives of New World saints reflect
criollo identity values and concerns. After all, the colonial-era hagiographer was not a monk living in cloistered isolation, but rather an active
member of the Spanish American community who was intimately
acquainted with its values and discourse. His views and concerns—
especially those of a patriotic nature—represented those of the broader community to which he belonged. Thus, his literary endeavor was
in many ways a dialogue between himself and his targeted readership,
the community of actual or potential devotees of his saint. It seems
safe to conclude that if he assigned to his saint a patriotic epithet or
urged pious persons to embrace the cult for patriotic reasons, it was
because he believed such an appeal would resonate with his audience.

That audience, of course, was made up of the relatively elite sectors of colonial society. Even when a hagiographer had the good fortune of publishing his text, the high costs involved usually kept the
number of printed copies to a few hundred. Such printed works, moreover, were expensive, limiting their circulation almost exclusively to the
wealthy sectors of urban society.[40] Can we even assume, then, that
hagiographic texts and the values they promoted penetrated to any significant degree into the middle and non-elite sectors of colonial society? Or would the influence of these costly and often erudite texts have
been limited to a narrow social elite of priests, female convent dwellers,
and wealthy families?

In point of fact, hagiographic literature influenced society in a
number of indirect ways through social interactions as well as literature, liturgy, and religious art. In the first place, the stories and religious
values contained in colonial hagiographies permeated society via the

everyday, informal social contacts between elites and non-elites. Ecclesiastical and civic leaders viewed such informal relations, which often occurred in domestic settings, as optimal for the dissemination of Roman Catholic doctrine, piety, and morality among lower-ranked social types, including indigenous household servants. In 1619, for example, the *cabildo* (city council) of Puebla chose Our Lady of the Immaculate Conception as spiritual patroness of their city and made provisions for celebration of her feast day. In the same act, the cabildo urged poblano elites "to hold to the pious opinion . . . that Our Lady the Virgin Mary was conceived without the blemish of original sin, teach it to their servants and children, defend it, and attempt to introduce it to the souls of all the faithful."[41] The same social dynamic is at work in a number of texts that I examine in later chapters. Juana de Caso, sister of Mariana de Jesús, provided pious instruction to the numerous Indian and mixed-race servants and dependents in her household (see chapter 5). By contrast, the beata Catarina de San Juan was on the receiving end of such instruction; as a domestic servant in urban Puebla, she heard prayers and readings from the lives of the saints in the home of her employers (chapter 6). Although the Jesuit hagiographers of Mariana de Jesús and Catarina de San Juan may have idealized actual events, it is reasonable to assume that some pious families among the socioeconomic elite did take seriously their religious duty of catechizing their household employees and dependents.

Members of the regular clergy employed other strategies for spreading post-Tridentine religious and social ideals. As early as 1578, for example, the Jesuits in New Spain established congregations of laypersons devoted to the Holy Virgin in her various advocations. These lay sodalities fulfilled religious, social, and educational roles in the urban centers of Spanish America. Non-elites as well as elites became members of such religious confraternities. Marian congregations and similar lay sodalities, although usually segregated along lines of race, occupation, and social status, provided opportunities for persons of all social levels to become immersed in the cult of the saints. They heard sermons, recited prayers, sang hymns, and participated in festival processions. As a result, they came in contact with much of the religious and social ideology contained in the Lives of Old and New World saints.[42]

The last point raises a related issue, namely the relationship

between hagiography proper and other texts, whether printed, oral, or iconographic. Hagiography proper influenced society at large not so much directly as indirectly, through its influence on religious histories and chronicles, sermons, art and iconography, and devotional prayers (including novenas). Consider, for example, the chronicles of the various religious orders. These texts, which were historical, religious, and propagandistic in nature, recounted the achievements of a religious order in a certain region. The chronicler usually reserved an entire section of his text for a series of brief vidas of his order's spiritual heroes. For example, in his *Tesoros verdaderos de las indias,* Juan Meléndez disseminates previously published hagiographic treatments of several Dominican holy persons of Peru, including Rosa de Santa María, Martín de Porres, and Fray Vicente Vernedo. Chronicles like *Tesoros verdaderos* exposed a slightly wider readership to abbreviated versions of the saints' virtues and miracles. More importantly, the religious chronicles fueled the imagination of colonial preachers, whose sermons acquainted the faithful with key episodes in the lives of the saints.

The sermon, in both its oral and printed forms, was a very common medium for disseminating key episodes from the less-accessible books of hagiography proper. The saint's Life and the sermon were, in a sense, symbiotic. Upon the death of a holy person who had already attained a significant reputation for sanctity, a member of the clergy would deliver a public funerary oration in his or her honor. This sermon was often published in economical book form, thus extending its influence beyond the funeral and preserving it over time.[43] Future hagiographers might use the printed funerary sermon as a primary source for their own narratives. As I shall show in chapter 5, both a Franciscan chronicler and a Jesuit hagiographer made such use of Alonso Rojas's printed eulogy of Mariana de Jesús. Similarly, authors of late-seventeenth- and eighteenth-century Lives of St. Felipe de Jesús had access to printed sermons by several high-profile Mexico City preachers, including Miguel Sánchez, better known today as a promoter of Our Lady of Guadalupe.[44] The relationship between hagiographer and preacher ran in the other direction as well; following a saint's beatification, preachers often drew the details for their feast-day sermons from published hagiographies. Through the sermon, both spoken and printed, vignettes from the saint's Life became familiar to individuals, including illiterates, who would never have had direct contact with a copy of the actual hagiography. Devout Catholics in Spanish colonies were familiar with specific episodes from Raymond of Capua's fourteenth-century Life of St. Catherine of Siena. In similar fashion, sermons celebrating Felipe de Jesús acquainted the faithful with stories from Baltasar de Medina's seventeenth-century Life of the novohispano saint.

Perhaps the most important "text" that mediated between the literary genre of hagiography proper and all social sectors of colonial Spanish American society was the religious iconography that figured so prominently in both public and private spaces. Statuary, painted canvases, and altarpieces *(retablos)* informed popular spirituality in at least three ways. First, pious art served as the visual focal point for prayer. The holy women whom I discuss in chapters 4, 5, and 6 had their most intimate and powerful religious experiences while in the presence of images of Jesus Christ, the Virgin Mary, and the saints. Second, these texts taught moral lessons like those emphasized in sermons and saints' Lives. In this vein, representations of the Virgin Mary or St. Rosa de Lima functioned as a sort of narrative, clearly illustrating the feminine virtues of obedience, modesty, and sexual purity. Third, the visual image linked the mass of believers to crucial episodes in the saint's life and, hence, to defining aspects of his or her sanctity. For example, a favorite theme for artist-devotees of St. Rosa de Lima, taken directly from the books of hagiography proper, is her mystical marriage to the Baby Jesus (see figure 2.2).[45] Indeed, even if social elites neglected their duty to catechize household servants and dependents, the abundance of religious images in the niches and oratories of their houses provided illiterate members of the household with texts they could see and understand.[46]

It is evident from my sources that non-elites knew how to recognize and replicate saintly behavior. Two of the holy persons examined in this study (Sebastián de Aparicio and Catarina de San Juan) came from non-elite origins and never learned to read. Nevertheless, they assimilated enough of the non-literary discourse on saints and heroic sanctity to emulate and display the moral and spiritual values represented in hagiographic texts.[47] The same can be said for Nicolás Ayllon, the Peruvian Indian who came to be venerated as Nicolás de Dios.[48] Similarly, non-elite witnesses who gave testimony before diocesan or papal investigators demonstrated an ability to recognize a liv-

FIGURE 2.2. "Mystical marriage of St. Rosa and the Christ Child, who is held by the Virgin Mary." This image narrates two famous episodes from the life of St. Rosa, portraying her both as devotee of the Virgin and Child and as spiritual protectress of Lima. Anonymous, oil on canvas, seventeenth century. From José Flores Araoz et al. *Santa Rosa de Lima y su tiempo* (Lima, 1995), 264. (Courtesy of the Colección Barbosa-Stern, Lima, Peru)

ing saint when they saw one, and were strong enough in their belief in the saint to go before ecclesiastical officials and give testimony. For example, an Indian servant in the household of St. Mariana de Jesús witnessed her mistress's austerities and conspired with her to conceal them. This Quechua-speaking domestic named Catalina was also the first to discover the lilies *(azucenas)* blooming in a spot where she had previously deposited Mariana's blood. Likewise, non-elites were among those who bore witness to the virtues and miracles of Sebastián de Aparicio. An examination of the testimonies of non-elite witnesses in the proceso documents reveals that they were familiar with much of the language of saints and sanctity.[49]

But even despite examples of how socioeconomic and racial non-elites came into contact with and adopted the ideologies that permeated the colonial-era vida de santo, there can be no denying that, ultimately, I am examining a dominant or elite discourse. My point has not been to postulate some blind, wholesale adherence by non-elites to the elite discourse found in saints' Lives and related cultural texts. However, in light of the heavy emphasis in recent scholarship on indigenous resistance to European cultural imperialism, I would remind the reader that in the urban centers of imperial and religious power, the rewards of assimilation were great while incentives to resist the dominant discourse were fewer.[50] The case of the nuns of Corpus Christi is illustrative. These indigenous women finally won support for a convent of their own in the early eighteenth century after arguing that they were just as capable of religious devotion and celibacy, if not more so, than the daughters of españoles.[51] As I shall show in the next chapter, ecclesiastical elites often grappled with how to handle the claims of sanctity made on behalf of socially marginal individuals who had mastered the dominant discourse too well.

Holy Immigrant

Old World Continuities
in the Lives of Sebastián de Aparicio

This chapter explores in microcosm the transference of Iberian people and culture to New Spain through a study of the life and hagiographic commemorations of Fray Sebastián de Aparicio, a Galician-born holy man who died in Puebla in 1600. The hagiographies that recount his life elucidate the broader process by which Spaniards adapted their Old World values and cultural forms to a New World context. In the first place, we discover the importance of cultural continuity, as Aparicio's hagiographers portray him as a pious replica of the quintessential medieval saint, St. Francis of Assisi. To these writers of sacred biography, most of them Franciscans, Aparicio's life is a familiar one; his faith, virtues, and miracles remind them of the founder of their religious order. Yet, as we will see, New Spain's unique physical and social environment shapes and transforms Aparicio's practice of the traditional Old World virtues, as well as his supernatural encounters with divine and demonic forces.

But the hagiographic accounts of Aparicio's life reveal more than the transference and adaptation of Old World cultural values and forms to New Spain. These Lives, examined alongside three sermons published in conjunction with Aparicio's 1789 beatification, reflect the Spanish preoccupation with origins and the ambiguous nature of criollo social identity. Like countless Iberian immigrants before and after him, Aparicio belonged to "both Spains," a fact that complicated his identity and multiplied his loyalties. But the same was true for New World criollos, who were forever Spaniards in exile. As this case may suggest, one must proceed with caution when contrasting Old World traditions with their New World adaptations, or peninsulares with their criollo offspring; the categories are not so clear cut.

In the remainder of this chapter, I present a composite narrative of Aparicio's life based on his numerous vidas, followed by a discussion of three seventeenth-century hagiographers and their particular contributions. Then, based on a reading of all three vidas, I elucidate how postconquest conditions in New Spain shaped the contours of Aparicio's sanctity despite its significant continuities with Old World patterns and models. Finally, with an eye to group identity formation in New Spain, I examine certain rhetoric contained in the hagiographies and sermons, noting how both criollo and peninsular writers describe this holy man in reference to their own communities of reference.

The Life and Career of Sebastián de Aparicio

Sebastián de Aparicio was born in the Spanish village of Gudiña, region of Galicia, in 1502.[1] His parents, Juan de Aparicio and Teresa del Prado, were Old Christians, free from the social and religious stigma attached to Jewish origins. Because the family was poor, Aparicio began working at a young age, first tending his parents' small flock of sheep, then farming on a small scale. He later moved to the city of Salamanca, where he served as a domestic servant in the household of a wealthy family. From Salamanca he continued southward to San Lúcar de Barrameda, near the southern seaport of Sevilla. In San Lúcar, Aparicio rose to the position of overseer *(mayordomo)* of farming enterprises for a wealthy *estanciero* of the region, a position he exercised so successfully that the man's estates flourished. From his salary as mayordomo, Aparicio supplied the needs of his elderly parents and set aside enough money to travel to New Spain in 1533, just twelve years after the dramatic defeat of the Aztec federation.

In the emerging Spanish colony known as New Spain, Sebastián de Aparicio became a successful, upwardly mobile entrepreneur. After a brief sojourn in the coastal port of Villarica (Veracruz), he moved to recently founded Puebla, where he began to cultivate wheat and maize. Not long thereafter, he began to breed and train cattle for domestic use in farming and transportation, perhaps the first Spaniard in the region to do so.[2] As a breeder of draft animals, Aparicio forged a partnership with a skilled cart maker and began to transport goods between Veracruz and the Valley of Mexico. Once he was financially able, he struck out on his own, serving the route between the viceregal capital of Mexico City and the Spanish silver-mining town of Zacatecas to the north. At the pinnacle of his success, the middle-aged Aparicio purchased a farm *(hacienda de labor)* near Mexico City and a ranch *(hacienda de ganado)* in Chapultepec, both of which prospered.

The wealth that Aparicio accumulated during his first few decades in New Spain became the basis for successive marriages to two impoverished young women, perhaps adolescents, both of whom died shortly after having married him. According to his personal testimony, each brief marriage was characterized by abstinence from sexual relations. Following the death of his second wife, Aparicio donated his personal property to the recently established female convent of Santa Clara (Mexico City). At the age of seventy-two, he entered the Convento de San Francisco de Puebla as a lay brother, making his profession of vows the following year (1575).[3] Recognizing both his technical skills and reputation for piety, Aparicio's religious superiors named him alms collector *(limosnero)* for the religious house, a role he exercised for the rest of his life. As limosnero, Aparicio traveled a circuit that included both urban spaces and rural hinterlands, interacting with peninsular and criollo *hacendados,* Indian farmers and laborers, black and mulatto artisans, and African slaves. Individuals of all these social sectors would later testify to his sanctity.[4]

When Aparicio died in 1600 at the age of ninety-eight, crowds of laymen and clerics thronged to the poblano convent of San Francisco, proclaiming his sanctity, invoking his intercession, and competing for his relics. An incipient local cult emerged, prompting Bishop Diego Romero and his successor to carry out diocesan inquiries in 1600–4 and 1608, respectively. In the course of these proceedings, numerous witnesses testified that God had miraculously preserved Aparicio's body from normal decay as a sign of divine favor. Moreover, devotees from all social categories began to attribute miracles to his intercession. On the strength of such evidence, Pope Urban VIII opened the first of several papal inquests *(proceso apostólico)* in 1628. In the nearly two centuries that transpired between his death and his papal beatification in 1789, devotees in New Spain and Europe produced numerous hagiographic accounts of his life in Spanish, Latin, and Italian. I turn now to these sacred biographies.

Sebastián de Aparicio: Hagiographic Traditions

Within two years of Aparicio's death, Fray Juan de Torquemada, O.F.M.—best remembered for his three-volume *Monarquía indiana* (1615)—published the first hagiographic account of his life.[5] Responding in part to the rarity of the Torquemada vida, Licenciado Bartolomé Sánchez Parejo[6] wrote *Vida y milagros del . . . padre fray Sebastián de Aparicio* in the 1620s.[7] A physician by training, this avid devotee of Sebastián de Aparicio had interests extending beyond pious topics to include everything from local history to natural science.[8] Bibliographers have attributed to Sánchez Parejo a treatise on the healing qualities of mineral water, as well as an essay on local history entitled *Tratado sobre la origen y nobleza de Puebla de los Angeles,* though neither is extant.[9]

Sánchez Parejo had begun on his own to collect data for a vida of Fray Sebastián around 1626, and when Urban VIII opened the papal inquest in 1628, he hurried to complete the project. Making use of records from the initial diocesan inquest of 1600–4, interviews with local religious who had known Sebastián de Aparicio, and the Torquemada vida, the physician-devotee completed the manuscript and presented it to the judges of the papal inquest on October 1, 1629. One copy accompanied the inquest documents that were sent to Rome while the other remained in the diocesan archives of Puebla.[10] The manuscript remained unpublished until 1965.[11]

A few decades after Sánchez Parejo, Fray Bartolomé de Letona, guardian of the Franciscan Convent of las Llagas of Puebla and official promoter *(procurador general)* of Aparicio's canonization cause, wrote a short Life entitled *Relación auténtica sumaria.* The modern editor of this work describes it as a biography "with a character all its own," distinct from the other Aparicio vidas. The *Relación auténtica sumaria* is unique with regard to its brevity, for it extends to only 108 pages. More unusual still is its function as a catalogue to the cumbersome diocesan and apostolic proceso documents. As the lead Franciscan promoter of Aparicio's cause, Letona's purpose is to facilitate the bureaucratic process and win papal officials to his side. His *Relación auténtica sumaria* provides readers in the Roman Sacred Congregation of Rites with a brief summary of Aparicio's life while rendering the massive inquest documents much more user-friendly. Letona smoothes the way for Aparicio's beatification by muting certain controversial issues that Sánchez Parejo had tackled head-on. The fact that Letona's 1662 manuscript remained unpublished would not have bothered him, for he clearly wrote the work as a guide to proceso documents, not as an inspirational vida for a general readership.

By the 1680s, although devotion to Sebastián de Aparicio was still strong in Puebla, the only published account of his life and sanctity was the increasingly scarce Torquemada vida. In 1687 this situation changed when a criollo named Diego de Leyba, O.F.M., published a two-part sacred biography entitled *Virtudes y milagros en la vida y muerte del V. P. Fr. Sebastián de Aparicio*. This Life was to become the most influential of all the Aparicio hagiographies. At the time of its publication, Leyba was minister-elect of the Franciscan province of Santo Evangelio de México and, like Letona before him, official promoter of Aparicio's cause for canonization. Perhaps more than any of the other Lives of Fray Aparicio, Leyba's *Virtudes y milagros* fulfills the four major hagiographic purposes examined in the last chapter. Together with the hagiographic text itself, the prefatory letters, authored by Leyba and other prominent churchmen of New Spain, make these purposes explicit. The Franciscan author edifies the faithful, honors the various communities who will share in Aparicio's eventual glory, flatters and recruits devotee-patrons, and persuades ecclesiastical officials of the authenticity of his saint.

While the impact of post-Tridentine reform on the novohispano church has not yet been adequately examined by colonial scholars, Leyba's *Virtudes y milagros* provides an intriguing example of how papal centralization of the canonization process was beginning to affect directly the form and content of the colonial Life. Pope Urban VIII's decrees of non cultu had been published in New Spain in 1664. At several points in Leyba's 1687 text, the criollo author directly responds to the papal regulations. For example, in the protesta (disclaimer) that precedes his main narrative, Leyba assures Roman officials that his use of the terms "blessed" and "saint" are honorific and tentative. Moreover, he submits his descriptions of apparent miracles to official evaluation. In

so doing, Leyba assumes an authorial posture that had become commonplace in the published saint's Life of his day.[12]

A second clear hagiographic response to the papal controls
appears in part 2 of *Virtudes y milagros*. Leyba's part 1 consists of four
sections *(libros)* that narrate Aparicio's childhood, his adult years and
marriages, his tenure in the Franciscan order, and his virtues and miracles. In part 2, he describes Aparicio's "happy transition" *(el feliz tránsito)* from mortal life, miracles attributed to his posthumous intercession,
and the efforts made up to that time to secure his canonization. In
Leyba's discussion of the canonization efforts, we find a posture that
was becoming much more common in his day; namely, an attempt to
explain away any apparent violations of the papal rules. Leyba inserts
into his discussion a list of questions that ecclesiastical judges in Puebla
had been instructed to ask in their interviews of the poblano faithful.
The list includes a question about whether local devotees had circulated and venerated painted images depicting Aparicio as a saint, a clear
violation of the non cultu decrees. In response, Leyba acknowledges
earlier indiscretions, but hastens to explain that poblano devotees had
responded to the publication of the papal decrees in 1664 by defacing
a painted image of Fray Sebastián kneeling before the Virgin of
Guadalupe and replacing his likeness with that of the universally recognized San Diego.[13] In addition, he adds, devotees painted a scene
from the life of San Paschal Baylon over a canvas that showed episodes
from Aparicio's life. "Thus it has remained," he assures Roman officials,
"until the church declares [Aparicio] a saint, as is expected."[14] Hopeful
that this demonstration of compliance with the church's antilocal measures will salvage the cause of a potential Franciscan saint, Leyba goes
out of his way to emphasize that Aparicio's devotees are willing to play
by the rules set down by the Sacred Congregation of Rites. His strategic response to the publication of Pope Urban VIII's decrees clearly
demonstrates how papal reform of the canonization process directly
influenced the writing of the saint's Life in the generations after Trent.

Continuities and Innovations
in the Hagiographic Tradition

Writers of New World hagiographies, whether criollos or peninsulares,
understood themselves to be writing new and glorious chapters in the

enduring sacred history of the church triumphant. Even so, they modeled their narratives after such Old World classics as Raymond of Capua's fourteenth-century *Life of St. Catherine of Siena* and St. Bonaventure's thirteenth-century *Life of St. Francis*. Furthermore, they portrayed their protagonists as reflections, even copies, of universally known Old World saints such as Ines of Montepulciano, Vincent Ferrer, or Francis Xavier. They did so for a number of reasons, one of which was the awareness that, according to Roman Catholic tradition and theology, heroic sanctity meant imitation of established models. Until Spanish America had its own native or at least local saints, writers of New World Lives had no option but to compare their holy persons to Old World saints.

Aparicio's hagiographers, most of them Franciscans, reflected in his sanctity the life of the founder of their order. Thus, for example, Diego de Leyba consciously and consistently juxtaposes events in Aparicio's life with episodes from St. Bonaventure's Life of St. Francis. In his prefatory protesta, Leyba offers an a posteriori justification for such comparisons: "In the first place," he notes, "I found sufficient basis [for such a comparison] in [Aparicio's] virtues and deeds, as the reader will soon discover." His second explanation, however, demonstrates the a priori principle that led him to see St. Francis in all aspects of Aparicio's life: "My Religious Order repeats [the following] antiphon to all the saints that have flourished in [the order]: . . . 'You, o blessed Saints of God, . . . imitated Saint Francis, etc.' It seems that the sanctity of all our Order's Saints is a reflection of their imitation of our most Holy Patriarch, and the Venerable Aparicio made great efforts to imitate him."[15] Leyba's argument, although somewhat circular in nature, illustrates Rubial García's assertion that post-Tridentine hagiographers were attentive to "the paradigmatic" *(lo modélico),* as well as to the historical person who lived and acted in place and time.

The Aparicio vidas narrate spirituality that is firmly rooted in the physical setting of the novohispano landscape where he lived and died. In New Spain, Aparicio's asceticism requires him, with occasional exceptions, to eat only what is available to poor Indians, namely corn tortillas and chili peppers.[16] In addition, the severe seasonal floods and hailstorms, so frequently described in the earliest Spanish histories of the region around Puebla, provide a context for his virtues and miracles.[17] Furthermore, Aparicio sees demonic apparitions and divine theo-

phanies of a decidedly novohispano quality: angels appear as Indians
in native dress, while demons take the form not only of the traditional female seductress, but also of the black man brandishing farming
tools as lethal weapons.[18]

Sánchez Parejo's description of Aparicio's interactions with a
stingy hacienda owner includes a reference to one such theophany (see
figure 3.1). The hacendado, it seems, had half-heartedly promised to
donate two fanegas of corn to the Franciscans. Yet every time Aparicio attempted to collect the grain, the man put him off. One Tuesday
during Lent, Aparicio stopped in at the hacienda and urged the man
to make good on his promise. Upon realizing that the elderly friar was
unaccompanied, the hacendado pointed to a mound of corn and, making no offer to help him load the grain, replied, "Father Aparicio, you
may take it now." But as the tight-fisted hacendado watched from his
house, he witnessed a miracle; as Aparicio began to load the grain onto
his shoulder, two men appeared out of nowhere to aid him. Sánchez
Parejo describes them as "well-built and eager Indians," identifiable by
the traditional white indigenous garments *(tilmas)* they wore. After filling Aparicio's cart, they disappeared as quickly as they had appeared,
leaving the hacendado astonished and ashamed. "From now on," he
promised Aparicio, "I will deny you nothing in my house."[19]

In hagiographic terms, this episode demonstrates for Sánchez
Parejo's readers that, in Aparicio's ability to convert stubborn, hypo-
critical hearts like that of the unwilling donor, his sanctity bears the
imprint of St. Francis. On a moral level, the anecdote of the stingy
hacendado displays the sanctity of Fray Aparicio as an antidote to
greed and closed-handedness toward God and his servants, the Franciscans. And yet there is something new here; exotic, angelic Indians
inhabit this otherwise traditional vignette, reflecting perhaps the Spanish preoccupation with the ethnic and religious "other."[20]

While the physical setting of New Spain—its foods, climate, and
exotic peoples—shapes the sanctity of Fray Aparicio, the region's
unique social conditions influence the practice and perception of traditional Roman Catholic sanctity at a more fundamental level. New
World conditions required new expressions of such enduring virtues as
humility, patience, chastity, and love for God and men. In a recent discussion of Francisco Losa's 1613 Life of Gregorio López, an Iberian-
born man who lived much of his life as a hermit in New Spain, Jodi

Los Angeles en figura de Indios, asisten al B.ᵗᵒ Aparizio, y le cargan la limosna en un Mulo

FIGURE 3.1. "Los Angeles en figura de Indios, asisten al Bᵗᵒ Aparizio, y le cargan la limosna en un Mulo." (Angels in the form of Indians aid Blessed Aparicio, helping him to load the alms onto a mule.) Illustration from Mateo Ximénez, *Colección de estampas que representan los principales pasos, hechos y prodigios del beato Frai Sebastián de Aparizio* (Roma, 1789). The 110 engravings are by Pedro Bombelli. (Courtesy of the Bancroft Library, University of California, Berkeley)

Bilinkoff argues that Losa constructs both López and himself as "much needed models of male behavior in a frontier society."[21] While the writing of the exemplary life was a "traditional Christian enterprise," she adds, "it was undertaken with special urgency in a society in which images of greedy and violent settlers and corrupt clerics dominated the cultural landscape." Bilinkoff's analysis provides a wonderful framework for understanding the New World narratives of Aparicio's life, especially in their description of the four decades that preceded his entry into the Franciscan order. While Aparicio replicates the life of St. Francis, his hagiographers portray him—entrepreneur, farmer, neighbor, and husband—in sharp contrast to prevailing social mores of postconquest New Spain.[22]

In 1533, Aparicio had immigrated to a land recently denominated New Spain, where transformations of all sorts were underway, some superficial, others irreversible and even devastating. Hernán Cortés's legendary defeat of the Aztec federation had been followed by the subjugation of indigenous populations beyond the Nahua core of Mexico's Central Valley. These Spanish victors, from the highest ranking to the lowest, sought to reward themselves with the economic and social spoils of conquest: land, tribute payments, and a steady labor supply, as well as a social rank and title beyond what they had enjoyed back in Spain. This small but growing Spanish population, which was characterized by its competitiveness, obsession with upward mobility, and disdain for labor, was given to periodic violence. More than one contemporary observer complained that every Spaniard in New Spain desired to be called a gentleman. This dog-eat-dog society, devoid of a spirit of social solidarity even between Spaniards, cried out for individuals to practice the Christian virtues.[23]

At the invitation of Cortés, Fray Martín de Valencia's twelve Franciscan "apostles" had arrived in 1524 to evangelize the region's indigenous peoples, followed by the Order of Preachers (Dominicans) two years later.[24] These two orders, along with the Augustinians who arrived in 1533, employed both time-tested and innovative methods in their efforts to effect major religious transformations. They founded new institutions and structures, such as the Indian doctrina, as well as the traditional urban *convento*. Some of the cities and towns where the mendicant orders settled, such as Mexico City–Tenochtitlán, rose on the foundations of pre-existing indigenous sites; others, including the city of Puebla, where Aparicio would live for many years as a Franciscan lay brother, were completely new settlements. While the contemporary observer may question the friars' evangelization project and the cultural assumptions on which it was based, there can be little doubt that these Spanish religious were devoted to their task. While they participated in the broader process of Spanish domination, they often found themselves at odds with laymen over the exploitative treatment of indigenous peoples. They objected to these abuses primarily on religious grounds, for the ultimate good in their view was the conversion and maturation of an indigenous church.

The response of the earliest Franciscans to the winner-take-all environment of the immediate postconquest period can be more clearly understood by examining their reasons for urging the Audiencia de México to found the city of Puebla in 1530.[25] According to Fray Toribio de Benavente, or Motolinía as he was popularly known, the Friars Minor pleaded with the audiencia judges "to found a town of Spaniards who would give themselves to cultivating the earth and making farming estates *(labranzas y heredades)* as is done in Spain." The objective, suggests Motolinía, was to "gather into towns the many Spaniards who were going about aimlessly, as vagabonds," waiting to be awarded their own allotments of Indians. If such men received land grants, they would develop a love for the novohispano patria and remain there rather than attempt to make a quick fortune and return to Spain. The foundation of towns like Puebla, Motolinía explains, would contribute to the friars' ultimate aims vis-à-vis the Indian population; a stable community of Spanish farmers "would provide the native peoples with a good example of Christianity and of work in the Spanish style."[26] In this particular case, Franciscan interests coincided with those of the Spanish crown and the royal appointees in the Audiencia de México, all of whom sought to diminish the power and influence of the ambitious *encomendero* class.[27] When Puebla was formally established with solemn ceremonies during Easter of 1530, Motolinía said the town's first mass.[28]

Motolinía's historical account of the foundation of Puebla points to the social ills among lay Spaniards that its founders sought to eliminate. The first was a lack of any long-term commitment to the land and its cultivation, exacerbated by a seignorial disdain for work. The second was a competitiveness and individualism that undermined social solidarity not just between Spanish victors and Indian subjects, but between Spaniard and Spaniard. Finally, the Spanish laymen's exploitative treatment of the local natives undermined the missionary orders' efforts to transform indigenous culture in terms of both production and faith.

As this discussion suggests, the interests of friars and Spanish laymen often collided, especially during the sixteenth-century era of institution building and legal codification. In order to achieve their goals as evangelizers, the mendicant orders sought royal support for the segregation of New Spain's indigenous peoples from the Spanish sector, a strategy that met with some success in the immediate postconquest period. In the last quarter of the sixteenth century, however, this strategy began to break down; King Philip II (reigned 1556–98) ordered the gradual transference of the Indian parishes (doctrinas) from mendicant to episcopal control, a process that continued throughout the colonial period despite mendicant efforts to slow it.[29]

As their ability to segregate their Indian neophytes from the influences and exploitation of Spanish laymen diminished, the friars resorted to a second strategy. In cities such as Puebla, where friars interacted with Spanish laymen in their convent churches as well as in the streets, they attempted to shape lay devotion and morality through preaching. During the seventeenth and eighteenth centuries, they found in Sebastián de Aparicio a perfect model for preaching to the competitive, status-conscious Spanish sector.

Consider for a moment Aparicio's credentials as a layman. Having lived much of his life "in the world" before joining the Franciscan order, he was a moral model with which a broad sector of novohispano society could identify.[30] Like other farmers, hacienda owners, and artisans, he had aspired to socioeconomic betterment, rising from day laborer to mayordomo to artisan-entrepreneur to landowner. He had dealt with intractable livestock, unpredictable weather, and dishonest competitors, not to mention constant requests for material aid from indigent persons. As hacendado, he had employed Indian laborers and exerted influence among his fellow landowners in strategic matters such as sowing, reaping, and marketing. As a man twice married, he had experienced conflict with in-laws over matters of dowry, inheritance, and his unwillingness to sire offspring. Even his life as a lay brother within the Franciscan order, characterized by constant travel and manual occupation, more closely approximated the piety of the local laity than that of his fellow friars. As Aparicio's seventeenth-century hagiographers narrated his pre-Franciscan years, and to some degree his years in the order, they created texts that preachers and iconographers could reinterpret in the future, thus exerting new influences on the piety and moral behavior of the Catholic faithful.

Aparicio's hagiographers portray him as a sanctified social climber whose hard work, charity, and social conscience were Christian antidotes for the sloth, selfish greed, and social oppression of the day. Sánchez Parejo calls frequent attention, for example, to his protagonist's energetic zeal for hard work. Beginning with his narration of Aparicio's professional ascent in Spain, Sánchez Parejo lauds his protagonist's aversion to idleness, describing him as "a man of steel." While overseer of the estancia near San Lúcar de Barrameda, Aparicio's "care and vigilance" resulted in record harvests and a raise in salary. In New Spain he abandoned grain farming for domestication of cattle, which better "employed his indomitable strength."[31] Sánchez Parejo even notes that when the aging Aparicio left the carting trade for the less grueling life of farming and cattle raising, he continued to toil and sweat, working alongside the indigenous laborers whom he employed.[32] In a society of status-conscious Spaniards generally contemptuous of manual labor but willing to expropriate the labor of others, Sebastián de Aparicio would have stood out as a pious man whose wealth was legitimate because he earned it with his own hands. His exemplary hard work, moreover, served as a tacit condemnation of the pretentious seignorial lifestyle to which so many Spanish immigrants aspired.

While Aparicio's hard work provided a counterpoint to *hidalgo* idleness, his willingness to give away his profits served as an exemplary antidote for selfish individualism. In this he imitated his Old World model, St. Francis of Assisi, whose life narrative centers around his decision to renounce his father's wealth, give his inheritance to the poor, and live a life of evangelical poverty. In a *novohispano* society deficient in social solidarity, Aparicio renounces his own personal wealth not only by eventually endowing the female Convent of Santa Clara, but also by joyfully aiding indigent persons in the decades prior to that pious act. By such actions, suggests Leyba, Aparicio proved that he was no lover of money.[33]

During his years as a cart builder and transporter of goods, Aparicio earned a reputation as a Good Samaritan who favored poor travelers with kindness and alms. As a fairly wealthy hacienda owner, he refused to hoard his wealth, preferring instead to give food and seed to needy neighbors, lend tools and money without interest, pay the obligations of debtors, and aid poor Indians, blacks, and castas.[34] This holy dissipation of his personal wealth contrasted markedly with the practices of the society in which he lived, where debtors were jailed, Indians were overworked, and competing neighbors and groups engaged each other in constant litigation. In an era when powerful hacienda owners not only withheld aid from smaller holders, but even attempted to usurp their lands, Aparicio spent his life "working for no other reason than to help those in need."[35]

For Aparicio's hagiographers, however, his decision to marry at the age of sixty, despite his previous commitment to practice perpetual chastity, was his most remarkable act of Christian charity.[36] As they point out, his motivations for contracting two successive marriages were the complementary desires of securing companionship for himself and rescuing impoverished young Spanish women from the predicaments *(estropiezos)* they would have faced outside of marriage.[37] Even prior to these marriages, note his hagiographers, the charitable layman had provided dowries for several such women: "With his gracious alms and kind gifts," explains Sánchez Parejo, "he remedied many daughters of poor men and put them in a [marriageable] state, turning them away from worldly temptations *(las ocasiones del mundo)*." His acts of charity were not occasional; Aparicio was in fact "unable to fully enjoy any day in which he did not exercise works of Christian kindness and fraternal compassion, giving no thought to the erosion of the fortune that he had acquired through so much hard work."[38] Sánchez Parejo's statement highlights not only Aparicio's socially conscious practice of Christian charity, but also the lack of desirable social options available to undowried Spanish women. He assumes the inevitability of sexual sin for any woman who is unable to "remedy" her situation through an advantageous marriage.[39] While similar social conditions existed in Spain as well as her colonies, the more volatile social and economic realities of New Spain exacerbated the problems faced by Spanish families and their daughters.

Thus, despite his marginal social origins, Aparicio's material success in New Spain made him a target for Spanish fathers seeking advantageous marriages for their daughters. The first of many offers came not long after Aparicio settled in Atzcapozalco, near Mexico City.[40] According to Sánchez Parejo, "a noble hidalgo of that town who was wanting in temporal goods" had secretly plotted with family members to corner Aparicio into marrying his daughter. To that end, the man made a social call to his hard-working neighbor. "Señor Aparicio," the man began, "It would please me greatly if you *(vuestra merced)* would do me the honor of coming to my house; I have a certain matter to discuss with you that interests both of us." On the appointed day, Aparicio arrived at the man's home only to find to his utter embarrassment that he had no other option but to sit right beside his host's attractive young daughter. Following a brief exchange of pleasantries, the would-be father-in-law got right down to business, declaring his desire for Aparicio to marry his daughter. For his part, Aparicio attempted to decline the proposal without causing offense. He offered numerous excuses, including the argument that, as "a man from the countryside," he could never please a city girl. As the girl's father repeatedly rebuffed his protestations, Aparicio, who was aware of the family's material straits, asked about the girl's dowry. To his consternation, her father immediately promised to hand over an estancia, along with some other lands. Unready to capitulate, Aparicio replied that, because he had land enough already, he preferred a cash payment. The ambitious father remained unflappable. He and his relatives proposed a payment of six hundred pesos, to be made immediately. It was at this point that Aparicio, now desperate for an out, declared, "I will match your offer with an equal amount." Having explained that he was not yet interested in marrying, Aparicio dismissed himself and went home. Though poorer by six hundred pesos, he had guarded his vow of perpetual chastity while providing material aid to a fellow Spaniard and his daughter.

Yet as I have already indicated, Aparicio's story does not end there. As the hacendado grew older, he began to feel the need for companionship. As a result, his feelings about marriage—though not about perpetual chastity—changed. At age sixty, he contracted the first of two short-lived marriages "for the sole purpose of sheltering the young girl under the shadow of his riches, just as he had agreed with her father." Hagiographer Torquemada reports that the girl must have been very young, for an older woman had once told him that Aparicio frequently took his young wife to her house for the purpose of learning female handicrafts like sewing. The implication, of course, was that the girl had not yet learned these skills. Indeed, she was so young, the woman had explained to Torquemada, that she would pilfer whatever monies she could from her elderly husband in order to buy toys.[41]

Aparicio chose to observe sexual continence within the sacramental institution of marriage—a practice that historian Dyan Elliott calls "spiritual marriage"—in imitation of Saints Joseph and Mary, as well as "other saints of the church." Although he took his meals with his young wife and rarely left her alone, observes Sánchez Parejo, Aparicio showed great prudence at bedtime: "He would put her to bed as if she were his own daughter and, having prayed the Rosary, . . . would lie down at the foot of the bed on a mat or a skin." Despite this exemplary treatment, however, the girl's parents soon began to complain, indignant that Aparicio should "disdain [their daughter] and pay her so little attention." Always the peacemaker, Aparicio reassured his parents-in-law of his best intentions for their daughter, who would inherit all his properties if she survived him. This reply did not sway the angry parents, who attributed his behavior not to the virtuous practice of chastity, but to a lack of natural feelings. However, not long after the parents threatened to annul the union, their young daughter died. As a result, Aparicio was freed from an unpleasant predicament.[42]

Aparicio married a second time at around age sixty-three, "proposing to maintain the same purity and chastity as in the first marriage."[43] This second union followed the pattern of the first: marriage to a poor girl in exchange for companionship, abstention from sexual relations, and complaints from in-laws who wanted a grandchild in order to secure Aparicio's inheritance for their lineage.[44] As with the first marriage, the second union did not last long; the young wife fell from a tree and died only eight months into the marriage.

Some years after Aparicio died and the church began to investigate his sanctity, questions arose as to whether this otherwise saintly man had violated the church's teaching on the procreative purpose of marriage.[45] For my purposes here, it is sufficient to note how Aparicio's practice of two mutually conflicting virtues—one a chaste denial of the flesh in imitation of the saints of old, the other a charity required by the absence of social solidarity in novohispano society—illustrates both continuity and discontinuity in New World modes of sanctity.

As a layman, Aparicio was a model of Christian virtue not only in his work ethic and charity, but also in his indirect contribution to the friars' program of conversion and acculturation of the indigenous peoples of New Spain. Although his hagiographers do not articulate Aparicio's virtue in these exact terms, their narratives are suggestive of how the virtues of laymen might contribute to the mendicants' goals.

The Franciscans who encouraged the foundation of Puebla in 1530 envisioned the introduction of Iberian farming know-how to the indigenous communities of New Spain. Rather than condone the practice of Spanish hidalgos living on the sweat of native producers, they sought to establish a town of Spanish farmers who would provide the indigenous peoples with "a good example of Christianity and of work in the Spanish style."[46] Their project found support with Vasco de Quiroga, a member in 1530 of the Audiencia de México, who began establishing experimental neo-utopian towns in 1532. Sebastián de Aparicio, who settled near Puebla soon after his arrival in New Spain, provided the sort of example that the friars desired. By producing both wheat and maize, the staple grains of Spain and Mesoamerica, Aparicio satisfied two groups of consumers while contributing to the hybridization of the novohispano economy. In addition, his hagiographers intimate that he was the first Spaniard in New Spain to breed and train cattle for domestic use.[47] The use of large animals for transportation and farming was unknown among the region's indigenous peoples; lacking draft animals and wheel technology, they had relied for centuries on human porters. The arrival of Spaniards and Africans would revolutionize transportation; Aparicio seems to have been an early participant in a transformation process that the mendicant orders favored.[48]

A central theme in medieval Catholic hagiography, particularly in the Lives and iconography of St. Francis of Assisi, is the holy person's ability to move persons and creatures around him or her to obedience, repentance, or greater piety. Sometimes that influence is described in terms of social influence: the saint does a good deed or speaks a word of exhortation and the hearers respond. In other cases, the holy person's ability to influence belongs to the realm of the miraculous. The hagiographers of Aparicio, intent upon portraying him as a latter-day version of St. Francis, describe similar demonstrations of spiritual power in the life of their protagonist.[49] On one occasion, as Aparicio and his Indian companion were returning to the Convento de San Francisco with a cartload of donated grain, they decided to take a rest, pausing unwittingly near an anthill. Upon noticing that ants were carrying off large quantities of grain, Aparicio warned them: "The wheat you have stolen belongs to St. Francis, so be careful." The very next morning, Aparicio found his cargo intact, without a single grain missing.[50]

Miracles like this, in which God empowers the saint to exercise spiritual authority over living creatures, is relatively common in hagiographic discourse and certainly not unique to the New World context. Nevertheless, Alex García-Rivera has argued that in the multiethnic, caste-conscious society of colonial Spanish America, this Catholic tradition took on new shades of meaning. García-Rivera highlights an episode in the life of St. Martín de Porres, a mulatto Dominican lay brother of seventeenth-century Lima, who through the spiritual power of his words moved a dog, a cat, and a mouse to eat from a common food dish without any conflict whatsoever. García-Rivera suggests that, given the social divisions in colonial Peruvian society and Fray Martín's frequent self-characterizations as "a mulatto dog," this episode of the coexisting creatures may represent the three major ethnic groups of the day, Spaniards, Indians, and blacks.[51] In similar fashion, Aparicio's ability to calm and command wild creatures is not limited to the thieving ants, singing birds, or angry bulls that one finds in medieval European discourse. In the violent and unstable social setting of immediate post-conquest New Spain, his power extended to a group of "creatures" on New Spain's northern frontier, namely, the seminomadic indigenous peoples known collectively as the Chichimecas.

The opening of the frontier route between Mexico City and the silver mines of Zacatecas after 1546 had brought Spaniards into contact with these indomitable peoples, whom the sedentary indigenous groups of central Mexico alternately disdained for their uncivilized customs and feared for their warlike ferocity. Around 1550, the Chichimecas began to make raids on Spanish silver traffic, thus posing a direct threat to the emerging colonial economy. While individual Spaniards met violence with violence, the colonial government failed to develop any consistent or organized response. After efforts at conciliation failed during the 1550s and 1560s, Viceroy Martín Enríquez implemented an unsuccessful policy of all-out war. In response, ecclesiastical officials who gathered in 1585 for the Third Mexican Provincial Council debated the morality of the anti-Chichimeca campaigns. Eventually, Spanish colonial authorities mitigated the Chichimeca threat through a policy of diplomacy and acculturation, including religious conversion.[52]

Aparicio's hagiographers explain how, as a carter in the region, his reputation for liberality and justice won him Chichimeca trust (see figure 3.2).[53] For example, the Chichimecas gave fruit and other gifts to their Christian friend and helped him with his work "without risk of being seized or mistreated by the Spanish soldiers who patrolled the land." With the advantage of hindsight, Aparicio's seventeenth-century hagiographers drew an important moral lesson; whereas most Spaniards had alienated the seemingly untamable Chichimecas by answering their threats with violence, Aparicio the holy man had subdued these wild creatures with "good works, attentive hospitality, and generous alms."[54] From the Franciscan perspective, Aparicio was not simply a peacemaker in the modern sense, but a contributor to their order's highest goal in New Spain, the conversion of the indigenous peoples.

Aparicio replicated the sanctity of St. Francis not only in his ability to tame wild creatures, but also in his capacity for softening the hard hearts of his fellow Christians.[55] Social conditions in New Spain provided him numerous opportunities to exercise this virtue. After his success and wealth won for him a position of influence in local society, Aparicio exercised that influence for pious ends. For example, he often intervened on behalf of Indians and blacks whose masters treated them unjustly. He would entreat such masters saying, "For God's sake, have mercy on these wretched ones who are temperamental *(antojadizos)* and will not wish to serve you any better than you treat them." More often than not, his admonitions "settled the masters' hearts and calmed their spirits, so that from then on [their Indians] received better treatment and reception than before."[56] In a chapter entitled "On the Zeal of Father Fray Sebastián for the Honor of God and the Well-Being of his Neighbors *(prójimos),*" Sánchez Parejo describes an intervention that occurred when a benefactress of the Convento de San Francisco stopped in to deliver her usual alms. The woman, a resident of nearby Cholula, owned one of the many *obrajes* (textile factories) of that town. Working conditions in these textile factories were notoriously bad for the Indians and poor castas who labored in them. When Aparicio saw the woman, he graciously received her pious gift but rebuked her with

Encuentra el Bᵒ en este viaje a los Indios Chichimecos, el los regala y ellos lo tratan bien

FIGURE 3.2. "Encuentra el Bᵒ en este viaje a los Indios Chichimecos, el los regala y ellos lo tratan bien." (Blessed [Aparicio] meets Chichimec Indians in his travels; he gives them gifts and they treat him well.) Illustration from Mateo Ximénez, *Colección de estampas que representan los principales pasos, hechos y prodigios del beato Frai Sebastián de Aparizio* (Roma, 1789). (Courtesy of the Bancroft Library, University of California, Berkeley)

words of spiritual warning: "Sister, sell your obraje now, for if you do not, you place your [eternal] salvation at risk." His words were efficacious, for without delay "she opened the door and released the Indians that she had maintained locked up in her obraje."[57]

By introducing Spanish methods of farming, cattle domestication, and wheeled transport, Aparicio the layman participated in the mendicant orders' larger goals of acculturating novohispano Indians to Spanish ways. His peaceful, winning ways with the Chichimeca peoples of the northern frontier offered an alternative to the military solution pursued by other Spanish laymen. And his defense of the socially defenseless, especially Indians, was consistent with the early Franciscans' self-perception as paternal protectors who shielded their spiritual charges from the exploitation and depredation of Spanish laymen.[58] In all these ways, the living example of Aparicio the pious layman was a fitting representation of Franciscan goals in postconquest New Spain. Of course, his seventeenth-century hagiographers explain his actions not in the modern secular language of social solidarity, but in terms of traditional Christian virtues.

Questions of Identity in the Lives of Fray Aparicio

The saintly persona emerging from the Lives of Fray Aparicio provides us with a clear example of how New World conditions shaped both the actual practice of Christian virtue and the hagiographic interpretation of the holy life. Yet to affirm that Aparicio's virtue has a distinctly novohispano flavor begs the sort of questions about identity and origins that are the focus of this book. Can Aparicio be treated as a local, novohispano saint? More importantly from a historical perspective, how did the Catholic faithful of Puebla, whether criollo or peninsular in origin, view him? To put it another way, which community (or communities) could claim his spiritual glory as its own? A consideration of the last question will reinforce my earlier assertion that place of origin played a crucial part in Spanish conceptions of individual or corporate identity, for both Iberians and New World criollos.

Anyone who searches Sánchez Parejo's *Vida y milagros* for declarations of criollo or poblano pride will be disappointed. That is not to say that patriotic motivations are irrelevant to his hagiographic project, but only that such motivations, if they do exist, are not easily discernible. There is a hint of local pride in Sánchez Parejo's brief description of the city of Puebla and the surrounding region.[59] Unfortunately, his *Tratado sobre la origen y nobleza de Puebla de los Angeles* has not survived; a glimpse at that local history might give some idea of how poblano localism informed his hagiographic project.

Various factors may explain the absence of criollo rhetoric in *Vida y milagros*. In the first place, Sánchez Parejo never published his manuscript. Had he done so, he might well have revised the text, thus rendering more explicit his various authorial aims. He certainly would have included in a published work the prefatory documents—prologue, letter of dedication, disclaimer, etc.—in which authors explain and justify their literary projects. A second explanation relates to chronology; while criollos were developing a stronger sense of self-consciousness by the 1620s, they were not as exuberant in their patriotism as they would be by century's end. Finally, a third and perhaps decisive factor has to do with the personal origins of his subject. Sebastián de Aparicio was Iberian by birth; much as they might desire to, the criollos of New Spain could not fully claim him as their own.

In contrast, Letona's 1662 manuscript guide to the proceso documents and Leyba's 1685 *Virtudes y milagros* contain tantalizing hints of how peninsulares and criollos viewed Aparicio's identity as well as their own. Letona, a native of the northern Iberian region of Vizcaya, had joined the Franciscan province of Cantabria (Spain) as a young man before transferring to the novohispano province of Santo Evangelio. The opening paragraph of his *Relación auténtica sumaria* contains the following statement: "And today, July 25 of this year of sixty-two, the celebrated day of the Apostle James, General Patron of the Spanish Monarchy and . . . of our saint [Aparicio], I begin [to write] his *relación*."[60] Having linked Aparicio and his cult to that of Santiago, Letona enumerates the regions and communities that had come to cherish him: "Galicia admired him in his earliest years. Mexico and its entire kingdom later experienced his virtues and charity for thirty-three years. The diocese of Puebla venerated him for thirty-four years as a famous universal benefactor of everyone in need." Recognizing that Aparicio's glory is a shared good, Letona predicts that the Kingdoms of Galicia and New Spain will look upon Aparicio with "singular devotion, . . . due to the interest and honor that will be theirs as a result of his canonization."[61]

Like Letona, the poblano author Leyba appeals to the sense of collective interest of his various constituencies of readers. Several of the prefatory documents in his *Virtudes y milagros* urge devotion from the various communities that can rightly take pride in this holy man. The four Franciscan signatories of the book's censura eulogize Aparicio as one "who honored Spain with his birth, our America with his life, the most religious Convent of Puebla with his death *(tránsito),* and the church with his incorruptible body." They rejoice, moreover, that Aparicio's elevation to the altar will "give glory to God, much distinction to our Sacred Religion [the Franciscan order], and to this Holy Province [Santo Evangelio] a son who proves its worth." That Leyba's primary appeal is to the collective pride of his own religious order is also clear in the aprobación, where Fray Francisco Sobrecasas notes how many saints have arisen within "the Province of the Sacred Family in Mexico" and lauds the order's saintly record throughout the world.[62]

Leyba attaches an intriguing appendix to the end of his Life, namely, a "Catalogue of Saints Born in Galicia" which he borrows from Fray Felipe de la Gandara's *Historia eclesiástica de Galicia.* Why, one may wonder, does a novohispano hagiographer include in his sacred biography an unnecessary feature that explicitly places the story of his protagonist within the sacred history of Galicia? Is this nothing more than a reflection of the fact that, since New Spain has no established saints of its own, the novohispano hagiographer must establish typological links between the New World saint and Old World precursors? Or, perhaps, does Leyba hope through this strategy to win potential devotees and patrons among the Iberian-born community in both Old and New Spain? Whatever the author's intent, his inclusion of this important paratextual element undermines any claim the criollo community of New Spain might wish to make on Aparicio's glory, while it reinforces the identification between this holy man and his Old World compatriots.

During the last half of the eighteenth century, some three-quarters of a century after Leyba published his text, the reform-minded Bourbon monarchy and the peninsular immigrant community began to reassert themselves in New Spain. While the crown began a systematic campaign to wrest administrative and fiscal control of its colonies from the criollo establishment, new waves of Iberian-born males crossed the Atlantic in search of economic opportunity. Historical studies of this period in New Spain have described the prototypical career path of the young Spanish immigrant who worked his way up through the family commercial business, branched into silver mining or finance, and eventually married into an established novohispano family.[63] As this pattern suggests, it would be misleading to overgeneralize about antagonisms between criollos and peninsular newcomers, for many first-generation criollos were the children of immigrant fathers, giving them natural linkages and affinities with the Iberian expatriate communities of Puebla, Mexico City, or Guadalajara. Even so, just as events in modern times have shown how political and economic clashes often awaken old ethnic antagonisms or provoke new ones, so also the anti-criollo policies of the Bourbon reformers gave rise to new criollo-peninsular antagonisms.

Textual evidence from this period suggests that peninsular elites in New Spain had patriotic reasons of their own for promoting the cult of Fray Aparicio. In New Spain, these immigrants and their children maintained their sense of Iberian identity by participating in corporations, often trade guilds or religious confraternities *(cofradía)*, that tended to consist of homogeneous social groups. The Congregation of Santiago was one such entity. Founded in Mexico City around 1769, this confraternity took an active role in the promotion of Aparicio's *causa* and in the proclamation of his beatification in 1790–91.

In 1769, Cuban-born José Manuel Rodríguez, whose parents were probably Iberian-born, published in Mexico City a Life of Aparicio entitled *Vida prodigiosa del siervo de Dios fray Sebastián de Aparicio.* By this date, positive steps in the beatification process had energized Aparicio's devotees for one final push toward their ultimate objective. Though Rodríguez was Cuban-born and thus technically a New World criollo, his literary product conveys no sense whatsoever of criollo pride. The first evidence that this work is in fact a piece of peninsular patriotism appears on the frontispiece, which bears the following inscription: "The natives and those with origins in the most noble realm of Galicia who reside in this royal city *(corte)* dedicate [this book] to the most Illustrious Señor D. Manuel Ventura Figueroa." In the dedicatoria, five representatives of the viceregal capital's Congregation of Santiago present their friend and patron, Galician-born Ventura Figueroa, with a virtual manifesto of peninsular, and more particularly, gallego pride. These five gallego transplants, including one Agustín de Quintela, seek the support of Ventura Figueroa for two reasons. First, as a well-connected member of the royal Council of Castile, Ventura Figueroa had already used his influence at Madrid and Rome to secure the foundation of the Congregation of Santiago itself, thus endearing him to the peninsular expatriate community of Mexico City. Second, they are certain that the "sentiment inherent in Patriotism" will sufficiently motivate Ventura Figueroa to aid Aparicio's causa. Referring to their would-be saint as "Honor and Glory of the Kingdom of Galicia," the gallego petitioners confess their own "desire to see such an illustrious Compatriot adored on the Altars in our own day."[64]

Devotees of Sebastián de Aparicio rejoiced in 1789 when Pope Pius VI beatified their saint, established his feast day on February 25, and permitted the observance of his cult in the dioceses of Mexico City, Puebla, Guatemala, Orense (Spain), and Astorga (Spain), as well as within the Franciscan order.[65] The contents of three celebratory sermons reveal how differently criollos and peninsulares viewed this happy development, however.

In October 1790, not long after official news of the beatification arrived in New Spain, solemn ceremonies were observed at the Franciscan Convento de las Llagas in Puebla. Two sermons preached on this occasion convey the criollo perspective. For example, in his *Panegírico sagrado del B. Sebastián de Aparicio* (published 1792), Mexico City native José Carmona, O.F.M., refers to Aparicio in the following terms: "Galicia's laudable honor, singular distinction of Mexico [City], and the most glorious splendor of this Noble City [Puebla]. Indeed, honor, distinction, and splendor of both Spains: the Old, which provided his cradle, and the New, which prepared his tomb."[66] In the Carmona text, Aparicio is no more gallego than novohispano, "the honor, luster, and splendor of both Spains."

A slightly different picture emerges from José Miguel Aguilera's *Elogio Christiano del B. Sebastián de Aparicio,* published in Mexico City in 1791. Aguilera, who dedicates his work to Pueblan Bishop Salvador Biempica y Sotomayor, divides his sermon into two distinct sections. In the first half (3–17), where Aparicio appears as a saint of the Church Universal, Aguilera locates Aparicio's practice of chaste marriage within a broader sacred history of this practice.[67] The emphasis of the preacher-author here is on historic continuity, as he presents Aparicio as participant in a previously authorized Christian tradition.

In the second half of his eulogy (17–23), Aguilera invites his audience-readership to recognize "our own particular interests": "It is impossible," notes this native of Tlayacapa, "that [Blessed Aparicio] should be indifferent towards the happiness of those of us who are fortunate enough to inhabit these lands."[68] The lands to which Aguilera refers include both Puebla and Galicia. Accordingly, the criollo author praises "happy Puebla de los Angeles, most fortunate of American lands, ever-fruitful church." But the Spanish preoccupation with origins seems to shape the sentences that follow, as the criollo author finds it necessary to affirm that the poblano church may indeed claim an Iberian-born saint as its own. Aguilera assures his criollo listeners that "Fray Sebastián is legitimately yours, truthfully yours, [since] you sheltered him in your breast with indescribable piety, [and helped make] the last third of his precious life so meritorious." Because the poblanos had received and nurtured Aparicio, argues Aguilera, "you have incontestable rights!"

But Aguilera is obliged to acknowledge that these "incontestable rights" to the glory and intercession of Aparicio belong to Galicia as well. Aguilera praises the remote northwest corner of Spain as "a region to which all of Spain is indebted for your temporal and spiritual felicity, which has given so many saints to the church, so many heroes to the world." "To you," he adds, "this America will be eternally grateful." Comparing Aparicio to a "textbook-perfect *(compendioso)* map" demarcating the straightest route to heroic virtue, Aguilera concludes: "For this reason, he is the delight *(delicias)* of the Church, glory of the Spanish Nation, splendor of Galicia, distinction of the Franciscan Religion, honor of the [Franciscan] Province of the Holy Gospel, firm support of the Kingdom of New Spain, and especially of Puebla de los Angeles."

In 1791, Aguilera dedicated his printed sermon to the poblano bishop Salvador Biempica y Sotomayor, a native of Galicia. Praising the recently appointed bishop as "brilliant and powerful Patron [and] Promotor of the glories of Blessed Sebastián de Aparicio," Aguilera describes the providential delays in the beatification process that had allowed a bishop from Aparicio's "distinguished birthplace *(cuna)*" to preside over the solemnities.[69] In Aguilera's portrayal of Blessed Aparicio as a shared spiritual good, I see more than the subjective even-handedness of a criollo Franciscan. In objective terms, the heightened presence of peninsular prelates in the americano church during the closing years of the eighteenth century made criollo hagiographers and preachers more beholden than in earlier years to their patronage and approval. Dependent upon the support of influential churchmen, this criollo preacher found it necessary to appeal to the self-interest and patriotism of a native of Galicia.

Finally, the text and paratexts of a 1791 sermon entitled *La sencillez hermanada con la sabiduría* give further hints as to why criollos may have doubted their community claims to Blessed Aparicio. Galician-born Agustín Quintela offered this panegyric in February 1791, an occasion on which the Real Congregación del Apóstol Santiago de Señores Gallegos celebrated the beatification of Sebastián de Aparicio.[70]

Here, as in the 1769 *Vida prodigiosa* whose dedicatoria Quintela had signed, the Congregación de Santiago claims Aparicio for natives of Galicia, wherever they might reside. This corporation, which itself underwrote the expenses of publication, dedicated the published sermon to "St. James the Greater, Apostle of Jesus, Patron of the Spains." To their patron saint Santiago, the gallego expatriates proclaim: "The applauded Hero, and the Body that celebrated him, all belong to you with an uncontestable right. We all belong to a Nation that is honored by your precious relics *(despojos);* all from a Country that sees and recognizes you as its adored Patron."[71] In the text of the sermon itself, Quintela builds upon this theme, frequently invoking the allegiance and pride of the gallego "nation." In his introduction, for example, an exuberant Quintela declares that "since you, Señores, have made me voice of the nation, I must eulogize the great Sebastián de Aparicio, . . . in whom you rejoice as a most noble Compatriot." Quintela concludes his oration by affirming that, by God's decrees, the rains, animals, and insects honor Sebastián de Aparicio, as do Saints Diego de Alcalá and Francis of Assisi and the city of Puebla. "These Decrees have filled you with joy, and rightly so, oh fortunate *(dichosísima)* Nación Gallega. . . . How great your joy must be in seeing the Church honor one of your sons!" Quintela assures the gallego expatriates of Mexico City that "the honors you have paid [Aparicio] . . . will give you merits beyond the bonds of homeland *(paisanage)* that unite you to him."[72]

In contrast to his contemporaries Carmona and Aguilera, Quintela proclaims the virtues of a gallego saint without references to Puebla or New Spain. In the late-colonial environment of increasing criollo frustration and heightened interethnic rivalries, the virtue of a holy man whose life had been rooted in "both Spains" would become a contested commodity.

Conclusion

Aparicio and his fellow Iberian immigrants in the conquest and post-conquest period belonged to two Spanish worlds. On the one hand, one might argue that Aparicio was more novohispano than peninsular; though a native of Spain, he lived most of his life in the New World. It was there, in the Valley of Mexico and the mountains around Puebla, that he made his wealth, redistributed it through various acts of charity, renounced it in order to take religious vows, and eventually gained a reputation for sanctity among the local populace. Indeed, he may have come to consider the New World, rather than his Iberian birthplace, as his sentimental home. Even so, Aparicio's Iberian origins made him a rallying point more for Spanish immigrants than for the criollo establishment of Puebla. As my reading of the vidas and sermons suggests, although the criollo elites of Puebla did join their Iberian-born neighbors in venerating Aparicio and pressing for his canonization, their claims on his honor and merit were limited. Because he had first seen the light of day in the Old World, he was and forever would be an Iberian or, more specifically, a gallego saint. Even so, during the seventeenth century the fertile spiritual soil of Peru produced a universally recognized flower of sanctity known as the Rose of Lima.

4

Heretics by Sea, Pagans by Land

St. Rosa de Lima and the Limits of Criollismo in Colonial Peru

St. Rosa de Lima (1586–1617) is perhaps the best known and most beloved of all Spanish American saints. Indeed, she was the only American-born Roman Catholic saint for almost two centuries.[1] Iconographic proof of her immense popularity during the seventeenth and eighteenth centuries is still evident in churches, convents, museums, and private art collections throughout the Americas, Europe, and the Philippines, and she continues to be venerated around the world.

Promoters of Rosa's causa met with much more immediate success than did the devotees of Fray Sebastián de Aparicio during the same period. Beatified barely fifty years following her death (1668), Rosa was canonized just three years later (12 April 1671). Even prior to her elevation to the altar by Pope Clement X, she was declared Principal Patroness of Lima and the Kingdom of Peru (1669), and subsequently (in 1670), of "all the provinces, kingdoms, islands, and regions of land in America, the Philippines, and the Indies."[2] In a letter of congratulation to the people of Lima in 1668, Pope Clement IX referred to her as "your Rosa, or better yet, our Rosa." Moreover, when the same pope declared Rosa de Santa María patroness of Lima and all Peru in 1669, he attributed his decision to "the personal friendship which united him to the Monarchs of Spain" and "the great royal services they have rendered to the Catholic Church, which are recognized every-where."[3] The royal services to which Clement IX alludes, the defense and propagation of the Roman Catholic faith, were well known, for the Spanish crown had for a century and a half made them the ideo-logical justification for its imperial project. The rapid rise of St. Rosa de Santa María to the status of spiritual patroness of Spain's overseas empire occurred in contravention of Pope Urban VIII's regulatory decrees, suggesting that Rome and Madrid were quite aware of the symbolic value of this American holy woman as a universal saint. For the staunchly Catholic Habsburg family, she symbolized the triumph of orthodox Spain and Austria over the Protestant heretics and Turkish Muslims that threatened their hegemony both in Europe and on the seas. Her fame also allowed the Spanish crown to advertise its success-ful fulfillment of its missionary role in the New World, where a Roman Catholic saint had now emerged. Finally, the choice of St. Rosa as patroness of the Spanish Empire strengthened sentiments of imperial solidarity within its various overseas dependencies.

Of course, the elevation of the young limeña to the altar as St. Rosa de Lima had important symbolic meaning for the criollos of Lima and Greater Peru, for it afforded them an opportunity to celebrate the glory of their homeland and its people. In this regard, Peruvian histo-rian Teodoro Hampe Martínez postulates an "undeniable link between the 'flower of Lima' [St. Rosa] and the unsettled environment in which protonationalism and criollo consciousness emerged."[4] Indeed, from the period of her canonization well into the nineteenth century, patri-otic religious writers throughout Spanish America celebrated St. Rosa de Lima as a symbol of criollo faith and virtue and as evidence that the americano church had come of age.

Even so, I agree with the assessment of D. A. Brading, who argues that although Rosa's seventeenth-century cult "offered grounds for patriotic pride, its message lacked any specifically Peruvian content."[5] In his view, the Rosa that emerges from the early hagiographies looks like any saint from any time or place. As a perfect reproduction of the Italian St. Catherine of Siena, she scarcely seems Peruvian or limeño at all, and like numerous beatas in early modern Spain, she is deeply devoted to both saints and sacraments, practices ascetic disciplines, dis-plays traditional Christian virtues, and receives mystical favors from Christ and the Virgin. For Brading, "the sheer normality of her type of sanctity confirmed the degree to which Lima was a Spanish city set down on the coast of the Pacific."[6] Even after her canonization, when Dominican chronicler Juan Meléndez and soldier-poet Luis Antonio Oviedo y Herrera narrate her life story within its proper Peruvian context, Rosa embodies the triumph of Spain's Roman Catholic mission in Peru and the protection of broader Spanish, as opposed to narrowly criollo, interests in that region.[7]

In this chapter, I examine these hagiographic portrayals of Rosa de Santa María within the wider historical context of the Spanish Empire and viceregal Peru during the seventeenth and eighteenth centuries. I argue that conditions particular to Peru shaped the emerging criollo identity by narrowing the ideological gulf between the region's criollo Spaniards and their Iberian-born counterparts. Around 1600, as the power struggles of the mid-sixteenth century between the Spanish crown and Spanish conquistadores faded away,[8] other threatening forces—Protestant pirates on the sea and superficially Christianized Amerindians in the altiplano—caused the "sons of the conquerors" to identify closely with peninsular Spaniards. With Brading, I acknowledge that cultural borrowing and imitation of Old World models affected this outcome. But such an affirmation begs the question of why Rosa's hagiographers, as well as Lima's criollo chroniclers in general, borrowed so heavily. This chapter will demonstrate how non-Spanish, non-Catholic forces threw peninsulares and criollos into each other's arms, shaping their understanding of St. Rosa as a primarily Roman Catholic rather than criollo saint.

Before turning to an analysis of the hagiographic traditions, I present a chronological narrative of St. Rosa's life and spirituality. This discussion will clarify the nature of her appeal among her contemporaries and illustrate how, in the eyes of her earliest devotees and hagiographers, she conformed to Old World ideals.

Isabel de Flores: Biographical and Spiritual Profile

Isabel de Flores, later known as Rosa de Santa María, was born to impoverished petty hidalgo parents in Lima in 1586. Her father, Gaspar de Flores, had migrated to Lima from his native Puerto Rico in 1548, only a decade and a half after the famous confrontation between Francisco Pizarro and Atahualpa.[9] Born around 1524, he was already around sixty years of age when Isabel was born. Amazingly, he outlived his famous daughter, dying sometime after 1618.[10] María de Oliva, a Spanish criolla and mother of ten, appears as a central figure in her daughter's Lives, though not always in a positive light.

An early and defining moment in Isabel's childhood involved a miracle that resulted in the changing of her name. Numerous witnesses later testified that, while Isabel was still an infant, one of her family's indigenous domestic servants saw her cheeks transformed into lovely roses (see figure 4.1). Thereafter, all of the family members except one began to call the young child by the name of Rosa. The dissenter was the child's maternal grandmother and namesake, who resented the abandonment of the name Isabel.[11] However, her resistance to the change ended abruptly a few months later when Toribio de Mogrovejo, archbishop of Lima, reportedly confirmed the young girl, miraculously, with the name of Rosa.[12] From that point on, family members and friends felt no misgivings about calling her Rosa, believing the name to have been divinely given.

The conflict between Rosa's mother and grandmother over her name was not an isolated event. Before long, the young prodigy's singular rejection of worldly interests put her at odds with most of her family, especially her controlling mother. Like St. Catherine of Siena, whom she sought to emulate from her earliest years, Rosa's relationship with her mother was characterized by constant confrontation and quarreling. In fact, Rosa's hagiographers explicitly describe María de Oliva as more physically abusive than the mother of the famed fourteenth-century saint.[13]

At age five, Rosa took a vow of perpetual chastity in imitation of St. Catherine. This vow came on the heels of a traumatic episode that had caused her to repent of her personal vanity. One day while Rosa was playing with her brother, the two began to throw mud at each other. When her beautiful hair became plastered with mud, she began to wail inconsolably. Recognizing this outburst as an act of female vanity, her pious brother offered a stern rebuke: "If you are crying because of your hair, you should know that on account of [beautiful] hair there are many souls in hell." Not long thereafter, Rosa cut off her hair in imitation of St. Catherine, one of many penitential acts that provoked María de Oliva to anger.[14]

FIGURE 4.1. The face of the infant Isabel de Flores is transformed miraculously into the likeness of a rose, prompting family and household members to call
her Rosa. Oil on canvas, attributed to Angelino Medoro. Property of Basílica-
Santuario de Santa Rosa, Lima. From José Flores Araoz et al. *Santa Rosa de Lima
y su tiempo* (Lima, 1995), 260. (From the Colección Arte y Tesoros del Péru;
courtesy of the Banco de Crédito del Perú)

This ritual debasement of her physical beauty was but one manifestation of her *recato,* an attitude of humility and sexual propriety much extolled by clerical writers and preachers of the era. Like other uncloistered women esteemed for their sanctity, including St. Catherine of Siena, Rosa rejected the various outward trappings of female beauty (clothing, hairstyle, feminine charm, etc.). Moreover, she began to resist going with her mother on social calls, fearing that men might look upon her with ill intentions or that her mother's female friends might call attention to her beauty. At one point, Rosa began to abhor such outings so much that she rubbed hot pepper *(ají)* on her eyes in order to make herself appear ill. When Rosa's suspicious mother discovered her daughter's secret by licking her cheek, another domestic conflict ensued.[15]

Like many parents throughout history, Gaspar de Flores and María de Oliva hoped to improve their social and economic status by arranging advantageous marriages for their children. In this regard, their family's plight was similar to that of the poor Spanish families who sought a marriage alliance with Sebastián de Aparicio (see chapter 3). From all accounts, Rosa's physical beauty, social charms, and reputation for piety made her an attractive candidate for well-to-do suitors. She demonstrated "ease and perfection [in] all skills *(adornos)* and activities *(ejercicios)* appropriate to her feminine sex: spinning, sewing, embroidery, weaving, [and] beautiful floral work."[16] However, having chosen an independent course in regard to marriage, Rosa made clear her indifference to her parents' plans. On one occasion when she refused the approaches of an eligible bachelor, her family members became so angry that her confessors had to mediate the crisis.[17] Young Rosa's dogged patience eventually won the day and her parents, persuaded by their daughter's clerical supporters, acquiesced to her desire to remain single. They even accommodated her desire for hermetic contemplation by preparing a simple four-by-five-foot hermitage in the garden *(huerto)* behind their house.[18]

In keeping with her vow of perpetual chastity and her devotion to prayer and asceticism, Rosa considered joining one of the local convents. Since her earliest years, she had worn the poor habit of St. Francis of Assisi, a practice not uncommon among pious laywomen of her day. As a result of her association with the Franciscans, she weighed the option of joining the convent of Santa Clara de Assisi which Archbishop Toribio de Mogrovejo and other elites founded when she was nineteen years old. Although her poverty might have made such plans impossible, a local gentleman offered to provide the necessary dowry payment, and the archbishop's niece, María de Quiñones, urged the virtuous Rosa to join her as one of the founding members. Lacking certainty that this was God's will, Rosa demurred. Soon thereafter, others began urging her to throw in her lot with the more rigorously disciplined discalced Carmelites, the order that Teresa de Avila had reformed in Spain a half-century earlier. In the end, however, she decided to join the convent of La Encarnación (Augustinian nuns). Afraid that her parents would oppose this decision, however, she asked her sympathetic brother Hernando to aid her flight, and together they quietly left home one day and headed for La Encarnación.[19]

En route to her would-be cloister, Rosa stopped to pray at the Dominican Chapel of Our Lady of the Rosary in hope of receiving divine confirmation of her decision to take the veil. In the event, she underwent an experience that altogether altered her plans. Having completed her prayers, Rosa attempted to stand up and proceed to La Encarnación, only to find "her entire body immobile *(yerto),* as if she were nailed to the ground."[20] Simultaneously, Our Lady of the Rosary revealed to Rosa in a vision that she should not enter the convent but should instead join the Third Order of St. Dominic. Only after Rosa vowed to return home and serve her earthly mother was she released from this rapt state.

Thus, Rosa desisted in her intention to enter a female convent, opting instead to live a life of intense spiritual devotion as a laywoman. Although she remained uncloistered and continued to support her aging parents with money earned through her sewing and embroidery, she also retreated daily to a tiny hermitage behind her family's home. There she sought mystical union with God while practicing acts of extreme asceticism—extreme fasts, self-flagellation, sleep deprivation—traditionally associated with Roman Catholic saints. Although Rosa and her later devotees understood her refusal to enter the convent as the result of a mystical vision, Rosa may have had other practical reasons for remaining uncloistered. Social expectations and community religious obligations within the wealthy convents often stood in the way of the sort of rigorous penitential life that an anchoress like Rosa longed to pursue. Regarding a similar incident in the life of Mariana de

Jesús, the Quito beata considered in chapter 5, John Leddy Phelan observes:

> She wanted freedom to follow her own vocation. Her refusal to enter either the Franciscan or the Dominican convent of nuns merits careful examination. Although the convents were not havens for licentiousness, neither were they centers of rigorous asceticism. . . . Although some nuns did devote themselves to acts of penitence and social charity, many more ladies lived behind the cloisters with all the creature comforts, including being attended by their own staff of servants. . . . Saint Mariana de Jesús and her contemporary, Rosa of Lima, were both women of intense religious vocations who deliberately avoided the cloisters. The convents, with their genteel atmosphere and comforts, if not luxuries, were not suitable places for those two baroque saints to pursue their spiritual development.[21]

While it is impossible to pinpoint the precise reasons for Rosa's decision to forego the cloistered life, it is clear that such a decision preserved for her a degree of independence that would have raised the hackles of many zealous clerics of her day. Since the late fifteenth century, reformers and inquisitors had become increasingly suspicious of female mystics in general, but especially those who moved about freely in society and refused to submit to the traditional authorities of priest, mother superior, father, or husband. Such concerns grew pronounced after 1530 due to fears of Lutheranism and certain types of mysticism *(alumbradismo)*.[22] Those who opposed the unsupervised religious activity of uncloistered women justified their position on the grounds that women were physically, psychologically, morally, and intellectually inferior to men, and hence more likely to fall prey to demonic ploys.[23]

Such was the ideological climate in Lima during Rosa's lifetime.[24] Indeed, Rosa's own siblings became concerned at one point that her rigorous fasts would arouse the suspicions of Lima's Holy Office of the Inquisition.[25] Local officials eventually did assign qualified experts to question Rosa at length about the origins, nature, and theological content of her mystical experiences. Among those assigned to the case were Dr. Juan del Castillo and Fray Juan de Lorenzana. Castillo was a layman and physician whose interests ranged from natural philosophy to mystical theology.[26] Lorenzana held several important posts within the Dominican province of San Juan Bautista del Perú as well as a number of academic chairs in Lima's Universidad de San Marcos.[27] Rosa's Dominican hagiographers describe in some detail the "examination of conscience" to which these experts subjected the young beata.[28] It is impossible to know just how precarious Rosa's position may have been at that time, for her posthumous reputation for sanctity allowed for a reinterpretation of the earlier, questionable events of her life.[29] Thus, when hagiographer Leonardo Hansen asserts that Juan del Castillo and Juan de Lorenzana never doubted the propriety of Rosa's motivations and mystical experiences, his assertion must be interpreted with caution. In point of fact, several beatas who had associated with Rosa in the home of Gonzalo de la Maza were brought before the Inquisition of Lima in the years following her death.[30]

In such a religious climate, then, it was essential that Rosa ally herself with individuals with reputations for virtue and sobriety if she wished to pursue her spiritual goals unhindered. Such considerations certainly played some part in her decision to form close ties with the Dominican order and the well-connected limeño household of Gonzalo de la Maza. In 1606, twenty-year-old Rosa took the habit of the Third Order of St. Dominic.[31] This agreement to live as a tertiary under a religious rule solidified her ties with the Order of Preachers and served as the basis for that order's later support for her canonization. The relationship also clearly influenced the nature of her religiosity, for throughout her life she venerated St. Catherine of Siena and Our Lady of the Rosary, both Dominican devotions. Furthermore, some of the more important episodes in which her sanctity shone through took place in and around the local Dominican church. Rosa's confessor Pedro de Loayza claimed to have heard her declare that she would gladly have joined a convent devoted to St. Catherine of Siena had there been one in Lima. Moreover, when the Order of Preachers did establish a convent under the patronage of St. Catherine just five years after Rosa's death, the success of the foundation was attributed to Rosa's prophetic prediction.[32] This accurate prophecy enhanced Rosa's reputation for sanctity and, as that reputation grew, the Convent of St. Catherine basked in her glory.

Some five years prior to her death in 1617, Rosa de Santa María found favor with an influential limeño couple, Gonzalo de la Maza and María de Uzátegui.[33] In a deposition before ecclesiastical officials following Rosa's death, Don Gonzalo explained that he and his wife had

known for some time of Rosa's reputation for virtue but had not met
her because they dared not interfere with her solitude. The couple's first
communication with Rosa had come about at her initiative, on an occasion in which she sought their aid in some unspecified charitable work.
After a chance meeting brought them together a second time, Rosa
began to spend much of her time in the Maza household.[34] In later testimony before church officials, Gonzalo de la Maza was careful to point
out that her entrance into his household did not come at the expense of
her parents' needs. On the contrary, while she spent much time in her
new benefactors' oratory and in the small hermitage provided for her
solitude and prayer, she also returned frequently to the home of her
parents, whom she continued to support financially through the sale
of her handmade embroidery.[35] Limeño society and its churchmen
could hardly present for imitation a Spanish girl who abandoned her
parents to poverty, not even if she had done so for the sake of prayer.

The relationship between Rosa and her wealthy benefactors must
have been one of mutual interest and support. Don Gonzalo and Doña
María provided material aid to this woman of limited means, along
with a safe and supportive environment in which to practice her intense
spirituality. Rosa brought into their home a religious influence and spiritual power that they desired for themselves, their daughters, and other
household members. A small but devoted spiritual following developed
around young Rosa in the Maza home as like-minded limeños, especially women, gathered there for prayer and pious conversations.[36]
These friends witnessed a number of the divine favors that Rosa
received during her lifetime and testified on her behalf during the
posthumous canonization proceedings. The association eventually
brought enduring fame for several of these individuals, who became
central figures in the hagiographic and iconographic record of Rosa's
life.[37]

Since Peruvian scholars have described Rosa's spirituality in some
detail,[38] I shall simply note here some of its more salient features: ascetic self-mortification; affective devotion to Christ, Mary, and the saints;
and imitation of established spiritual models. Through the ascetic
denial of sensual urges (food, sleep, sexuality, etc.) and the harsh discipline of her flesh, Rosa de Santa María sought both to mortify her
earthly desires and to atone for sins, whether her own or those of her
fellow limeños. The aforementioned episode in which she cut her beau-

tiful hair is but one example of this penitential ethos. At age fifteen, she vowed to abstain from eating meat and to live on bread and water. Thereafter, despite her mother's attempts to make her eat vegetables and soups, as well as her confessors' insistence that she eat meat during periods of illness, Rosa spent long periods of time in rigorous self-denial, including an entire Lenten season in which she ate nothing but orange seeds. She would often test her resolve during family mealtimes by serving the plates of her siblings in order to "inflame" her own appetite.[39]

Like many penitents in the history of the church, Rosa wore cilices and chains underneath her garments in order to punish her flesh and kill all bodily desire. She astounded admirers by wearing a metallic "crown of thorns" under her hair in order to partake in the suffering of Jesus Christ. In addition, her flagellation of her own flesh became so severe on occasion that family members began to worry about her health and her reputation. In a similar vein, Rosa constructed special beds that functioned as instruments of torture rather than places of comfortable repose.[40]

Over time there developed various traditions linking Rosa's acts of penitence with her role as spiritual protectress of Lima. According to one such legend, her prayers and rigorous acts of penitence had saved the city of Lima from God's impending judgment when she was about twenty years old. On that occasion, Fray Francisco Solano, a future saint who was renowned for the persuasive power of his sermons, warned that Lima would be destroyed by an earthquake if its residents refused to repent of their religious and moral apathy.[41] Moved by love for God and her patria, Rosa began to flagellate herself so violently that "those of her household thought she was going to beat herself to pieces."[42] In the event, Father Solano's prophecies of doom failed to materialize. With time, devotees of St. Rosa attributed the salvation of Lima to her intervention.[43]

Rosa's spirituality was characterized not only by rigorous asceticism, but also by an intensely affective devotional life that centered on the persons of Jesus Christ (especially the Christ Child), the Virgin Mary (Our Lady of the Rosary), and a number of favorite saints. Rosa exhibited a commitment to prayer and contemplation at an early age. At the age of five, she began to repeat the prayer "Blessed be God, and May He Reside in My Soul."[44] When she was twelve or thirteen years old, God began to grant her numerous supernatural favors *(mercedes)* via unitive prayer.

One such miracle occurred in the home of Don Gonzalo and Doña María just four months before Rosa's death. As previously noted, Rosa spent much time in the Maza household praying before various images in the household chapel. Once while in prayer before a painted image of the face of Christ, Rosa uttered the following petition: "Lord, cause all people to serve you. . . . Give some reason, my Husband, for all to melt away in loving you." Immediately, those who were present, including the pious benefactors of Rosa, observed in amazement that the image of Christ began to perspire, exhibiting a "beautiful dew or mist."[45] Convinced that a miracle had taken place, the witnesses called a number of individuals who might confirm their hopes. Among those summoned was Angelino Medoro, the Italian artist who had painted the work. The fact that pious laypersons in Rosa's prayer circle took steps to rule out natural explanations for this rare phenomenon points to their inclination to view her even prior to her death as a special conduit for God's power. The miracle of the sweating Christ convinced Rosa's earliest devotees, laypersons as well as clergy, that her prayer life was not only within the parameters of what the church allowed, but that it was extraordinarily pleasing to God.

The most famous miracle associated with Rosa's prayer life served to confirm that this beautiful, uncloistered woman's observance of sexual chastity had won her the favor of Jesus Christ. Rosa, who frequently prayed before images of the Virgin and Child in the Dominican church and the Maza home, developed a strong affective tie with the Christ Child (Niño Jesús). He would pay her spiritual visits while she sat with her sewing—often sitting on a pillow by her side—or engage her in conversation as she tended to household chores, thus allowing her to pursue the priorities of both Martha and Mary.[46] With time, she later told her confessors, he began to speak to her in visions, saying, "Rosa, my beloved, marry me." One Palm Sunday as Rosa prayed before a statue of the Virgin and Child in the Convent of San Domingo, the Niño Jesús again expressed his desire to have Rosa as his spiritual wife. In response to this proposal of mystical marriage, Rosa fashioned a wedding ring that would symbolize the union. However, when she asked Fr. Alonso Velázquez to perform the nuptials on Easter Sunday by placing the ring on her finger, he voiced misgivings about what people would say if they saw the ring on Rosa's finger. Undaunted, she responded that because this marriage was the will of God, only those whom he permitted would be able to see the ring. Miraculously, this prediction proved true, for although she wore the ring from that point on, her mother never saw it. In contrast, the more sympathetic María de Uzátegui was able to see the ring once Rosa called her attention to it.[47] The miracle of the wedding ring, a motif from Raymond of Capua's *Life of St. Catherine of Siena*,[48] signified for Rosa's devotees that Christ recognized the young virgin's bodily purity and desired spiritual union with her.[49] This episode also became a favorite theme for Rosa's iconographers, who popularized it among the faithful through their paintings, sculptures, and bas-reliefs (see figure 2.2).

Finally, Rosa's spirituality was not only both ascetic and affective, but also highly imitative in nature, a fact that she and her hagiographers frequently emphasized. While her contemporaries considered her sanctity to be rare, they did not view it as novel or creative. On the contrary, her hagiographers note how she learned principles of contemplative prayer from the writings of Teresa de Avila and Luis de Granada, as well as from Francisco Losa's 1613 Life of Gregorio López.[50] Most significant, however, was her conscious imitation of St. Catherine of Siena. Inquisitorial records of the period reveal that several beatas closely associated with Rosa had read Raymond of Capua's *Life of St. Catherine of Siena*.[51] One hagiographer observed that Rosa memorized Fr. Fernando del Castillo's Life of the Sienese saint "in order to not deviate in even one point from the path that her seraphic teacher *(maestra)* had walked."[52]

The Order of Preachers sought consistently to demonstrate the similarities and connections between their order's most prominent female saint, Catherine of Siena, and Rosa de Lima. For one thing, they misidentified the date of Rosa's birth as April 30, 1586, in order to make it coincide with St. Catherine's feast day.[53] And during the 1669 solemnities surrounding the formal proclamation of Rosa's beatification in the cathedral of Lima, a Dominican preacher noted that if Rosa was not greater than St. Catherine of Siena, neither was the latter "holier *(más santa)* than the Virgin Rosa."[54] While the last statement might have provided limeños and inhabitants of Peru in general with a sense of pride in their patria and its native-born saint, it also contains hints that criollo identity was being articulated in reference to Old World identities rather than independently of them.

However, even as Rosa's hagiographers portray her as an exact copy of the fourteenth-century Catherine, their silence in regard to one particular theme in her forerunner's hagiographies illustrates the limitations of the comparison. In his Life of St. Catherine, Raymond of Capua vigorously defended her activity in the world. Following her spiritual marriage to Christ, Catherine began to circulate freely, attracting to herself "disciples" of both genders. Her devoted hagiographer condemned the distrustful attitudes of those who suspected this pious, uncloistered woman of engaging in illicit sexual activities. In contrast to her fourteenth-century model, Rosa's religious activity appears to have been much more circumscribed. Although men were among those who met for prayer in the Maza home and looked to Rosa for spiritual inspiration, it is significant that her hagiographers stopped far short of defending her right to circulate freely or exercise spiritual authority over men and women. On the contrary, Loayza praises her for "never appear[ing] in the door, at the window, or at fiestas, not even general processions, but only those [associated with] her Father St. Domingo."[55] This fact reflects, of course, the greater social and religious limitations on women during Rosa's era, especially in the Hispanic world, which exalted female virginity not only as a spiritual virtue, but also as a means for guaranteeing limpieza de sangre.[56] It also suggests that, try as they might to define their saint or themselves in reference to European standards (whether Iberian or Italian), criollo laymen as well as clerics would find this project limited by the realities of their unique social world and historical experiences.

The death of Rosa de Santa María at the age of thirty-one on August 24, 1617, brought an immediate outpouring of emotion and faith on the part of the limeño faithful.[57] The throngs that entered his home to view Rosa's body, noted Don Gonzalo de la Maza, were so large that "had the house not had two doors and patios so that people could enter through the one door and exit through the other, there would have been chaos."[58]

That St. Rosa quickly became a prominent feature of the cultural landscape of Lima is evident in the personal diary of Josephe Mugaburu, a peninsular Spaniard and military man who lived most of his life in Lima. In periodic journal entries spanning more than four decades

(1640–86), Mugaburu frequently describes religious ceremonies and processions. He notes, for example, the religious observances that accompanied major moments in the growth of the cult of St. Rosa, including the local announcement of her beatification (December 1668), the singing of mass at her former residence (February 1669), and numerous celebrations that followed her first feast day (August 1669). In August 1669, he observes, Rosa was named patron saint of Lima by Viceroy Lemos and various corporate entities. On November 13, 1669, Viceroy Lemos, his wife, and their children attended a play about St. Rosa's life. In December of the same year, limeños celebrated St. Rosa with bullfights, *cañas* jousting, and processions, displaying her portrait prominently above one of King Carlos II under a canopy near the local city hall. In September of the next year, residents of Lima turned out for a masquerade for St. Rosa at the port of Callao.[59]

Rosa's fame spread quickly following her formal beatification, canonization, and selection as patroness of Spain's overseas empire; by century's end she had devotees throughout the Roman Catholic world. This was an age—the late seventeenth century—in which Rome and Madrid faced mounting threats to their religious and imperial hegemony in Europe and beyond. Even for criollo lovers of their Peruvian patria, St. Rosa would not be a religious weapon to be wielded in polemics against the Iberian metropolis.

Rosa de Lima: Hagiographic Traditions

Shortly following the death of Rosa de Santa María in August 1617, local church officials began to question witnesses regarding Rosa's life, death, and miracles. During this first stage of the canonization proceedings, known as the proceso ordinario, seventy-five witnesses appeared before Baltasar de Padilla, a canon in the local cathedral chapter, and notary Jaime Blanco, an ordained priest from Catalonia. Among those who testified were Rosa's parents, a brother, Don Gonzalo de la Maza and Dona María de Uzátegui, the beatas María Antonia del Castillo and Luisa de Melgarejo, a domestic servant named Mariana de Oliva, Dr. Juan del Castillo, Fr. Juan de Lorenzana, and several other clergymen and confessors. These individuals had experienced Rosa's sanctity during interactions at the Flores and Maza residences or in the confessionals of nearby churches, and were able to give in-depth accounts of her penitence, mystical experiences, and miracles, as well as her attitudes of humility, obedience, and charity. After the proceso ordinario was closed in April 1618, a copy of the resulting records was remitted to Europe with the annual fleet.[60] Fray Pedro de Loayza, a Dominican priest who had been one of Rosa's confessors, consulted the proceso ordinario documents in order to write the first Life of Rosa de Santa María in 1619, entitled *Vida, muerte y milagros de sor Rosa de Santa María.*[61]

In response to petitions from the Dominican province and with the approval of the Sacred Congregation of Rites, Archbishop Hernando Arias de Ugarte of Lima called for the opening of new investigations in 1630. In the course of this proceso apostólico (1630–32), forty-seven witnesses, including twelve who had participated in the proceso ordinario more than a decade earlier, gave depositions before investigators. When copies of documents from this two-year investigation were forwarded to the papal curia in 1632, a manuscript copy of the Loayza hagiography was among the voluminous papers.[62] As Rosa's causa for beatification raced forward, a German Dominican named Leonardo Hansen wrote and published a second vida, this time in Latin, based on the Loayza Life and the proceso apostólico of 1630–32. His Latin-language *Vita mirabilis* became the most influential of the Rosa hagiographies, one followed by subsequent hagiographers and iconographers.[63]

The fact that the Loayza and Hansen Lives lack "specifically Peruvian content" is hardly surprising, for both authors wrote to satisfy Dominican rather than criollo concerns.[64] Loayza, a personal spiritual director of Rosa's who wrote shortly after her death, was more concerned with the authenticity of her spiritual life than with the patriotic symbolism of her persona, hence the absence in his manuscript of explicitly criollo concerns and rhetoric. Furthermore, Leonardo Hansen was a German Dominican who was much more interested in Rosa as a replica of his order's St. Catherine of Siena than as a symbol of americano achievement.

As Elisa Vargas Lugo has noted, however, by the last quarter of the seventeenth century, criollos of Lima had begun to portray St. Rosa as *their* saint. In the 1680s, for example, limeño Juan Meléndez inserted a narrative of the life and miracles of St. Rosa de Lima into his three-volume *Tesoros verdaderos de las indias,* a history of the Dominican province of San Juan Bautista del Perú.[65] The *Tesoros verdaderos* is primarily an attempt to set the record straight regarding the primary role of the Order of Preachers in the early conquest and evangelization of Peru.[66] But Meléndez's pro-criollo agenda is also clear, beginning in his letter of dedication to the book's patron, Father Antonio de Monroy, Mexican-born master general of the Order of Preachers. In the letter, Meléndez rejoices that his *Tesoros verdaderos* should be published under the patronage of "the first . . . from among the *Spaniards born in the Indies* to be included [among] the famous Caesars of the Religion of Guzmán."[67] Referring to himself as "another son of the Indies," Meléndez observes that Monroy's elevation to the Dominican order's highest post "has set straight the world's misconception by making known that there is much that is good in the Indies."[68] By inserting the Life of St. Rosa into such a textual context, the criollo writer offers specific proof of the goodness of his land and its native Spanish children. Even so, Meléndez closely follows Leonardo Hansen's narrative; while the *Tesoros verdaderos* is mildly pro-criollo in tone, its lengthy Life of St. Rosa is highly derivative, and "lacking in any specifically Peruvian content."

The generic quality of the Rosa narrative gave way in 1711 to one marked by a strongly Peruvian flavor. In that year, Iberian-born Don Luis Antonio Oviedo y Herrera (1636–1716) published a lengthy epic poem entitled *Vida de la esclarecida virgen Santa Rosa de Santa María, natural de Lima y patrona de el Peru, poema heroyco* (hereafter, *Poema heroyco*).[69] In octet verse, Oviedo y Herrera intersperses the best-known episodes of Rosa's life among major defining moments in viceregal Peruvian political and military history. For example, between descriptions of Rosa's penitence and reception of mystical favors, Oviedo y Herrera narrates Pizarro's capture of the Incan prince Atahualpa in 1535, subsequent civil wars between the Spanish conquerors of Peru, and assaults on Peruvian coastal cities by English and Dutch pirates. But the soldier-poet also "interweaves history with fiction,"[70] imagining scenes in which a pagan necromancer (Bilcaóma) reminds an imprisoned Incan ruler (Yupangui) that the time of his liberty is near, while the Devil tempts the Queen of England with the enticements of Peru's vast silver wealth. On one level, the *Poema heroyco* pits Rosa the spiritual athlete in a cosmic battle with the Devil (Luzbel) for Peruvian souls, both Spanish and indigenous. In this sense, the sanctity and patronage of

Rosa de Lima signify the triumph of Spanish (and Imperial) Catholicism over the tenacity of native idolatry and the insidious threat of Protestantism. On another level, however, Oviedo y Herrera's Rosa protects Peruvian Spaniards and their capital city from the very real military threats that they constantly face:

> *He who gives law to all laws*
> *And boasts of bringing armies down,*
> *Will not allow them to destroy the City of Kings,*
> *For it has Rosa as its Star and crown.*[71]

Presenting St. Rosa as preserver of Lima and of Spanish Peru as a whole, Oviedo y Herrera reinterprets her to reflect the struggles and lessons of nearly two centuries.

That Oviedo y Herrera should interpret the significance of Peru's spiritual patroness in military terms is not surprising. Son of a knight of the order of Santiago, he fought in Spain's European military campaigns against Dutch separatists before going to Peru as commander of a company of cuirassiers in 1668. Shortly after his arrival in Upper Peru, he assumed a number of public appointments, serving for a time as *corregidor* of Potosí. In the latter post, his role was to keep the mines of Potosí producing silver for the imperial economy by procuring a steady labor supply, keeping the peace, and enforcing royal tax laws. As soldier, royal administrator, and devout Roman Catholic, the peninsular Oviedo y Herrera had much in common with criollo devotees of St. Rosa de Lima, whose lives were marked by the challenges and threats posed by anti-Spanish Protestants and Andean Indians.

By recognizing Oviedo y Herrera's poetic attention to such unresolved tensions in Peruvian history as vengeful Incan rulers and threatening Protestant corsairs, the modern reader is able to identify similar themes in the Loayza and Hansen Lives, details that might otherwise go unnoticed. In the remainder of this chapter, I examine these two long-term sources of Spanish apprehension in mid-colonial Peru—highland Indians and seafaring Protestants—and how these tensions intersect with the hagiographic traditions of St. Rosa de Lima, growing stronger by the time of Oviedo y Herrera's *Poema heroyco*.

On the occasion of Rosa's beatification in 1668, Pope Clement IX sent a congratulatory letter to ecclesiastical officials in Lima. Praising Rosa as the Peruvian church's "first fruits of sanctity," and exalting her "heroic virtues" and "heavenly splendor *(resplandores)*," he presented the limeña saint as "clear proof of the authenticity of the Catholic faith . . . in those warm *(cálidas)* lands."[72] While americanos like Juan Meléndez might interpret such a statement as an endorsement of criollo spiritual achievement, it was more problematic for them to make triumphalistic claims of evangelistic victory among the region's indigenous peoples. In a letter of 1632 in which civil *alcaldes* and *regidores* of Lima requested canonization of their beloved Rosa and her designation as local patroness, they contrasted the fragrant virtue and religious purity of the Rose with the "thorny" *(espinosa)* idolatry of the indigenous peoples. The Indians of Peru would certainly benefit, noted the limeño petitioners, from the canonization of a person from their own land, whose example "would help greatly toward their complete conversion."[73] As these statements suggest, Spanish elites in Peru were painfully aware of indigenous resistance to Catholic evangelization efforts, a lesson learned not only in remote tropical regions such as Marañón, but also in locations much nearer to the ecclesiastical jewel of Lima.[74] The same awareness and preoccupation seems to have affected pious urban laywomen like Rosa de Santa María and Mariana de Jesús (chapter 5). According to hagiographer Leonardo Hansen, "whenever [Rosa] looked towards the mountains that fill the interior of equatorial America (América Meridional), she felt immeasurable pain in her pious heart, weeping over the perdition of the souls of so many barbarians, blinded by idolatries inherited from their ancestors, captives of the Devil."[75]

A closer look at the Loayza and Hansen Lives of St. Rosa reveals subtle evidence of these Spanish concerns about the Amerindian church in Greater Peru. For example, most of Rosa's hagiographers refer to her confirmation at the hands of the famed Archbishop Toribio de Mogrovejo. Hansen briefly describes the event in order to prove the miraculous origin of her epithet when the saintly prelate allegedly confirms her by the name of Rosa, not Isabel. With time, this event seems to have taken on a fuller significance. The confirmation of young Rosa in 1597 took place in Quives (or Quibi), an indigenous village located northeast of Lima, near the confluence of the rivers Chillón and Arajuay.[76] Gaspar Flores had moved there from Lima with his family in order to take up duties as overseer of an obraje that processed silver ore. The majority of the local population, and therefore of his labor force, was Amerindian. According to a legend added later to the story of Rosa's confirmation, the local Indians had not fully embraced Christianity. Thus, when the archbishop made his second pastoral visit there in 1597, the local parish priest warned him about the continued idolatry of his flock. Upon entering the village chapel, the archbishop was disappointed to find that only three children had been brought for baptism. To add insult to injury, when the disheartened prelate left the chapel following the baptismal ceremony, local Indian children followed him through the village shouting, "Big Nose! Big Nose!" In response, rather than bless the children, Toribio choked away tears while prophesying, "Wretched ones! You will not go beyond three!" This reference, presumably to the three children who had welcomed baptism, was in fact a prediction that the village itself would not last more than three years. Indeed, later tradition reported that earthquakes, collapsed mines, crop failures, and flooding left the village virtually depopulated within three years.[77]

The accretion of these later legends to the story of Rosa's confirmation has very little to do with the persona of the saint herself. The tale may have originated in the hagiographic accounts of the life of Archbishop Mogrovejo, who was also a candidate for canonization by the middle of the seventeenth century.[78] What this expanded version does reveal is how Spaniards' ambivalence about the religious condition of the Amerindian majority colored their interpretations of the role and significance of St. Rosa.

Observers of the era recognized that the poor spiritual harvest among Peru's indigenous peoples was not simply a product of the intransigence of idolaters. Another key factor was the reluctance of criollo and peninsular preachers to leave the comforts of the urban university, cathedral, or convents in order to seek converts, a problem with which Rosa and her hagiographers were familiar. According to Pedro de Loayza, Rosa's zeal for the conversion of souls led her to plead with the preachers she knew to go out and "bring *(reducir)* to God all of the idolaters of this land." She also urged them to focus their academic studies toward this end.[79] According to Hansen, the pious beata often stated that if she were not a woman, she would give all of her efforts to converting the most savage and cannibalistic of peoples, even at the cost of her own sweat and blood. Furthermore, she longed to adopt an orphaned boy and instill in him a desire to preach among the Indi-

FIGURE 4.2. The Virgin and Christ Child appear mystically to Rosa in the presence of indigenous converts, who appear to venerate all three holy persons. Anonymous oil on canvas, eighteenth century. Property of the Monastery of Santa Teresa de Jesús, Cuzco, Peru. From José Flores Araoz et al. *Santa Rosa de Lima y su tiempo* (Lima, 1995), 178. (From the Colección Arte y Tesoros del Perú; courtesy of the Banco de Crédito del Perú)

ans, although she was never able to fulfill this dream.[80] Even so, in the various Lives of Rosa de Lima, the problem of the unconverted peoples of Peru provides a context for her prayers and acts of devotion (see figure 4.2).

For most Spaniards, however, the continued paganism of the Andean peoples represented not so much a personal opportunity for penitential self-sacrifice as a public threat to the socio-political order. The dangers posed by Túpac Amaru in the 1560s and his namesake in the 1780s were not isolated events;[81] in fact, indigenous chiefs *(caciques)* led numerous rebellions during the middle decades of the seventeenth century, the period of Rosa's initial rise to fame. These uprisings, which had a negative impact on commerce and the reliability of forced labor, created a tense situation in the colony.[82] If Oviedo y Herrera's St. Rosa protected the viceroyalty from the demonic machinations of past Incan necromancers and rulers, this was not simply a historical achievement of a remote past; rather, it was an ongoing patronage against the living threat of Indian apostasy and rebellion.

A second major source of apprehension in mid-colonial Peru was the ongoing maritime pressure exerted by Spain's Northern European rivals for empire. Beginning with Francis Drake in the 1570s, English and Dutch corsairs posed a continuous threat to Spanish shipping between the Strait of Magellan to the south and Nombre de Dios (Panama) in the north, as well as to the security of coastal cities in the region.[83] Of course, this was a tension felt throughout the empire, from the Spanish Netherlands to Asturias, from Acapulco to the Philippines, and from Florida to Cartagena. Yet an examination of seventeenth-century printed histories for Greater Peru gives the impression that the Protestant maritime threat in that vicinity permeated all aspects of life: administrative, military, commercial, and religious. Not surprisingly, it shaped the way limeño criollos conceived of themselves and their holy persons.

The threat of piracy and invasion left a significant mark on the limeño imagination, including that of Josephe Mugaburu, a career soldier who served for a number of years in Lima's port of Callao. A glance at his diary entries for the years 1671 and 1686 demonstrates how responses to the coastal threat punctuated the local calendar. In January 1671, the year of St. Rosa's canonization, news reached Lima of the sighting of enemy vessels in Valdivia, Chile. The next month, word came that English Captain Henry Morgan had captured the Spanish fort on the Chagres River in Panama. Responding to a request for help from the Audiencia de Panamá, the viceroy dispatched ships and soldiers three different times between March 4 and April 4. Meanwhile, back in Lima, civil and ecclesiastical officials led local residents to the Church of San Domingo, from whence they bore images of St. Dominic and Our Lady of the Rosary through the streets in solemn procession. Mugaburu observes that "all types of people, friars, clerics, seculars, and women were saying the Rosary aloud throughout the procession," adding that "such a multitude of people praying to Our Lord through the intercession of His Holy Mother for a successful outcome at Panama had never before been seen."[84] The temporary English occupation of Panama impeded sea traffic between Spain and Lima for several months. As a result, news of the canonization of St. Rosa was delayed, eventually arriving over land from Quito, not via the normal maritime route, on May 18, 1671.[85]

The threat to Lima itself was so acute in 1686 that viceregal and municipal officials sought to direct all human resources toward the cause of public defense. Josephe Mugaburu records a decree of March 17 according to which all bricklayers and laborers were required immediately to cease work on all other construction projects in order to help build a new wall around the city. On May 22, the viceroy, duque de La Palata, issued a proclamation ordering all able-bodied men, without exception, to enlist for military service within four days. In both cases, public officials prescribed the payment of harsh fines for noncompliance. In the case of the enlistment decree, the officials declared that lower-status citizens who shirked their public duty would be exiled for two years to the fortress at Valdivia, where they would help defend the far southern limits of viceregal Peru.[86]

The maritime threat is also a major theme in printed histories of the era, including Fray Buenaventura Salinas y Córdoba's *Memorial de las historias del nuevo mundo Piru*. In a lengthy chapter on the tenures and achievements of the Peruvian viceroys, the Lima-born author evaluates each viceregal administration according to two criteria: its efforts to defend Lima and Callao from its enemies and the value of its silver remittances to Spain. The two matters were closely related, of course, a point that Salinas y Córdoba is wont to emphasize. He remarks, for example, that the heavy financial cost of repelling the Englishman

Richard Atkins in 1594 had diminished the value of silver remitted to the royal treasury. In reference to the Dutchman George Spielbergen's attempted assault on Lima two decades later, Salinas y Córdoba praises the marqués de Montesclaros for having sent a large sum of silver to Spain despite the costs incurred in the defense of Peru's coastline. The Franciscan reserves his highest accolades for the marqués de Guadalcazar, the viceroy responsible for defending Lima during a three-month blockade of Callao by the notorious Dutchman Jacques L'Hermite in 1624.[87] Describing the viceroy as "Father, Tutor, and Defender," Salinas y Córdoba credits him with the successful defense of the region, aided of course by God, "the sons of this land," and Spanish soldiers trained in Flanders.[88]

Printed religious histories of Peru such as Diego Córdoba Salinas's chronicle of the Franciscans in Peru (1651) also include frequent discussions of the maritime and coastal depredations of heretic pirates. Córdoba Salinas lists several of the more famous Dutch incursions and, in a mildly defensive tone, claims that "on occasions in which armadas have gone out from our port of Callao . . . [members] of the Order of Our Father St. Francis have offered themselves for the common good."[89]

This constant reality of the Dutch and English threat in Peru shaped the reputation of St. Rosa, especially as it developed over the course of the seventeenth century. One of the more famous episodes in the history of Dutch piracy in Peru, already alluded to previously, occurred in 1615, just two years prior to the death of Rosa de Santa María. In June of that year, a fleet commanded by George Spielbergen sunk the galleon *Santa Ana,* a Spanish crown ship, near the port of Cañete. Viceroy Juan de Mendoza y Luna, marqués de Montesclaros, had divided the small fleet at his disposal into two squadrons, sending one to confront Spielbergen while preparing the other to transport the annual silver shipment to Spain via Panama. Spielbergen's fleet proceeded to blockade Callao, the port serving Lima. When the news came that Dutch forces were disembarking and would soon enter the capital itself, the viceroy dispatched ground forces to Callao, while the archbishop of Lima ordered that the consecrated Host be uncovered in the churches and that prayers be offered on behalf of the city. While the seventeenth-century sources praise Rosa for her willingness to die defending the consecrated body and blood of Christ from heretics bent on sacrilege, a later tradition credited her with saving the city itself from destruction through the efficacy of her intercessory prayers. The absence of the latter claim in the seventeenth-century hagiographies, as well as in the testimonies given during the proceso apostólico, suggests that as the worsening maritime threat coincided with papal confirmation of Rosa's sanctity, her devotees concluded that St. Rosa had guaranteed their survival all along.

Eyewitness Gonzalo de la Maza and all of Rosa's various hagiographers confirm that she regarded the Dutch incursion of 1615 as a religious challenge to Catholic orthodoxy on the one hand and as an opportunity to die as a martyr for Christ on the other. When Lima's men hurried to Callao to repel the intruders, claim the witnesses, Rosa proceeded to the Chapel of Our Lady of the Rosary, where years earlier she had received the vision that dissuaded her from entering a convent and where two years later she would make marriage vows to the Niño Jesús. According to Maza, Rosa later told him that she had gone there because "it appeared God was offering her the occasion to give her life for the sake of her husband." She went so far as to cut her confining clothing with shears in order to gain greater ease of movement should it become necessary to climb up on the altar and "defend the Most Holy Sacrament from the enemies of the faith."[90] The brevity of Pedro de Loayza's description of the episode warrants that it be quoted in full: "She desired to be a martyr, and thus, when the Dutchman came to Callao, she rejoiced greatly that she should merit death as a martyr on behalf of her Husband. Thus, she explained to her mother that she cut her scapulary so that she might better do battle and win, right alongside the Most Holy Sacrament that was uncovered, and that there she longed to die."[91]

In both Loayza's and Maza's account, the emphasis is on Rosa's desire for martyrdom and on the pirates as a religious threat. Leonardo Hansen and Juan Meléndez, who wrote several decades later, also emphasize St. Rosa's willingness to die in defense of the Eucharist, though they add details not mentioned in the earlier accounts.[92] Hansen, for example, quotes one Francisca Hurtado de Bustamante to the effect that Rosa had also aspired to die a martyr's death among savage Indians.[93] According to Hansen, Rosa planned to beg the heretics not to kill her with one blow but to dismember her slowly, piece by piece, for she hoped in this way to delay their advance upon the altar and her beloved Husband. Both Meléndez and Hansen recount how Rosa rallied many terrified women and children to the Chapel of the Rosary, where she inflamed their zeal for martyrdom through impassioned speeches. Hansen may well have gleaned such details from testimony offered by Rosa's devotees during the course of the proceso apostólico of 1630–32. What is absent from both the Hansen and Meléndez accounts, however, is any suggestion that Rosa prayed for the deliverance of her city. In fact, such an assertion would have run contrary to each writer's claim that Rosa longed for martyrdom. Indeed, they note how bitterly disappointed she felt upon hearing that the Protestants had cut anchor and fled the port.

Interestingly, however, Luis Antonio Oviedo y Herrera, in his *Poema heroyco* written at the beginning of the eighteenth century, attributes the delivery of Lima in 1615 to the prayers of St. Rosa de Lima; in fact, he claims that everyone had attributed the flight of the Dutch forces to her intercession. In one sense, it is tempting to attribute such a claim to poetic license; after all, Miguel Núñez de Roxas praises the former corregidor of Potosí for "interweaving history with fiction."[94] On the other hand, it is possible that Oviedo y Herrera was drawing on oral legend, promoted perhaps by local Dominicans, according to which Santa Rosa had saved the city with her prayers.

The desperate situation of Lima during Rosa's lifetime and the decades that followed her death makes this possibility quite plausible, for the people of Lima increasingly resorted to all available resources in their struggle for survival against the Dutch and English threats. Peter T. Bradley's research on maritime defenses in viceregal Peru has shown that building and maintaining a fleet sufficient to the challenges posed by foreign intruders was a chronic problem during the seventeenth century. Requests from the viceroys of Peru for royal aid (ships, funds, etc.) rarely brought the desired results, a factor which, according to Bradley, contributed to local efforts at self-sufficiency:

> One cannot escape the conclusion that financial limitations imposed from Spain, in the interests of keeping silver shipments at the highest possible levels, played a significant part in the development of the [Peruvian] armada. Every effort was made to pare down costs to a minimum . . . until the entire responsibility for sea defense passed into the hands of private commercial interests.[95]

As Bradley makes clear, the merchants and administrators of Lima faced great challenges in their efforts to keep silver remittances high. Because the Spanish crown demanded silver remittances from its Peruvian colony, it was reluctant to allow its administrators to spend much of the profit on the sort of land and sea defenses that would in fact guarantee the safety of those shipments. Like settlers on other American frontiers of the Habsburg Empire, the Spaniards of Lima were left more or less to their own devices.[96]

Under such conditions, religious chroniclers credited local holy persons associated with their respective orders with the preservation of Lima during the decades of duress. For example, Córdoba Salinas claims that when Spielbergen entered Callao in 1615, Doña Isabel de Porras reported a vision in which Our Lady of Mercy appeared in a cloud, protecting the city by covering it with her "white robe." When the Dutch cut their anchors and fled in haste, he notes, everyone in Lima and Callao felt the effects of Doña Isabel's vision.[97] For our purposes in this chapter, it is significant that, although Franciscans Córdoba Salinas and Salinas y Córdoba both refer briefly to a pious beata named Rosa de Santa María, neither links her reputation for sanctity with the invasion of Callao in 1615. This leads to two possible conclusions: Either partisan mendicant rivalries kept these Franciscan writers from crediting a Dominican tertiary with saving the city through her prayers, or the oral legend of St. Rosa's intercessory prayer was not yet circulating in Lima by 1650. The latter possibility seems quite likely, since neither Hansen nor Meléndez, the latter a native of Lima, mention this episode in their late-seventeenth-century vidas.

In a recent study of Carlos Sigüenza y Góngora's seventeenth-century *Infortunios de Alonso Ramírez,* a prose work characterized by a rather subtle criollo agenda, Kimberle S. López assesses the identity of the work's protagonist, Alonso Ramírez:

> "The main Other against which the captive Puerto Rican defines himself is the British buccaneer; curiously, the main point of contention in this alterity is not the fact that the corsairs are outlawed, but the fact that they are Protestant, which in the Hispanic rhetoric of the Counter Reformation constitutes heresy. Thus, in the vocabulary of the *Infortunios,* the terms English, pirate, and heretic are treated as synonyms. . . . For the purposes of *Infortunios,* then, religion is a more accurate cultural marker than nationality."[98]

Sigüenza y Góngora, who was fully conscious of criollo-peninsular alterity, allows the presence in his narrative of the Protestant Other to diminish the cultural distance between the criollo Ramírez and peninsular Spaniards. In similar fashion, I have argued, the pressures of non-Spanish, non-Catholic forces on the Spanish sector of mid-colonial Lima forged a special solidarity between criollo and peninsular.[99] In response to the constant specter of heretic pirates and quasi-pagan Amerindians, Peruvian Spaniards came to understand the significance of St. Rosa in terms of these historic challenges and to seek her intercession against them.

The ideology of Roman Catholic Spain as converter of pagans and guarantor of Roman Catholic orthodoxy found expression in the persona of St. Rosa de Lima, whom hagiographer Antonio de Lorea (d. ca. 1687) described as an effective combatant against "idolaters" and "heretical iconoclasts."[100] Indeed, Rosa's religious iconographers presented her as the embodiment of both ideals. Italian Lázaro Baldi, for example, depicted Santa Rosa in her evangelistic role vis-à-vis pagan, nonwhite peoples of the New World. In one painting, Indians and blacks kneel in veneration before a benign St. Rosa, who cradles the Christ Child in her arms.[101] In the other, which Baldi painted for the Dominican church of Santa Maria Sopra Minerva in Rome, a more militant Rosa destroys the Indians' pagan altars using their own stone idols.[102] Like peninsular and criollo mendicants who evangelized among Peru's Amerindian population throughout the colonial period, St. Rosa the icon found herself caught between the desire to nurture and persuade on the one hand and the need to extirpate idolatry by force on the other.

A second pictorial theme associated with the cult of St. Rosa de Lima by the eighteenth century was one in which she held the Eucharist aloft while a sword-wielding Spanish monarch fends off turban-clad Turks bent on profaning the Host (see figure 4.3).[103] On the European continent as well as in the Mediterranean, the Ottoman Turks had posed an immense threat to imperial Spain beginning in the reign of King Philip II (1556–98) and continuing through the seventeenth century and beyond. The iconography of St. Rosa de Lima as defender of the Eucharist reinforced Spanish and papal hopes that the religious superiority of their cause would assure them favorable outcomes against the Protestants of Northern Europe and the Muslim Turks to the east.

FIGURE 4.3. "St. Rosa defends the Eucharist." Oil on canvas. Cuzco school, anonymous, eighteenth century. From José Flores Araoz et al. *Santa Rosa de Lima y su tiempo* (Lima, 1995), 141. (Courtesy of Museo Pedro de Osma, Lima, Peru)

Yet while the papacy and the Spanish crown interpreted and promoted the persona of St. Rosa de Lima according to their respective
needs and purposes, so did Rosa's limeño devotees, both peninsular and
criollo, among whom there emerged a third iconographic tradition. In
keeping with the theme of St. Rosa as preserver of Lima against the
depredations and sacrileges of Spielbergen's Dutch pirates, her hand
holds a ship's anchor on whose flukes rest the city of Lima (see figures 1.1 and 2.2). In St. Rosa's hand, the anchor, which historically signified salvation, reinterpreted the flight of Spielbergen in 1615, placing
a greater emphasis on Rosa's preservation of the city than on her
defense of the Eucharist. Of course, all three artistic visions were
mutually compatible. St. Rosa was the pacifier of the region's indigenous peoples, defender of its Roman Catholic orthodoxy, and preserver of its capital city, Lima.

Conclusion

Peru's diverse ethnic groups contested her identity and spiritual protection during the seventeenth and eighteenth centuries. Peninsulares,
criollos, Indians, and mestizos competed with each other, notes Ramón
Mujica Pinilla, to become "legitimate heirs of the righteous empire of
St. Rosa, Aurora of the Indies." Each of these social sectors has
attempted, at some point in time, "to appropriate St. Rosa as its own
as a means of consolidating its political sovereignty."[104]

Peru's highland indigenous peoples, including those who claimed
direct descent from the Incas, frequently turned to St. Rosa as a mark-
er of their identity and guarantor of their causes. During the years of
her beatification and canonization, caciques from Jauja petitioned royal
authorities for the right to found an order of noble gentlemen for
"descendants of the *ingas* and *moctezumas*" under the spiritual patronage of St. Rosa de Lima. In 1671, the year of her canonization, their
request was denied. Even so, when an indigenous rebellion broke out in
the region of Acobamba in 1743, both Spanish and indigenous forces
looked to St. Rosa as protector of their cause.[105]

Belief in the restoration of an Incan New Age persisted in and
around Cuzco from the 1560s to the early nineteenth century. There is
a literary reference to this almost messianic expectation in a 1723 edition of Garcilaso de la Vega's *Comentarios reales de los incas,* edited by

Gabriel de Cárdenas. In his prologue to the new edition, Cárdenas alludes to a prophecy about the imminent restoration of Incan rule in the region of Cuzco, a fact to be achieved with the assistance of England. Although it is impossible to determine whether such local rumors directly shaped Oviedo y Herrera's literary imagination when he sat down to pen his *Poema heroyco,* such influence seems likely given his tenure as corregidor of Potosí. Oviedo y Herrera was not the only one to link the persona of St. Rosa with the ideology of Inca restoration. But whereas he portrayed the limeña saint as the one who opposed and defeated such anti-Spanish machinations, certain indigenous prophecies of the late eighteenth century linked her name to the cause of Incan restoration. For example, both she and St. Francisco Solano were rumored to have prophesied that an Incan restoration would occur in the year of "the three sevens" *(los tres sietes)*; that is, 1777. José Gabriel Túpac Amaru, the rebel leader who rose up against Spanish rule in 1780, believed not only in this prophecy attributed to St. Rosa, but also in the forecast that England would come to his aid against Spain.[106] Following the outbreak of his rebellion, Spanish officials in Cuzco began to investigate the origins and spread of the prophecy of the three sevens.[107] This episode illustrates two features of the colonial-era identity and cult of St. Rosa de Lima: it was hotly contested between competing groups (especially Indians and Spaniards), and it was closely linked in the minds of both Spaniards and highland Indians to their historic power struggles. Both features of the cult of St. Rosa de Lima would persist into the period of Peru's independence struggle and beyond.[108]

Hagiography in Service of the Patria Chica

The Life of St. Mariana de Jesús, "Lily of Quito"

With the canonization of St. Rosa de Lima in 1671, pious criollos throughout Spanish America acquired a new religious point of reference. Although Pope Clement IX described the new saint as "our Rosa,"[1] a reference to her significance for the whole of Latin Christendom, many self-conscious americanos believed that she was *their* saint. For some, including an eighteenth-century writer who described St. Rosa as "lustrous honor of New Spain,"[2] she represented the greatness of criollos in general. Devotees of americano holy persons who had not yet been beatified found new reason for optimism. Sor Antonia de San Juan, mother superior of Puebla's Convento de Santa Clara, expressed such a hope in 1715. Writing on behalf of the causa of a locally born Conceptionist nun named María de Jesús Tomellín, she asked Rome "to grant to the city of Puebla its own criolla and patrician, just as Peru has St. Rosa."[3] Perhaps most important, however, St. Rosa provided pious criollos with a model of Roman Catholic sanctity that had roots in their native soil and in their social experiences. No longer content simply to imitate Old World originals, criollo holy women and their male hagiographers were free after 1670 to pattern both life and pious text after a New World exemplar.

Nowhere does the theme of St. Rosa as spiritual prototype figure more prominently than in Jacinto Morán de Butrón's *La Azucena de Quito* (The Lily of Quito), the first published Life of St. Mariana de Jesús (1618–45), a native of the northern Peruvian city of Quito (see figure 5.1).[4] In his introduction to this work, which he wrote during 1696–97, the Jesuit author (1668–1749) establishes a providential link between Lima's "Rose" and Quito's "Lily":

> Divine Power endowed America with the most admirable Rose, . . . planted in the lands of His Indies. He [then] decided to transplant [the Rose], for His own glory's sake, to the paradise of His delights. This kingdom [i.e., Peru] wept in the absence of the Rose, as daytime mourns the absence of sunshine, and as Judea [mourned] without Moses. But if in the latter case God ended the tears and sobs [by granting] new succor and gifts, certainly He did not, upon taking the Rose from this realm, leave it without . . . protection and patronage. For not even a year passed between the transfer of St. Rosa from Lima to heaven and the birth of the Venerable virgin Mariana de Jesús y Paredes, most beautiful of flowers and purest of lilies, who became a substitute for the Rose and a perfect representation of her virtues.[5]

Morán's use of the Rose/Lily metaphor is much more than a convenient play on the two beatas' popular epithets; it informs his hagiographic strategy from beginning to end. Morán compares these holy women's religious practices and mystical experiences, as well as the selfless actions by which each miraculously saved her patria from disaster.

Through a close reading of *La Azucena de Quito,* in this chapter I explore criollo notions of group identity and origins, concluding that American-born Spaniards did not identify themselves simply as members of some pan-Criollo brotherhood that defined itself in opposition to Amerindians, Protestants, or peninsular Spaniards. Rather, their primary sense of homeland, and thus of group loyalty, was much more local. In short, most Spaniards in the Americas, whether americanos or not, identified themselves most closely with a *patria chica,* or "small homeland." As this chapter will show, Jacinto Morán de Butrón, a

FIGURE 5.1. "B. Mariana de Jesús de Paredes y Flores llamada La azucena de Quito." (Blessed Mariana de Jesús de Paredes y Flores, called the Lily of Quito.) Frontispiece from Jacinto Morán de Butrón, S.J., *Vida de la B. Mariana de Jesús de Paredes y Flores, conocida vulgarmente bajo el nombre de la Azucena de Quito* (Madrid, 1854). (Courtesy of the Bancroft Library, University of California, Berkeley)

native of the Imperial Spanish administrative region of Quito (in northern viceregal Peru) and a lifelong member of the corresponding Jesuit province, fills his text with this parochial sense of local identity. By favorably comparing his patria's Lily with Lima's St. Rosa, Morán makes a subtle case for the greatness of Quito. Furthermore, his efforts to account for the Lily's relatively unknown status vis-à-vis the more famous St. Rosa lead him to lament the unappreciated status of his own patria in relation to illustrious Lima, the royal and ecclesiastical center of viceregal Peru. In the end, he intimates that the secondary status of both Mariana and Quito is the result not of some objective inferiority, but of poor advertising.

In the pages that follow, I present an overview of Mariana's life, with some preliminary attention to the hagiographic traditions that developed following her death. I then examine *La Azucena de Quito*, pointing to the historical and regional factors that shaped the hagiographer's narrative strategies.

Mariana Paredes y Flores: Biographical Sketch

Mariana Paredes y Flores was born in Quito to relatively prosperous hidalgo parents, Jerónimo Zenel Paredes y Flores and Mariana Jaramillo de Granobles, in 1618.[6] According to witnesses, numerous signs of divine approval accompanied her birth and persisted throughout her early childhood. Following the premature deaths of her parents, Mariana entered the home of her older sister and brother-in-law, Jerónima de Paredes and Cosme de Caso, who raised the extraordinary girl as their own daughter. In the home of her sister and brother-in-law, Mariana exercised a powerful spiritual influence over their daughters, Juana and Sebastiana, both of whom would later gain reputations for sanctity due to their close association with their famous aunt. Although Mariana had taken a vow of perpetual chastity at age seven, and despite the urging of Don Cosme de Caso, she refused to enter a convent. Instead, at the age of twelve she withdrew into seclusion in a room provided for that purpose by her adoptive parents.[7]

Regardless of motivation, however, Mariana de Jesús was similar to Rosa de Lima in that she lived the life of an uncloistered beata, devoted to charity, prayer, and a rigorous asceticism. A prominent element of her spirituality, reflecting the baroque excess of the era, was the Passion of Christ, symbolically represented by symbols of suffering and death. Like many Roman Catholics throughout the ages, Mariana considered it an honor to shed her own blood in imitation of her Savior, for this allowed her to identify with his suffering. Thus, she often prevailed upon the family's Indian maid, Catalina, to beat her naked shoulders and back with a whip, always vigilant to have the resulting bloodstains wiped from the walls lest she be discovered. During her frequent illnesses, Mariana insisted on being bled in a sort of penitential ritual that eventually contributed to her posthumous reputation for sanctity.[8] Eventually, her fascination with death led Mariana, as a reminder of the insignificance of earthly things and as a stimulus to greater acts of penitence, to place symbols of death, such as human skulls, in her personal quarters.[9]

Mariana's spiritual life centered upon the Jesuit church located near her home. There she received the sacraments, sought the wisdom and spiritual guidance of her confessors, and participated in such religious sodalities as the Confraternity of the Holy Trinity and the Congregation of the Slaves of the Virgin of Loreto. Under the influence of Jesuit preachers, she came to hold the Sacred Heart of Jesus in great devotion. Jesuit historians have identified Mariana de Jesús as a founding member of the Association of the Holy Christ of Consolation (later, Congregation of the Good Death), and credited her with having rekindled local devotion to Our Lady of Loreto.[10] In terms of interior devotion as well as exterior participation in the spiritual life of the community, Mariana appears to have conformed to the clerical, and especially Jesuit, ideal for beatas.

Following Mariana's death in May 1645, she was buried in the same Jesuit church where she learned and exercised her devotion.[11] Father Alonso de Rojas, S.J., who had served for a time as Mariana's confessor, delivered a panegyric in her honor. This *Sermón,* which was published the following year in Lima, exercised a fundamental influence on all subsequent accounts of the beata's life, including Morán's *La Azucena de Quito.*[12] The Rojas *Sermón* praises Mariana's lifelong practice of self-mortification, evidenced by a rigorous daily schedule that mixed intense devotional activity with the ascetic suppression of bodily cravings for food, drink, and sleep. Calling attention to Mariana's aspiration to martyrdom, Rojas describes how she filled her personal chambers with several realistic reminders of life's brevity. This practice, which the

Jesuit preacher describes as Mariana's "antidote" against the poison of sin, freed her from feminine vanity and strengthened her resolve to keep her childhood vow of perpetual virginity. Thus, on one occasion she turned away a would-be seducer with the reply, "I am learning to die." By enumerating Mariana's virtues, Rojas not only proves her sanctity, but also offers the women and girls of Quito a model for living: "Learn, girls of Quito, from your fellow countrywoman, [to prefer] holiness over beauty, virtues over ostentation."[13]

This Jesuit preacher's emphasis on Mariana's ascetic renunciation of the flesh, and specifically of her own female beauty, merits further attention, for it makes Mariana's body, rather than her words, the locus of her spiritual authority. Since the Middle Ages, ecclesiastical restrictions on female religious activity had increased to the point that devout nuns and beatas could neither preach nor carry out missionary functions among non-Christian peoples. Denied the opportunity to serve God and the church in these ways, pious women expressed their faith by exercising control over their own bodies. By denying themselves the sensual gratification of a healthy diet, adequate sleep, or sexual relations, these women turned their bodies into religious texts. Indeed, male clerics who promoted the spiritual reputations of such female ascetics often described this female exemplarity as a wordless sermon. In his thirteenth-century account of the life of Elizabeth of Spalbeek, for example, Philip of Clairvaux warned that her corporeal experiences had left the most rustic of Christians without excuse:

> No human . . . can prevaricate, however illiterate and simple he or she may be, and say: "I cannot understand such profound mysteries, because I am not lettered," or "because this is a closed book for me." For now this illiterate man or woman can read, not in parchments or documents, but in the members and the body of this girl, as a vivid and unmistakable Veronica, a living image and an animated history of redemption, as if he or she were literate.[14]

Although the charismatic or non-institutional authority exercised by the female penitent was distinct from the more objective, sacramental authority of male clerics, the two were not at all irreconcilable. Indeed, by associating themselves with the sanctity of the female holy woman, ordained priests enhanced their own religious status.[15] In Philip of Clairvaux's thirteenth-century Life of Elizabeth, notes Wal-

ter Simons, Philip "frequently reverts to the analogy between her bodily enactment of the Passion story and a priest's exposition of the
Gospel" in order to defend Elizabeth's religious practices from potential censure by ecclesiastical authorities.[16] In a similar fashion, Alonso
de Rojas describes Mariana's last days of physical suffering and death
as a spiritual work by which she complemented and lent support to
his own sacramental ministry.

Over several years, popular acclamation of Mariana's sanctity led
to official investigations into her sanctity, the most important being
the proceso apostólico of 1670–78.[17] As occurred in the case of St.
Rosa, numerous members of the local community, both social elites and
low-status household servants, testified before ecclesiastical investigators about Mariana's faith, works, and miracles. The list of eyewitnesses included Mariana's niece and great-niece, Madre Andrea María de
la Santísima Trinidad and Madre Catalina María de los Angeles (both
Carmelite nuns); a childhood friend named Doña Escolástica Sarmien-
to; and household servants María and Catalina Paredes, the latter of
whom aided Mariana in her secret penitential acts. Other prominent
locals—family members, clergymen, and a physician acquainted with
Mariana's health problems—also offered testimony, just as in the case
of St. Rosa. Yet in one important respect the beata of Quito was very
unlike St. Rosa of Lima: her cause for canonization did not meet with
rapid success. Rather, the "humble, shy Lily" remained unknown,
locked, as it were, "in the . . . closed bud."[18] She was eventually beatified in 1850, however, and canonized a century later.

Mariana de Jesús: Hagiographic Traditions and Strategies

Mariana's eventual Jesuit hagiographer, Jacinto Morán de Butrón y
Guzmán, was born in 1668 in Guayaquil, the principal port city for
the administrative region of Quito.[19] He was the firstborn son of Don
Jacinto Morán de Butrón y Rendón and Doña María Ramírez de
Guzmán y Mestanza, both criollos. At the age of sixteen, young Jacinto traveled to Quito to begin a novitiate in the Jesuit house, but did
not make the Jesuit profession of four vows until some twenty years
later in the city of Riobamba. Thereafter, he held a number of posts
in the Jesuit provinces of Quito and Nueva Granada, including preacher, lecturer in the Universidad de San Gregorio (Quito), vice-rector of

the *colegio* of Popayán, and rector of the colegio of Panama. He spent the last twenty-three years of his life in Guayaquil, where he died in 1749. Because of Morán's authorship of *La Azucena de Quito,* as well as several other unpublished works of regional history, one twentieth-century Ecuadorian scholar labeled him "the initiator of historical studies of our fatherland *(patria)*."[20]

In 1695, while studying at the Jesuit colegio in Ibarra (province of Quito), Morán experienced a "vocational crisis," which may have been the result of his family's financial difficulties. In the event, one of his Jesuit superiors, Father Ignacio Altamirano, decided to reinforce Morán's spiritual commitment by ordering him to read Father Alonso de Rojas's *Sermón.* Inspired by the reading, Morán went on to examine carefully the voluminous proceso apostólico of 1670–78. From this stage it was a logical step for Altamirano to request that Morán, so recently and intimately acquainted with the two most important primary source documents, compose a long-overdue biography of Mariana de Jesús. The proceso was Morán's most complete source for testimonial information concerning the details of his subject's life. The *Sermón* gave him thematic foundations upon which to build.

In keeping with the multifaceted nature of hagiographic writing, Morán attempts to achieve several interconnected goals in *La Azucena de Quito.* First, in order to convince Rome that Mariana de Jesús is a saint deserving of official recognition, he offers a number of proofs, including the existence of an enduring and widespread popular devotion. Second, he seeks pious patrons for the Lily's causa from the various regions of greater viceregal Peru. But he also writes to stake a claim to her sanctity on behalf of Quito and the Jesuits of that region. In *La Azucena de Quito,* Mariana de Jesús reflects the status and achievement, indeed the maturity, of Morán's home region and his religious order.

As a Jesuit, Morán writes to defend his order's interests and to promote its pastoral priorities. As late as the mid-1690s, fully a half-century after Mariana's death, the Jesuits of the province of Quito had not completed or published a hagiography in her honor.[21] In the meantime, their religious rivals, the Franciscans, had staked their own claim to her reputation for sanctity. Fray Diego Córdoba Salinas included brief biographies of Mariana de Jesús and her nieces in his history of the Franciscan province of Peru, citing the *Sermón* of Alonso de Rojas, S.J., as one of his principal sources. Córdoba Salinas also cites a letter from fellow Franciscan Fr. Juan Cazco, who claimed to have seen a written request in Mariana's own hand for entrance into the Third Order of St. Francis, as well as a written copy of her profession as a Franciscan tertiary.[22] This Franciscan account uproots the Lily of Quito from the Jesuit soil in which she had developed, as well as from her quiteño patria; instead, she emerges as a spiritual fruit of the Franciscan province of San Francisco, which had its administrative center at Lima. By the 1690s, this fact had become a source of embarrassment and indignation for members of Quito's municipal council and its Jesuit province, which helps to explain the urgency of Morán's hagiographic endeavor. I will return shortly to this frustrated publication history, for the failure to publish any accounts of Mariana's life, which some were blaming on a lack of devotion, shapes Morán's hagiographic text. In his efforts to account for the hagiographic lacuna, the Jesuit writer betrays an awareness of Lima's cultural and institutional hegemony over Quito.

An explicit Jesuit polemic is evident from the opening paragraphs of *La Azucena de Quito*. In fact, Morán's title symbolically locates Mariana within specific geographic and religious contexts: "The Lily of Quito, Who Germinated in the Florid Field of the Church in the Western Indies of the Realms of Peru, and Whom the Company of Jesus Cultivated by its Diligent Teaching." Morán's Lily belongs to Quito, the western Indies, and Peru, but also to the sons of St. Ignatius.[23]

In his main narrative, Morán explicitly denies the Franciscan claims by emphasizing Mariana's devotion to the Jesuit order, which she frequently referred to as "my mother." Mariana dropped her family surnames for the title "de Jesús," Morán explains, to demonstrate the crucial role that the Jesuits had played in her spiritual development. Morán lauds his own order "for being the only one that cultivated, watered, and harvested this Lily," and reinforces his point by enriching his narrative with brief biographies of her Jesuit confessors, including such well-known clerics as Juan Camacho and Hernando de la Cruz. In a chapter entitled "Su devoción a Cristo sacramentado y a los santos," he seeks to prove conclusively that Mariana's connection to the order of St. Francis was incidental. Having described Mariana's strong affective ties to Jesuit confessors and saints, he argues that she wore the Franciscan scapulary and sash only because her Jesuit confessor suggested she do so. Indeed, the whole matter was so insignificant to Mariana that she did not go to the Franciscan church to receive the emblems, but sent someone else in her place.[24]

But Morán is not simply a Jesuit polemicist; he also directs his attention to his order's pastoral priorities. Referring to Mariana's exemplary life as "a silent sermon"[25] Morán gives her vida a markedly moralistic tone. Transcending both the hagiographic and the historical, he seeks to inspire his readers to virtue, as well as to provide future preachers with a useful source for hortatory. In his original prologue, Morán explains the multifaceted nature of his text:

> I will not deny that the historical is mixed with the laudatory *(panegírico)*, and the narrative with moral instruction, but in this regard neither my feelings nor my heart could be contained. Besides, being a Jesuit requires as part of the vocation that the finality of one's writing be no other than the benefit of souls. Those who aspire to virtue will find [what they need] by looking attentively at the works of Mariana.[26]

Jacinto Morán de Butrón writes not only as a Jesuit, but also as proud native of Quito. In this capacity, he presents Mariana as a sign that his own patria has come of age. Morán achieves this goal by presenting his subject's spiritual stature in relation to the recognized spiritual grandeur of St. Rosa de Lima. For Morán, the remarkable similarities between the Lily and the Rose made his hagiographic task an easy one.

Morán notes at least four parallels between Mariana de Jesús and Santa Rosa de Lima—their popular titles, religious exercises, mystical experiences, and special salvific relationship with homeland or patria. He makes a great deal, for example, of the similarities between the two women's popular titles, La Rosa de Lima and La Azucena de Quito. In both cases, a miraculous sign led to the replacement of their given names with the name of a flower. Moreover, on each occasion an Indian servant played a key role in the name change. I have already described how an Indian maid's astonishing vision led the family of Isabel de Flores to begin calling her Rosa. Whereas Isabel became Rosa in infancy, Mariana de Jesús received her popular epithet posthumously. During her final illness, when Mariana's physicians were bleeding her each day, the Indian maid Catalina poured the collected blood into a pit in the family's garden. Shortly after Mariana's death, Catalina and other witnesses found lilies miraculously blooming in the very spot; devotees were soon referring to the deceased beata as the Lily of Quito. The miracle of the lilies, as well as the floral epithet that resulted from it, allowed Morán to argue for a providential connection between Mariana and St. Rosa. At several points in his narrative, Morán makes that divine link explicit:

> When a very beautiful child was born in Lima and given the name Isabel at her baptism, . . . God willed that they should change her name from Isabel to Rosa. . . . [And] it appears that He arranged in Quito, even though this Venerable virgin was called Mariana during her lifetime, that following her death she should be even more applauded and celebrated. He ordained that a lily should be formed from her blood as a sign to us, that we should change her name and call her our Lily; having given Lima a Rose, He granted to Quito a Lily.[27]

In keeping with this observation, the quiteño author quotes classical and biblical sources to show that everyone associates the lily with the rose.[28] Morán extends his comparison of Rosa and Lily to the two beatas' ascetic and virtuous lives, observing, in the words of Pliny, that "lilies are planted, cultivated, and grow like roses."[29] In the opening pages of *La Azucena de Quito,* Morán testifies that "when I read through the authentic Procesos of [Mariana's] life, aware of the virtues of Rosa, I discovered great similarities between the two, for [in Mariana] I saw Rosa's graces and perfection represented in living form." "Indeed," he adds, "were the Venerable virgin Mariana de Jesús to have no other praiseworthy credentials than to have followed in the footsteps of the illustrious virgin Santa Rosa de Santa María, her sanctity would require no other applause, nor its narration any further adornment."[30]

Morán argues that these similarities in religious observation and virtue were far from coincidental. On the contrary, when Mariana was yet a very small child, Cosme de Caso had returned home from Lima with news about Rosa, who had only recently died. Morán describes what transpired after Mariana's adoptive father told her all about Rosa's heroic virtues: "Even though at that time [Rosa] had not been canonized by the Holy See, Mariana's love for her was so great that she built an altar of devotion [to Rosa] in her own heart." Just like Rosa before her, Mariana took a vow of perpetual chastity years before reaching adolescence. Like Rosa, Mariana imitated St. Catherine of Siena. Moreover, the quiteña resembled her limeña predecessor by practicing a piety marked by "drops of blood, tears, acts of penitence, abstinence, and austerities." Commenting on Mariana's particular devotion to the Eucharist during Holy Week observances, Morán offers yet another comparison with Rosa de Lima: "I am unsure if, during her days in the Jesuit Church, our Lily did less than the finest Rose did in Lima's convent of the Rosary; but I am certain that both of them, kneeling attentively, desired to drink all of the blood of the innocent Lamb." As is clear from these examples, Morán portrays Mariana's spirituality as an outgrowth of her devotion to Rosa de Lima. Rosa was the teacher, Mariana the disciple; Rosa the original, Mariana a perfect copy.[31]

Ultimately, however, divine providence was the source of each woman's sanctity, not human will or effort. To put it another way, God had ordained the path of both Rosa and Lily and had chosen to shower them with divine favors. As previously mentioned, Morán attributes the timing of Mariana's birth in Quito to God's desire to grant the people of Peru a replacement for their beloved Rosa.[32] Moreover, just as God prevented Rosa from taking the nun's veil, he also blocked Mariana's entrance into the Convento de Santa Catalina de Sena.[33] Divine guidance enabled Mariana to prophesy accurately that the house of Cosme and Jerónima de Caso would someday shelter a community of discalced Carmelite nuns; Rosa had similarly foreseen the establishment of a convent in the home of her patrons. And as he had done for their beloved Catherine of Siena, God not only showered Rosa and Mariana with special spiritual favors, but also miraculously nourished their bodies for long periods with no other food but the consecrated Host.[34]

Finally, in order to strengthen the parallels between the Lily of Quito and the Rose of Lima, especially as representatives and patronesses of their respective patrias, Morán calls attention to Mariana's death, by which she atoned for the sins of Quito and preserved it from God's temporal judgment. In making this comparison, Morán assumes his readers are familiar with similar acts of heroism attributed to Rosa de Lima. As noted in chapter 4, hagiographic and oral traditions credited St. Rosa with penitential acts of public service, one in which her self-flagellation averted the disasters predicted by St. Francisco Solano and another in which her defense of the consecrated Host turned away Spielbergen's Protestant pirates. With one or both of these pious traditions in mind, Morán de Butrón narrates how the Lily of

Quito gave her life in expiation for the sins of her compatriots, thereby becoming "liberator of her patria [and] redeemer of her brethren." Therefore, he asserts, "just as Lima owes its freedom from devastation to Santa Rosa, one can conclude that . . . Quito owes its continued existence to Mariana."[35]

Mariana performed this act of public devotion in the Lenten season of 1645, a dramatic time for the residents of Quito and the surrounding region. Once again the volcanic peak known as Pichincha was ominously active, threatening destruction of life and property. When word reached Quito that an earthquake had destroyed the city of Riobamba, quiteños began to fear their city would be next. To make matters worse, an epidemic of measles and diphtheria began to afflict both Spanish and Indian populations to such an extent that "one could see nothing but cadavers in the streets."[36]

This sort of public security crisis, which was rather commonplace to the inhabitants of the region, was ripe with religious significance. As city council (cabildo) records from this period reveal, it was customary on such occasions for clerics and civil rulers to carry religious images in procession through the streets of Quito.[37] Penitents filled local churches in order to make confession and receive the Eucharist, while zealous clergymen preached passionate sermons that warned of impending doom. In reference to the crisis of 1645, Morán describes an episode in which an Indian fanned the flames of public hysteria by running through Quito's dark streets warning at the top of his lungs that disaster would strike the city at midnight.[38]

One day, in the midst of this emotional angst and religious frenzy, Father Alonso de Rojas, who would a few months later offer the oratory at Mariana's funeral, said mass before an anxious crowd in the Jesuit church. Crying aloud to God in the presence of the faithful, Father Rojas pleaded that his own life be accepted as expiation for the spiritual and temporal salvation of the people. But even as he reached the dramatic climax of his prayer, young Mariana de Jesús, who was kneeling near the church's main altar, silently directed her own request to God: "My confessor is so necessary for the conversion of souls; . . . My own life is superfluous. At this moment I offer my life to you, my God, dear Husband of my soul, so that in Quito your anger may cease and your rigors soften, and that you may free my beloved countrymen . . . from the pestilent scourge . . . and ruinous tremors."[39]

In the end, it was the young virgin's selfless offer that placated God's wrath; she was struck by fever as she returned home from mass that very day, and died within two months. The seismic tremors ceased immediately, however, and by Easter Sunday the pestilence was but a memory. Recounting this episode some fifty years after it occurred, Morán aims his message at both quiteño and non-quiteño audiences. He reminds the former group of their indebtedness to Mariana, the "liberator" and "redeemer" of their patria. To his non-quiteño readers, especially those Peruvian devotees of St. Rosa who may be unaware or unconvinced of Mariana's sanctity, he argues that Quito has in the Lily what Lima enjoys in the Rose.

Yet to recognize Morán's use of the Rose/Lily metaphor is to beg the related question of why he employs this strategy. One could reasonably argue, of course, that he does nothing new. After all, as noted in chapters 3 and 4, Roman Catholic hagiographers had for centuries described their protagonists as copies of previous models. Thus, it would seem, Mariana's late-eighteenth-century hagiographer makes a very standard argument for sanctity by association, noting the similarities between his local popular saint and an officially recognized predecessor. However, this explanation proves inadequate upon closer examination of Morán's narrative. Further, when the textual evidence is considered in the light of Lima's historic hegemony over the secondary provincial cities of Peru, it leads to the conclusion that the author is writing more than hagiography.

Before proceeding, then, it is imperative that I consider the hegemonic relationship between Spanish America's viceregal capitals, Lima and Mexico City, and secondary urban centers like Quito, for the Spanish colonial administrative structure tended to privilege the former vis-à-vis the latter. In terms of civil administration, the viceregal capitals were the seats of royal Spanish authority. The creation of colonial structures in Peru dates to the 1530s, when conquistador Francisco Pizarro chose to establish the new "City of the Kings" (Lima) on the coast of Peru, rather than in Cuzco, Jauja, or Quito, traditional centers of Inca rule. The importance of Quito, however, was clear from the beginning, prompting Pizarro to create a governorship *(gobierno)* there in 1534.[40] When the Spanish crown began to create secondary administrative districts known as audiencias, Quito was among the first to attain such status (1563).[41] The urban-centered audiencias—which handled most legal, military, and administrative matters for their hinterland regions—often came into conflict with the higher-ranked viceroys over matters of jurisdiction, rank, and protocol. During the seventeenth century, as the power of Spanish royal institutions waned while that of influential criollo families increased, regional audiencias like that of Quito began to exercise greater autonomy at the expense not only of Madrid, but of the viceregal capitals as well.[42] This development increasingly exacerbated tensions between Lima and the provinces.

Ecclesiastical organization, in terms of both the secular clergy and the mendicant orders, placed Quito in a secondary position to Lima. Under the terms of the *patronato real,* King Charles V created episcopal sees in the viceregal capitals in the 1530s.[43] Quiteño aspirations to similar ecclesiastical status met with mixed success; in the same year that Quito gained a bishop (1546), Lima became archdiocese of Peru. As such, Lima enjoyed a greater episcopal income, a larger cathedral chapter, and higher status than the second-tier episcopal sees.

The administrative structure of the major male religious orders reinforced Lima's primacy over the secondary urban centers. Whether headquartered in Madrid or in Rome, these orders divided their New World operations into administrative units called *provincias.* Within viceregal Peru, each order imitated the civil and episcopal structures by establishing its first Peruvian institution in Lima. For example, the Franciscans established the province of Los Doce Apóstoles de Lima before creating the provinces of San Antonio (Charcas), San Francisco (Quito), and Santa Fe (Bogotá). For their part, the Dominicans and the Jesuits followed the same pattern.[44]

The elevation of St. Rosa to a unique liturgical position in the Spanish Empire effectively reinforced this notion of Lima's superiority over the secondary cities of Greater Peru. Whereas holy persons from other regions remained relatively unknown as a result of papal regulations against unofficial cults, St. Rosa's presence was palpable in Chile and Quito, as well as in New Spain. Novohispano devotees of the first americano saint encountered her in diverse printed texts (vidas, sermons, poems), in church art and altars, and in the female convents bearing her name.[45] As previously noted, moreover, her canonical success frequently inspired promoters of other potential New World saints, and explicit references to that success appeared in their hagiographic texts and sermons.

Even so, only one criollo hagiographer bases his literary project on a sustained comparison between his subject and St. Rosa, and that author is a quiteño whose saint and patria languish in Lima's shadow. In *La Azucena de Quito,* Morán seeks to bring both Lily and Quito out of the shadows, to advertise their true excellence. From the opening pages of his narrative, Morán defends Quito's material, spiritual, and cultural accomplishments against those who despise it as a backwater. For example, in response to European critics, he denies that Quito's southerly location is disadvantageous.[46] To the contrary, his native region is rich in minerals and "fruits," the garden *(vergel)* of the Indies. In his other descriptions of Quito, however, Morán betrays the fact that his primary point of comparison is Lima, whose specter lurks in the background. Praising Quito's architecture as "sturdy and first-class," Morán points out that within ten years of its foundation as a Spanish city, it had built a cathedral, divided itself from the archdiocese of Lima, and begun to support a bishop with large revenues. Furthermore, notes Morán, quiteño devotion to numerous pious cults and careful maintenance of holy sites and sanctuaries had prevented their land from suffering the "unfortunate types of destruction that is lamented in many regions of the Indies."[47] In his declaration that Quito's "pulpits and learned chairs *(cátedras)* need not envy the brilliance of others," we find an implicit reference to Lima. Finally, in one of his clearest expressions of quiteño envy, Morán discounts the relative paucity of books on quiteño religious history, asserting that "the lives of those who earned reputations for heroic virtues and public acclaim as saints [in Quito] would not fit into a large volume." The lack of such printed volumes, he explains, is due to "this region's lack of a printing press by means of which it might shed public light on its own honors."[48]

Morán's lament about a limited quiteño literature related directly to his immediate task, namely the defense of Mariana's public reputation for sanctity through the publication of her Life. He was aware that Lima enjoyed hegemony over Quito in the strength and reputation of its cultural institutions. The prestigious Universidad de San Marcos had been founded in Lima as early as 1551, while Quito had managed only recently (1680s) to establish its own colegio and university.[49] The viceregal capital was also home to a licensed printing press, something that Quito still lacked at the turn of the eighteenth century. As a result, Peru's seventeenth-century criollo literature was almost exclusively

limeño in its flavor. Those early articulators of criollo pride encountered in the previous chapter—Fr. Buenaventura Salinas y Córdoba,
O.F.M., Fr. Diego Córdoba Salinas, O.F.M., and Fr. Juan Meléndez,
O.P.—were born and educated in the viceregal capital.[50] Through their
efforts, Lima developed a reputation as the Peruvian producer of saints,
while the pious heroes of the secondary regions remained unknown.

In his role as hagiographer, Morán feels compelled to explain why
a Life of the quiteña saint has been so long in coming, for the half-century delay reflected very badly on both Mariana and her devotees. In
a brief prologue that he wrote in 1697 to accompany the hagiographic text in a printed edition, Morán explains that three potential hagiographers had been unable, due to burdensome administrative duties or
untimely death, to write and publish her Life. At the same time, he
praises the efforts of the Quito city council and the Jesuit province to
promote Mariana's cause for canonization and preserve documentary
evidence pertaining to her life.[51]

As Morán prepared his manuscript for publication a few years
later, he called on fellow Jesuits Diego Abad y Cepeda, Juan Calvo,
and Isidro Gallegos to testify in writing to the orthodoxy and spiritual
usefulness of his narrative. In their "Parecer" (Opinion), the three
authors employ Morán's Rose/Lily metaphor, observing that "Mariana de Jesús, called 'Lily of Quito,' . . . seems to us a very close likeness to the fragrant flower of the Kingdoms of Peru, Rosa de Santa
María." Divine Providence, which earlier had raised up Rosa as "queen
for the glory of the Indies," had now cultivated the Lily "as her sister in
customs, for the honor and adornment of these provinces." The enthusiasm of the three Jesuits is tempered, however, by the observation that
although the two saints "were born practically in the same garden *(un
mismo jardín)* and time period *(edad del tiempo),*" they remain different
in one important respect. Whereas the Rose has won fame throughout
the church, "this humble, shy Lily" remains "imprisoned in the closed
bud of ignorance."[52]

Ironically, Morán's *La Azucena de Quito* remained unpublished for
another quarter-century, as he and his agents met with one setback after
another. By the time his efforts bore fruit in 1724, he had managed to
publish a very abbreviated *Compendio* (1702), but had also lost two manuscripts in the process, one among the personal papers of a deceased
patron and the other at sea.[53] In the prologue to his 1724 edition of

La Azucena de Quito—which begins with the phrase, "Seventy-six years
have passed since the death of the Venerable virgin Mariana de Jesús"—
Morán justifies the tardy publication of Mariana's Life.[54] Between 1699
and 1702, he explains, efforts to publish the work in Lima had met with
limited success (i.e., the *Compendio*), since "costs there are very high"
and the region around Quito relatively poor. This factor, along with the
deaths in rapid succession of three leading Mariana patrons—including Captain José Guerrero de Salazar, who arranged publication of the
Compendio and was collecting alms for Mariana's causa in the city of
Cuzco at the time of his death—had greatly hampered progress toward
publication. As a result of these misfortunes, Morán confesses, "If
[Mariana's] cult did not wane, for it flourishes still in these realms,
patronage of it was suspended, the manuscript book of her life was
lost, and her causa was forgotten."[55]

As Morán goes on to explain, following the setbacks of 1699–1702,
the Jesuit province of Quito had sent a second copy of the manuscript,
along with funds to cover publication costs, to Spain in 1706 aboard
the galleon *El Gobierno*. These efforts had been frustrated, however,
when English pirates captured the ship and its contents. As a result,
Morán explains, he had been forced to take up the pen and "test fortune
once again." As in his earlier, unpublished prologue, Morán defends
Mariana's devotees from charges of "carelessness or neglect," praising
the Jesuit province and the city council of Quito for taking care to preserve the essential original documents. For Morán, only the conver-
gence of several unfortunate circumstances, one of which was "the lack
of a printing press in these parts," had prevented the publication of
Mariana's Life.[56]

The successful publication of *La Azucena de Quito* in 1724 was the
result of great persistence on the part of the Jesuits of Quito, as well as
the financial support of Don Pedro de Zumárraga, archdeacon of the
Cathedral of Quito. In his letter of dedication (dedicatoria) to Zumárraga, a descendent of the famed first bishop of New Spain, Morán
praises him for devotion to St. Rosa de Lima, whose altar he had placed
in the Quito cathedral at his own personal expense. After flattering
Zumárraga for his famous lineage and faithful ecclesiastical service in
the diocese of Quito, and noting the numerous parallels between St.
Rosa and the Lily of Quito, Morán pleads with him to do for the Lily
what he had already done for the Rose. The persuasion campaign

apparently worked, and Zumárraga paid the publication costs of *La Azucena de Quito.*[57]

Conclusion

Twentieth-century Jesuit historian José Jouanen once suggested that it would be impossible to write the history of the Jesuit province of Quito without including the life of St. Mariana de Jesús.[58] For Jacinto Morán de Butrón, writing the Life of Mariana de Jesús provided an opportunity for celebrating the merits of Quito.

American-born Spaniards did not always craft group identities in opposition to peninsular Spaniards, Amerindians, or even Protestant rivals for empire; they sometimes defined themselves in more local, civic terms; that is, vis-à-vis rival criollo communities. As a native-born son of the region of Quito, Morán narrates Mariana's life in a way that reflects this very sort of regional self-consciousness. In the preceding pages, I have argued that Morán's comparison of his local saint, who lives in the shadow of the widely recognized St. Rosa de Santa María, reflects his indignation over the unappreciated status of his own patria in relation to Lima.

However, while Morán exalts his saint and his home region, he does not place Quito at odds with Lima; on the contrary, his broad use of regional terminology reflects a complex sense of group identity. Like Mariana, Morán is quiteño, peruano, and americano. Thus, he sees her sanctity, like that of St. Rosa, as a credit to the "New World," the "Western Indies," and "this hemisphere."[59] Moreover, when Morán states that quiteños view their Lily as "the glory of this Province [Quito] and a new coat of arms *(blasón)* for the realms of Peru," he implies a broader Peruvian loyalty.[60] He also recognizes the primacy of St. Rosa, and by implication of the city of Lima, at several junctures.[61]

Morán's metaphoric Rose and Lily—like the two holy women they symbolize—germinate, bud, and bloom in the fertile soil of mid-colonial Peru. Yet while the criollo hagiographer must account for the sanctity of his Lily and demonstrate her merit in relation to St. Rosa, he does not feel any compulsion to defend her origins nor to argue that a woman of her social status could comprehend the matters of God. This would not be the case for the hagiographers of Catarina de San Juan, a dark-skinned domestic servant. It is to her intriguing case that I now turn.

"Very Good Blood"

Reconstructing the Asian Identity of Catarina de San Juan

Catarina de San Juan, a domestic servant and religious visionary of Asian origins, died in the city of Puebla in 1688. She had arrived in New Spain aboard the Manila galleon around 1619, at approximately ten years of age. Despite Catarina's lowly social status, many poblanos sought her out in her later years for healing, advice, intercessory prayer, or a glimpse into the future. Following her death, they thronged to the Jesuit church to view her body and to hear a son of St. Ignatius give a sermon-eulogy in her honor. Before long, devotees were venerating Catarina de San Juan as a saint. They unofficially transformed two of her former dwellings into shrines and began to circulate printed images of her physical likeness despite Pope Urban VIII's general prohibitions against unauthorized popular veneration. Within four years of Catarina's death, two of her former confessors attempted to foment this local devotion by publishing hagiographic accounts of her life.

The main sources for Catarina's life are three published texts, namely, a funeral sermon by Francisco de Aguilera, S.J., and hagiographies by Alonso Ramos, S.J., and José del Castillo Grajeda. For his *Sermón,* Aguilera consulted the notebooks of Father Ramos, who had served as Catarina's confessor for the last fifteen years of her life. Despite its derivative character, this brief text is instructive for the way

Aguilera elaborates on details from Catarina's story for purposes of exemplarity and moral exhortation. Ramos, rector of the Jesuit Colegio de San Ildefonso (Puebla), published a Life of Catarina in three parts. The first volume, published in Puebla in 1689, was entitled *Primera parte . . . de los prodigios de la omnipotencia y milagros de la gracia en la vida de la V. sierva de Dios Catarina de San Juan, natural del Gran Mogor* (hereafter *Primera parte*) (see figure 6.1). Two subsequent volumes appeared under the titles *Segunda parte . . .* (1690) and *Tercera parte . . .* (1692).[1] In recent years, Ramos has attracted scholarly attention as Catarina's hagiographer, due in part to the ill fate suffered by his *Primera parte,* which Spanish and Mexican inquisitions banned during the 1690s.[2] In 1692, a parish priest named José del Castillo Grajeda, who had also served as Catarina's confessor, published the shorter and more cautious *Compendio de la vida y virtudes de la venerable Catarina de San Juan.*

Even a cursory reading of these narrative accounts of Catarina's life raises intriguing questions about the protagonist's exotic origins. While hagiographies of nuns and beatas from this period contain countless descriptions of graphic spiritual visions, amazing feats of ascetic endurance, and nature-defying miracles, one rarely encounters in these texts tales of the holy person's childhood like those that characterize the Catarina narratives. I still remember my initial astonishment when I began to peruse the opening chapters of the Ramos Life in the Bancroft Library in June 1996. None of my extensive reading in medieval and early modern Roman Catholic sacred biography had prepared me for what I found there. Catarina appears as an exotic Asian daughter of royalty, her mother an Arabian princess and her father a ruler of the great Mughal Empire of northern India. The story of how she ends up in New Spain is equally fantastic. Kidnapped by pirates from her homeland, the preadolescent Catarina changes hands several times, pursued for her enticing beauty by lascivious sailors, ship captains, and merchants. Through a series of miraculous interventions by Christian saints, however, the otherwise defenseless Catarina arrives in New Spain in an immaculate sexual condition, a condition that she protects and preserves for the rest of her life, even as a married woman.

In my view, these narrative portrayals of Catarina as a kidnapped princess who maintains her virginity against all odds are highly improbable accounts, less valuable as records of actual historical events than for what they reveal about novohispano social values in the late

PRIMERA PARTE
DE
LOS PRODIGIOS
DE LA OMNIPOTENCIA,
Y MILAGROS DE LA GRACIA.
EN LA
VIDA DE LA VENERABLE SIERVA DE DIOS
CATHARINA DE S. JOAN.
NATURAL DEL GRAN MOGOR, DIFUNTA
EN ESTA IMPERIAL CIUDAD DE LA PUEBLA DE
LOS ANGELES EN LA NUEVA ESPAÑA.
ESCRITA
POR EL PADRE ALONSO RAMOS PROFESSO
de la Compañia de IESUS su vltimo Confeffor, Natural de Santa
Eulalia en la Vega de Saldaña, y Reynos de Caftilla la Vieja.
DEDICALA
AL ILL.^{MO} Y REV.^{MO} SEÑOR
DOCTOR DON MANUEL FERNANDEZ DE
SANTA CRVZ, COLEGIAL, QVE FVE EN EL MAYOR DE
QVENCA DE SALAMANCA, Y CANONIGO MAGISTRAL
DE LA SANTA IGLESIA DE SEGOVIA. CONSAGRADO
DESPVES EN LA PRELACIA DE QVATRO IGLESIAS,
PRIMERO DE LA DE CHIAPA: DESPVES DE GVADALA-
XARA, Y ACTVAL OBISPO DE LA PVEBLA DE LOS AN-
GELES, HABIENDO SIDO ELECTO ARZOBISPO DE
✠ MEXICO: DEL CONSEJO DE SV MAGESTAD. ✠

CON PRIVILEGIO
En la Puebla, en la Imprenta Plantiniana de Diego Fernandez de Leon. Año de 1689.

FIGURE 6.1. Title page from Alonso Ramos, S.J., *Primera parte de los prodigios de la omnipotencia y milagros de la gracia en la vida de la V. sierva de Dios Catarina de San Juan, natural del Gran Mogor* (Puebla, 1689). (Courtesy of the Bancroft Library, University of California, Berkeley)

seventeenth century.³ In the pages that follow, I propose a number of reasons why Catarina and her clerical promoters reconstruct her origins as they do, arguing that their narratives reflect Spanish preoccupations with family lineage, social hierarchy, and ethnic purity. Catarina and her hagiographers recognized that it was extremely problematic to claim that someone of her social and physical type had been a frequent object of male sexual desire, had successfully resisted those sexual advances, and had received divine favors in the form of visions, ecstasies, and spiritual transports. Indeed, as Catarina's reputation as a visionary grew during the later years of her life, she often lamented to her confessors that people she passed on the street sometimes called her "that lying *china* bitch."⁴

In response to the significant challenges arising from her marginal social status, Catarina and her hagiographers construct for her a less problematic identity or, to put it differently, a more impeccable pedigree. Rather than ask their readers to trust the angelic claims of a dark-skinned servant woman, Catarina's hagiographers portray her as a fair-skinned princess. Catarina emerges not as a marginal social type with much to gain in social and economic terms from developing a personal following; instead, she is a woman of elite, well-connected origins who abdicates her natural earthly status in order more fully to love and serve her divine spouse.

Ramos's Life of Catarina de San Juan, like other similar works written by confessor-hagiographers who knew their subjects personally, presents the historian or literary scholar with a complex problem of authorial voice: the hagiographer is technically author of the work, but does his narrative reflect his own voice or that of the protagonist who first described her experiences to him? An answer to this dilemma must recognize that although Alonso Ramos claims to recount details from Catarina's childhood, adult years, and interior mystical life just as she had described them to him in the confessional *(al pie de la letra)*, he does not in reality present her account "word for word." On the contrary, his authorial presence in the text is constant, marked by moral preachments to his readers as well as his knowledge of Roman Catholic doctrine, printed histories of the Jesuits in India, and rules governing female mystical activity. Thus, the surviving account of Catarina's lineage, early life, and conversion is the collaborative product of penitent and confessor, composed of her own sketchy memory, personal religious desires, and performance goals and the historical, hagiographic, and professional concerns of her confessors. It is, in the words of Alan Soons, the "intersection between two conceptions of the world."[5] Even so, the voice of the writer ultimately prevails, for his role "involves the selection and ordering of the events into a coherent narrative, and the infusion of meaning into these events through his discursive interpretation of them."[6] Like Sigüenza y Góngora in the *Infortunios de Alonso Ramírez,* Ramos includes, transforms, and omits elements from Catarina's story in accordance with his own objectives. Thus, while I recognize the complexities of voice inherent in a text like the Ramos Life, I treat the narrative, at least in its surviving printed form, as the construct of its Jesuit author.[7]

In what follows, I present a chronological narrative of Catarina's life and mystical experiences based on the printed sermon and hagiographies, followed by an analysis of the hagiographic strategies of Ramos and Aguilera.[8]

Catarina de San Juan: Biographical Sketch

Catarina de San Juan claimed to have been born in India around 1607. Her parents named her Mirrha, literally "bitterness," an omen of events to follow. (It was only at the time of her Catholic baptism that young Mirrha adopted her Christian name of Catarina de San Juan; for sake of clarity I refer to her here as Catarina.) Her mother, Borta, was an Arabian princess and her father the Mughal ruler of a territory bordering on "Arabia Felix."[9] Ramos theorizes that Catarina's paternal grandfather may have been the great Mughal ruler Akbar (1556–1605), a pious Sunni Muslim whose lively interest in matters of religion and cosmology led him to sponsor debates with the Portuguese Jesuits at his court in Fathpur Sikri (near modern Agra).[10] This assumption on the part of Ramos was a logical one, for he had read of Mughal history in the writings of early Jesuit missionaries to India.

In his treatment of Catarina's religious origins, Ramos borrows extensively from these printed letters, treatises, and histories.[11] Sixteenth-century Jesuit missionaries to Asia, like their contemporaries in Spain's New World colonies, had searched diligently for evidence that Judeo-Christian faith and practice had preceded them. They enthusiastically reported discoveries of monotheism (worship of "the God of

Abraham"), Christian symbols (crosses, baptism, etc.), and even faith communities (for example, the "Thomas Christians" of Kerala, southwest India). Ramos and Aguilera enthusiastically build on their fellow Jesuits' assumptions about pre-European faith foundations and the imminent victory of the Christian evangelistic project in India.

Ramos points out that although Catarina's parents never fully embraced Christianity during her early childhood, they did show numerous signs of a predisposition to the faith. Borta saw visions of the Virgin Mary, to whom she developed a strong devotion, while Catarina's father prohibited idolatry in his home, practiced monogamy, and did penance when one of his sins became public knowledge.[12] Although Catarina's father believed in the God of Abraham, he could not accept the notion of an incarnate God nor comprehend the doctrine of the Trinity.[13] In the end, however, both Catarina and Alonso Ramos were convinced of the ultimate conversion of both of her parents to Christianity. In one vision, Catarina saw their souls in heaven, while in another St. Francis Xavier transported her spiritually to her homeland, where she witnessed the baptisms of scores of people.[14]

That Catarina may have been introduced to Christianity while still a child in India is entirely plausible. Following the visit of Vasco da Gama to Cochin in 1498, the Portuguese quickly established themselves as traders on the Indian coast. At Cochin they had encountered the ancient Nestorian community of 'St. Thomas Christians' and by 1503 had built a temple of their own. A few years later Governor Afonso de Albuquerque supervised the construction of Santa Catarina Martyr, the first of many Portuguese churches in Goa. Portuguese secular priests, Franciscans, and Dominicans had flocked to the west coast of India soon afterward; and beginning in 1542 the Jesuit followers of Father Francis Xavier had undertaken a major effort to convert both Muslims and Hindus to their faith in any Indian state that would tolerate their presence. By 1549, Francis could report that Jesuit missionaries were located strategically in major coastal cities throughout the Portuguese sphere of influence.[15]

By the early seventeenth century, many Indians had been exposed to Catholic symbols, ritual, and faith, at least in those regions subject to direct Portuguese administration or evangelization.[16] As Portuguese men established formal or informal sexual unions with Indian women, the latter became primary targets for religious conversion. These gen-

erally low-caste Indian women found that by accepting Christian baptism and Portuguese names they might strengthen their ties to the out-
siders, and thereby achieve something of an elevation in social status.
In Goa, laws were passed requiring any resident with an Indian wife
to teach her the Paternoster and Ave Maria. It became common practice
to reward female converts with a gold coin and a length of valuable
cloth to compensate for their lost family ties and employment possibilities. These formerly Hindu women must have found the doctrinal
elements of their new religion rather incomprehensible, but probably
felt quite at home with its paintings and images, its periodic religious
processions, and the smell of incense that filled its churches.

The Virgin Mary favored Catarina throughout her early childhood
in India, including during an episode in which she saved her from
drowning. On the occasion, three angels warned her parents that their
daughter, although favored by God, would eventually be separated
from them forever.[17] Soon thereafter her father's realm came under
siege from new Turkic invaders, forcing him to evacuate his capital for
an unnamed coastal region. One day as Catarina and other children
played along the seaside, she was seized by Portuguese marauders and
carried away, never to see her parents or home again.[18]

The story of Catarina's life from the time of her kidnapping until
her arrival in New Spain is a litany of suffering and uncertainty from
which two themes constantly emerge. One involves a young girl whose
physical beauty makes her a desirable commodity in the estimation of
numerous men; the other involves the unprotected child, bereft of family and homeland, who comes to see her physical, sexual, and spiritual
survival as a sign of God's favor.

As a captive aboard the pirates' vessel, Catarina's life became a living hell. After her captors stripped her of the elegant clothes and jew-
els to which she had grown accustomed, she wept in the hull of the
ship as she "considered how her wealth had been converted to naked-
ness, her nobility into slavery, her esteem into scorn, and her freedom
into chains."[19] Catarina soon attracted the attention of several pirates
aboard the ship, and when swords were drawn over who should have
her, she herself was wounded. The captain, who had intentions of his
own, used the injury as a pretext for keeping her as his ward. When the
ship arrived at the southwest Indian port of Cochin and local magistrates received word that the vessel contained a number of children

who were being held illegally, the captain used subterfuge to retain Catarina and several of the others in his care. In the months that followed, however, Catarina changed hands a number of times, as several men of wealth attempted to purchase her. At Cochin, a Muslim merchant's scheme for an eventual marriage to Catarina failed when his envious female friend attempted to kill her by throwing her into the sea. The ship captain who had formerly held Catarina seized her once again and sailed to Manila, capital of the Spanish Philippines. In Manila, a Japanese merchant offered him two shiploads of goods in exchange for the child.[20] Finally, the governor of Manila attempted to purchase Catarina for the viceroy of New Spain. At the last minute, however, a representative for a wealthy poblano merchant named Miguel de Sosa bought her from her Portuguese captors, promising as part of the deal to take a dozen unsold slaves off their hands. The parcel of Filipino and Asian slaves was then shipped to Acapulco on the annual Manila galleon, and from there, following the annual trade fair, to their new masters' homes in the Mexican highlands.[21]

Amidst the physical and emotional suffering of this transoceanic odyssey, Catarina experienced an important milestone in her spiritual journey. At Cochin, where the kidnappers allowed Catarina and the other captives to be baptized by the local parish priest, her lifelong friendship with the Jesuit fathers began when one of them gave her prebaptismal instruction.[22] Following her baptism and the adoption of her new Christian name, Catarina saw a vision in which Saint Anne, the Virgin Mary, and the Christ Child (Niño Jesús) received her with much affection. For Catarina, this was an important confirmation of her new spiritual status, for prior to her baptism she had seen a similar vision in which the very same figures rebuffed her attempts to embrace them. Now, on the contrary, she saw visions of Mary and Jesus assuring her that they would be her substitute mother and father.[23] In later years, despite all she had endured during the months (or years) between her kidnapping on the Indian coast and her arrival in Puebla, Catarina viewed that period as one filled with signs of divine providence. She attributed the maintenance of her virginity and numerous rescues from life-threatening situations to divine aid.[24]

Catarina's arrival in the home of Miguel de Sosa and his wife Margarita de Chaves was, in her estimation, a deliverance from suffering and a new beginning. Her new masters treated her as a daughter rather than as a slave, looking after her in times of illness, insisting that she take meals with them, and taking her along on visits to the homes of friends. But for Catarina, who was already an earnest Catholic, this special treatment became a burden, for it prevented her from devoting herself to prayer and penitential exercises. When she unburdened her heart to them in this regard, they stopped insisting that she accompany Doña Margarita on her social calls and made their private chapel available for her devotional needs.[25]

Catarina received occupational training from Doña Margarita and other women in her home.[26] Soon she excelled in cooking and the milling and preparation of chocolate, skills commonly exercised by indigenous women in New Spain, as well as in spinning and sewing, an economic activity generally dominated by Spanish women.[27] Thus, as a young dark-skinned woman employed as a domestic servant, Catarina was one among thousands of women whose work was essential to the urban economy in colonial New Spain. In a period when female domestic servants were often suspected and accused of stealing, Catarina's masters rewarded her thrift, efficiency, and honest management of household petty cash and candle supplies by elevating her above her fellow servants to the role of housekeeper *(ama de llaves)*.[28] This combination of skills and thrift, notes hagiographer Ramos, enabled her to survive on her own later in life.

Catarina's conversations with her confessors reveal much about the pious religious environment in which she was acculturated to New Spain. Miguel de Sosa and Margarita de Chaves must have seen to her confirmation by Bishop Mota y Escobar and, as was often customary for wealthy masters, they served as her godparents *(padrinos)*. Their private chapel, with its various images of Christ and the Virgin Mary, provided a spatial and visual context for her spiritual development.[29] Miguel de Sosa had funded the construction of a hermitage in the garden *(huerta)* of the local discalced Carmelite convent of Santa Teresa.[30] Furthermore, Doña Margarita had made arrangements that, should she survive her husband, she would enter the same religious house, which she did following his death in 1624. It may well have been through their influence and connections that Catarina began to frequent the Jesuit church nearby and to confess to Jesuit fathers.[31]

Catarina's ties to the Jesuits were at least threefold. First, she served the Jesuit colegio by baking the bread for the Host to be used in the sacrament of the Eucharist. Second, she frequented the Jesuit church, where she heard mass, listened to sermons, and became familiar with Jesuit devotions such as the Passion of Christ, the Virgin Mary in various advocations, and the Cinco Señores (Sacred Family). Finally, she developed strong spiritual ties with her confessors, a series of relationships that was to last her entire life.[32]

One of the clearest manifestations of the Jesuit imprint on the life and faith of Catarina was her strong emotional bond with the Virgin Mary. The Jesuits in New Spain and elsewhere were very active in the promotion of Marian cults and devotions during the seventeenth and early eighteenth centuries.[33] The well-known promotion of the apparitions of Our Lady of Guadalupe was but one case among many. Jesuit priests encouraged the growth of Old World cults to Nuestra Señora de Loreto and Remedios, as well as the proliferation of such New World advocations as Nuestra Señora de Itzamal, Nuestra Señora de Ocotlán, and Nuestra Señora de Cosamaloapan. Father José Vidal, S.J., fomented the cult of the Virgen de Dolores, whom he praised as "confidant for domestic problems and resolute defender of the maintenance of family honor."[34] In printed accounts of New World Marian apparitions, as well as in sermons dedicated to the Virgin, Jesuit writers stressed themes such as Mary as mother, the importance of feminine modesty *(recato),* and the spiritual superiority of virginity, all themes that seem to have made a strong impression on Catarina.

Devotion to the Virgin Mary must have played a crucial role in the successful transition of Catarina, a young girl with no family, to life in New Spain. It appears that she took a formal vow in order to join a congregation of laypersons devoted to Nuestra Señora del Pópulo. In addition, counted among her few material possessions was a modest image of Our Lady of the Rosary, to which she regularly prayed. But the Virgin was more to her than simply an object of veneration or petition, for Catarina saw numerous visions in which Mary called her "my daughter," or said, "I am your mother." Most significant, perhaps, is the fact that Catarina's recollections of her childhood, especially those involving her own mother, bear the imprint of the Virgin's presence and favor.[35]

According to Ramos, Catarina took a vow of perpetual chastity at the age of three, resolving to wed Christ alone.[36] Although this claim seems implausible, it is apparent in retrospect that Catarina's sub-

sequent exposure to the cult of the Virgin Mary—with its emphasis
on female sexual purity, feminine sorrow, and the maternal protection
of the afflicted—helped her cope with personal experiences of sexual
objectification and, perhaps, victimization. Such a conclusion finds support in Castillo Grajeda's narrative of Catarina's life. On one occasion
during her childhood in India, he reports that she secretly made her
way to a quiet place in order to commune with Christ and escape the
unwanted attentions of her male admirers. Upon falling into a trance,
she heard St. Anne, mother of the Virgin Mary, say to her, "Child, what
are you doing out here?" To this young Catarina replied, "Señora, I am
here crying to myself because I am very afraid of men."[37] There were
clearly connections in Catarina's mind between her devotion to the
holy Mother and Grandmother and her own sexual survival.

Miguel de Sosa died just a few years after Catarina entered his
home. His will provided that, following two years of service to his
widow Margarita de Chaves, Catarina would be free to leave or to enter
the poblano convent of Santa Teresa, an option for which he
bequeathed her a dowry of one hundred pesos. In fact, soon after his
death, his widow entered Santa Teresa. According to the biographers of
Catarina de San Juan, the nuns of Santa Teresa recognized her remarkable spiritual devotion and urged her to enter the convent as well, even
offering to provide her with a private cell, but she declined their offer.
There are several reasons, however, for doubting that such an invitation
was ever extended. In the first place, by the 1620s the constitutions of
female convents such as Santa Teresa clearly prohibited the admission
of castas as novices. Second, the small sum that Miguel de Sosa
allegedly bequeathed to Catarina was much less than the two or three
thousand–peso dowry usually required for admission. Third, all these
events are reported to have occurred just a few years after Catarina's
arrival in New Spain, when her reputation as a visionary probably had
not yet developed. Despite all this, however, Margarita de Chaves may
have persuaded the nuns of Santa Teresa to allow Catarina to enter
their community as a lay sister. Whatever the case, she did not enter the
cloister but continued to live and pursue her spiritual goals on her own.

Soon after these events, Catarina accepted a position as domestic
servant in the house of an exemplary parish priest named Pedro
Suárez.[38] Suárez served for a time as confessor for María de Jesús
Tomelín del Campo (1579–1637), a member of the poblano convent

of Nuestra Señora de la Concepción whose reputation for sanctity convinced the Holy See to open canonization hearings.[39] Through Father Suárez, Catarina may have entered into conversations with this holy woman.[40] It is difficult to know how seriously to take such claims given that hagiographers often attempted to demonstrate links between their protagonists and other individuals of recognized sanctity.[41] If this relationship did in fact develop, however, Catarina must have learned much about religious devotion, asceticism, and prayer from Madre María de Jesús.

In the home of Pedro Suárez, Catarina met her future husband, a "chino" (presumably Filipino) named Domingo, who took a fancy to the household newcomer and began to lavish his attentions on her.[42] Father Suárez, who was attempting to establish a home for poor girls, needed a married couple to oversee the new institution. Hoping to employ Domingo as his fiscal manager, Suárez sought to arrange for the marriage of his slave to the unattached Catarina.[43] While Domingo embraced this opportunity with enthusiasm, Catarina refused to discuss the matter, devoted as she was to lifelong chastity. In response to her resistance, however, Father Suárez urged her confessors to command her, as a matter of obedience to the church, to marry his slave. For reasons I will revisit later, Catarina's confessors prevailed upon her to consent to the union. On May 1, 1626, at approximately twenty years of age, Catarina de San Juan entered into holy matrimony with the chino slave Domingo.[44]

In his *Primera parte,* Ramos records the following inscription for May 1, 1626, from the Libro de Matrimonios in Puebla's cathedral church: "Domingo Suárez weds and agrees to care for Catarina de San Juan, *china, india,* born in India, etc." Conscious of the need to clarify these ethnic labels, Ramos explains that "in these parts, those who come from the Orient via the Philippines, transported here by our Portuguese, are called 'chinos' of India."[45] Even so, we should not too readily assume that Domingo the "chino" slave was from Asia, nor that he and his "china" wife shared matching ethnic origins to go with their matching ethnic labels. Hagiographer Ramos, who consistently refers to Domingo as "chino," may have presumed he was from Asia, considering how Ramos himself defines this ethnic descriptor. But the seventeenth century was a time of transition in the conceptualization of ethnic and social typologies in New Spain. Patricia Seed's study of race and division of labor in Mexico City has demonstrated that by the mid-eighteenth century racial definitions were based more on social than phenotypic criteria.[46] In a discussion of race and status *(calidad)* in late-eighteenth-century Parral (northern New Spain), Robert McCaa notes: "Calidad, typically expressed in racial terms (e.g., indio, mestizo, español), in many instances was an inclusive impression reflecting one's reputation as a whole. Color, occupation, and wealth might influence one's calidad, as did purity of blood, honor, integrity, and even place of origin."[47] These observations find confirmation in the "casta art" that became popular in late-eighteenth-century Mexico City.[48] In the numerous artistic cycles that portray diverse socioethnic types, two patterns are discernible. First, there is no consistency in the application of these ethnic labels; the categories are completely fluid and subjective.[49] Second, the chinos and chinas portrayed in these paintings display no evidence of Asian origins or phenotype (see figure 6.2). Thus, while it is entirely possible that either or both Catarina and Domingo originated in Asia and came to New Spain via the Manila galleon, we cannot be certain, based on terminology alone, that this was the case. The seventeenth century was probably already witnessing a gradual shift in the use of the term chino, which was becoming less associated with things Asian and more associated with social types, including domestic servants.

Catarina's marriage to Domingo turned out to be a disaster, especially in relation to the domestic harmony and monogamy that the church sought to promote in New Spain. Caught between the virtues of obedience to her confessors and faithfulness to her vow of perpetual virginity, Catarina had agreed to marry Domingo, at least in her own mind, under the condition that they abstain from sexual relations. Following the wedding, Domingo claimed never to have agreed to such terms. Neighborhood matchmakers, who recognized the difficulty of their case, refused to become involved, leaving the couple to fight it out in a prolonged domestic conflict. When Domingo continued to demand his conjugal rights, Catarina placed an image of Christ in the bed between them, thus enabling herself from that day forward to sleep "less vigilantly." For his part, Domingo soon established relations with

FIGURE 6.2. Casta art of late-colonial New Spain. "De Chino e India, Genízara."
(A chino male and Indian female produce a mixed-blood baby.) Attributed to
Francisco Clapera, 1775. (Courtesy of the Denver Art Museum and the Col-
lection of Jan and Frederick Mayer, 190.1996.14)

another woman, eventually bringing children from the irregular relationship into Catarina's house in order to torment her. At the same time, he accused her of being an imposter *(embustera)* who engaged in sorcery *(hechicería)* and invented false visions. In short, he made her life miserable.[50] Despite this constant conflict with her husband, however, "she did not stop considering [him], in the approximately fourteen years she lived with him, as her superior and head, serving as his slave."[51]

Despite all this, Catarina used her connections with influential churchmen to acquire a *mandamiento de amparo,* which would enable her ne'er-do-well husband to "trade and make contracts" in New Spain in order to support her. Rather than provide for Catarina, however, Domingo made deals and contracted debts "as if the King and the Royal Treasury were his guarantors." Within two years, he fled to the mountains outside Puebla in order to escape his angry creditors, venturing into the city from time to time to receive material aid from his long-suffering wife. Following Domingo's death, his creditors began to pressure Catarina, threatening to have her jailed if she did not pay his debts. At this critical juncture, however, she prayed for relief to an image of the Savior in the church of San José; soon thereafter, her debts were miraculously forgiven.[52]

Sometime after Domingo's death, Captain Don Hypólito Castillo y Altra and his wife Doña Juana Mexia Moscoso invited the impoverished beata to reside in their home.[53] Catarina's prospective benefactors urged her to sleep upstairs with their small children, but she would agree to enter their home only on the condition that she reside downstairs with the other servants. During the last decades of her life, and perhaps prior to her move into the Castillo y Altra home, she must have employed her skills in spinning, sewing, and confectioning chocolates in order to provide for her own material support.[54] But as a result of poor eyesight and declining health, she increasingly subsisted on alms supplied by her benefactors, often in exchange for her spiritual services.

Catarina's connection to the Castillo y Altra household is reminiscent of the relationship between Rosa de Santa María and her well-to-do benefactors Gonzalo de la Maza and María de Uzátegui. In both cases, social elites provided material support and a residence for a poor beata who was beginning to attract a spiritual following. Like Gonzalo de la Maza, Don Hypólito became one of the principal witnesses to his protégé's spiritual gifts following her death. He claimed, for example, to have overheard Catarina tell a household employee that the annual fleet would arrive safely in Veracruz on the October feast day of Santa Teresa, a prophecy that proved accurate. Don Hypólito and Doña Juana personally benefited from Catarina's spiritual power and insight; indeed, her prayers aided Doña Juana in her hour of death. Catarina subsequently counseled Don Hypólito regarding remarriage and, when he became critically ill, accurately forecast that not he, but his oldest son, would die.[55]

The elderly and infirm Catarina died on January 5, 1688. In keeping with visions she had seen and reported to Father Ramos prior to her death, a great multitude thronged to see her body and honor her life. One notable absentee was Bishop Fernández de Santa Cruz, who was not in Puebla at the time of Catarina's death. Following her funeral, at which Francisco de Aguilera delivered the aforementioned sermon-eulogy, Catarina de San Juan was buried in the Jesuit church where she had worshipped and made confession for years.[56]

Catarina de San Juan: Hagiographic Strategies

During the last decade of Catarina's life, a treatise on prayer by the then-deceased Miguel Godínez was published in Sevilla. The Jesuit author, a renowned theologian, latinist, and churchman during his career, had directed the spiritual lives of well-known women in the city of Puebla a few decades earlier. In his *Práctica de la theología mystica,* Godínez warned his readers to scrutinize the extravagant spiritual claims of "pitiful women [with] a great appetite for honor, . . . since it is not God's habit *(estilo)* to appoint such low persons *(personas viles)* to the office of secretary of state."[57]

A few decades after Godínez wrote these words, an illiterate domestic servant named Catarina de San Juan claimed that Jesus Christ, the Virgin Mary, and numerous other saints had blessed her with extraordinary mystical favors. Over several years, Catarina described such wondrous experiences to her confessors. On one occasion as she venerated an image of Jesús Nazareno, Christ descended from the cross, warmly embraced her, and spoke to her "in a lover's tone."[58] Catarina's visions and transports extended not only to celestial, but to earthly matters as well, "as if the entire world were within her purview."[59]

She saw and intervened against dangers on the sea, in the royal court and family, and within the Spanish Empire. In August 1678, for example, Catarina accompanied the Virgin Mary in flight as she rescued the annual fleet from a hurricane off the coast of Puerto Rico.[60]

Alonso Ramos, who belonged to the same religious order as Miguel Godínez, recognized the obstacles he would face in attempting to promote Catarina's spiritual claims through the medium of sacred biography. First, he had to get his manuscript past the calificadores of the Holy Office, who had the authority to approve or ban hagiographic literature. Second, he needed to persuade diocesan and papal officials to open canonization proceedings. Third, he had to win the support of New Spain's social elites, on whose favor and financial support the future of her cult and causa depended. To achieve all three ends, Ramos and his cowriters—the authors of the numerous, lengthy *cartas, pareceres, aprobaciones,* and *advertencias* that precede the main narrative text in his first two volumes[61]—seize upon a dual strategy. On the one hand, they counter the notion that she was a self-aggrandizing charlatan by emphasizing her humility. On the other hand, they ennoble and whiten her personal origins, thus demonstrating that, in objective social terms, she was not only a woman who had nothing to gain by inventing false spiritual favors, but also one whom men would have desired. Just as important, by ennobling and whitening her origins, they cast her as a woman capable of maintaining her vow of chastity.

In the "Carta y discurso preocupativo" that prefaces Ramos's *Primera parte,* Antonio Núñez de Miranda, S.J., best known today as the rejected confessor of Sor Juana Inés de la Cruz, anticipates potential objections to Catarina's mystical claims. "Is it not mindless credulity," he rhetorically asks Ramos's readers, "to believe such wondrous things about a poor 'china' slave simply because she imagined and recounted it?"[62] In essence, Núñez y Miranda argues that, while God rarely favors persons like Catarina with "wondrous things" *(maravillas),* in her case he made exceptions. Nevertheless, Núñez's words of caution turned out to be prophetic; when the Spanish Inquisition issued its ban on the *Primera parte* in 1692, it condemned the work not only for containing blasphemies, but also for the author's "vain credulity."[63]

Ramos employs the theme of Catarina's low status to hagiographic advantage. In a *dedicatoria* to Gaspar de Sandoval, viceroy of

New Spain, he offers his addressee an alliance of mutual benefit. Filling the letter with references to the viceroy's noble lineage, honor, and high rank, Ramos symbolically contrasts Sandoval's status with the humble and defenseless condition of Catarina de San Juan. Ramos identifies Catarina with the stellion lizard *(estelion)*, the animal which the Hebrew King Solomon described as the smallest and weakest of all creatures.[64] Quoting Solomon's command to "let the lizard nest in the King's hand and dwell in his house," Ramos urges Gaspar de Sandoval to grant Catarina refuge in the viceregal palace; i.e., to patronize and defend her cause for sanctity, beginning with underwriting the publication costs of her vida. Describing Catarina as one whose prayers had protected previous viceroys, the Spanish monarchy, and imperial maritime commerce, he concludes, "And who can doubt that the one who thus employed her prayers [while] on the earth, motivated solely by her charity, will, now that she is indebted *(empeñada)* as a result of your Excellency's patronage, reciprocate from heaven with special favor?" In this way, Ramos establishes a theme of mutual dependence and support that he hopes will influence the way pious lay readers interpret and respond to his vida of the beloved holy woman.

Father José Vidal continues the theme of God's favor for the lowly in his parecer (opinion), but here his purpose is moral exhortation. Vidal opens his parecer with the observation that Catarina, as one "outstanding in all the estates," "is a practical model" from whom all can learn, "from the poorest slave to [those who claim] the highest condition of nobility, and from the most perfect Religious to the most degenerate of spirit." Vidal warns his readers, moreover, against overly concerning themselves with Catarina's "favors," for God demands virtues not wonders (maravillas).[65] Noting that Ramos interweaves a narrative of Catarina's virtues "with serious and devout commentaries," Vidal expresses hope that those readers who may have become inured to other forms of teaching will sit up and take notice of her exemplary life. Utilizing the common biblical theme of God's exaltation of the weak as a means of confounding the powerful,[66] Vidal attempts to shame his lax, well-to-do readers into religious devotion: "For what a turn of events it will be on the day of judgment to see seated on the Throne of Glory one who was a china, pagan, slave, outcast, ignorant; and to see damned to hell those who in this life were so satisfied with its momentary goods that they completely forgot about Eternity."[67] No longer, warns Vidal, can one's "estate" or condition as a woman justify impiety, for Catarina has been exemplary as virgin, wife, and widow.

Both Ramos and Castillo Grajeda describe Catarina as one who was resigned to her lowly status, noting how she denigrated herself alternately as "china dog," "poor bozal," "china slave," or "one baptized standing up," the latter a reference to her original non-Christian origins.[68] Catarina's humble self-estimation, observes Aguilera, enabled her to trust her confessors: "She called herself a vile worm *(gusanillo vil)*, unworthy even to crawl along the ground, an untamed beast who needed three confessors, one to bridle her *(enfrenarla)*, another to saddle her *(enjalmarla)*, and yet another to spur her on *(picarla)*."[69] José del Castillo Grajeda highlights her unpretentious nature, noting the simple, ungrammatical quality of her speech. His brief *Compendio* reads like an interview, with Castillo Grajeda alternating Catarina's spare, awkward words with his own interpretation of their meaning.[70] The picture that emerges reminds one of St. Teresa de Avila (d. 1582), the Spanish religious reformer and mystic who denigrated herself in writing as "a poor little woman" *(mujercilla)*, or of St. Martín de Porres (d. 1639), the Peruvian Dominican lay brother who constantly belittled himself as a "mulatto dog."[71]

On the other hand, Catarina's promoters are not content to assert, in effect, that "she was nothing and she knew it." Indeed, they characterize her as a beautiful young princess—*somebody* by the world's standards—whose humility led her to forfeit her natural status in order to become a slave of Christ and the Virgin. Having been thus transformed into a "nobody"—that is, a poor china slave—Catarina embraced her own nothingness.

By focusing on Catarina's royal origins, Ramos and Aguilera suggest that she would have had no reason to invent false mystical experiences. Yet their attention to Catarina's abnegation of her natural earthly status serves other important purposes, as is clear in their descriptions of her resistance to male sexual advances. Ramos in particular recognizes the challenges inherent in representing a poor china like Catarina as both sexually desirable and steadfastly chaste, no small challenge in light of novohispano canons of female beauty and notions of casta moral weakness. The Ramos text reveals his own misgivings— and by implication, those of his readers—about whether Catarina could have aroused the sexual interests of so many men, especially those of high social rank. The old beata also seems to have been aware of this contradiction, for as she told Ramos, "everyone tells me I look like an ugly old 'china.'"[72]

In principle, Ramos and Aguilera could have attempted to reconcile the objective facts (Catarina's undesirable physical features) with subjective claims (her sexual desirability) by arguing that the years had not been kind to her. After all, she was more than eighty years of age by the time she died in Puebla. It would not have taken a creative genius to say, in essence, "She was a real looker when she was younger." However, these Jesuit writers pursue a different line of argument, and their descriptions of Catarina's horrible maritime adventures and her tumultuous marriage to Domingo reveal much about novohispano ideas about race, gender, and casta sexuality.

In accounting for Catarina's sexual desirability, they employ a motif that is common in other Christian sacred biographies; that is, the devout virgin's prayer that God change her appearance in order to make her less attractive to men.[73] In this regard, Catarina told Father Ramos that sometime after her marriage to Domingo, God granted her prayer to be made ugly. Unlike the vast majority of holy virgins described in medieval and early modern hagiography, however, Catarina's transformation is a racial one. Ramos notes that, prior to the divine intervention, she was a woman "of rare beauty, her color more white than brownish, her hair more silvery than golden, with a wide forehead and bright eyes."[74] Such beauty, he continues, served as her dowry, for even men of high rank, unaware of her noble origins, found her extremely desirable. But when God answered her prayer for deliverance from the attentions of such men, he did so dramatically:

> In very short order, her flesh began to dry out and wither; her facial features changed; her hair became darker and the color of her face like that of the chinos; as a result, she began to appear more like an old woman than a young girl; more ugly than attractive; more like a brown-skinned china than a white, fair-haired Mughal woman; more like a nut-brown Indian, that is, one of the darkest in all of the Occident, than like a white, beautiful Orientess from the region of Arabia Felix.[75]

This statement is a striking lens through which to see the relationship in the minds of New World Spaniards between physical beauty and racial phenotype.

Sometime after she was made ugly, Catarina saw a vision in which Christ appeared accompanied by three beautiful virgins, two of them white, and one of them dark *(trigueña)*. In a sort of spiritual beauty contest, Christ the judge *(Arbitro)* declared the dark-skinned contestant more beautiful than the other two. When Catarina asked Christ to identify the three, he responded: "Look, this beautiful white woman is St. Ynes, this other white beauty is St. Catharina [Martyr?], and the dark one is you. You are the most beautiful." The Lord expressed this preference, adds Aguilera, "because one never hears about these two purest of virgins having asked to lose their [physical] beauty, as the dark-skinned one did." Aguilera, whose hortatory purpose is to stir the consciences of women "who lose God in order to preserve their fleeting *(caduca)* beauty," reminds his listener-readers of the traditional Christian moral that "a pure soul is more beautiful than a very lovely body." Yet while her panegyrist does not explicitly say so, this centuries-old religious value takes on new social and cultural overtones in the case of the dark-skinned china. In words that Aguilera himself gives to her, Catarina could rightly proclaim, "I am dark *(morena)*, but as beautiful as tabernacles of Cedar, and as the tents *(tiendas)* of Solomon, whose beauty is known only to those who penetrate their interiors."[76]

If, as Alonso Ramos claims, this story of a physical transformation from "beautiful white Orientess" to "nut-brown Indian" originated with Catarina herself, it is a compelling statement of how her yearning for acceptance in her adopted land led her to judge herself by its norms of "genuine" beauty. Catarina certainly seems to have understood the importance in New Spain of bloodline, for as an adult she remembered childhood episodes in which people gazed upon her and remarked, "This child has royal blood."[77] This conviction remained with her for a lifetime; as an adult in Puebla, she sometimes responded to detractors with the retort, "I have very good blood in these veins."[78]

In recapturing Catarina's noble origins, Ramos has one further aim, which has less to do with her physical appearance and desirability than with her moral character. His discussion of her prayer for physical transformation, appearing as it does in the context of her marriage to Domingo, enables him to explain why her confessors pressed her to marry despite her earlier vow of perpetual chastity: "Judging that she would behave like a slave," Ramos proposes, "they feared some unsteadiness or lewdness on her part." These well-intentioned clerics, who "assum[ed] she was weak-willed in her purposes, persisted in their opinion that she should marry."

Why, one might ask, would these peninsular and criollo priests have had such low expectations for Catarina? Why assume that at worst she would practice "lewdness," at best be subject to "unsteadiness" and a "weak will"? If the marriage union of Catarina and Domingo came about as Ramos narrates, it reflected not only the general clerical practice of regularizing marital unions whenever possible, but also the prevailing social preconception that perpetual virginity was not viable for an individual of Catarina's racial and social status.[79]

Not many years after Catarina's death, an intense ideological debate raged in Mexico City around the possible establishment of a nunnery for the daughters of New Spain's indigenous elite, those known as caciques.[80] Critics of the proposed Convento de Corpus Christi protested that while some native indias of New Spain were virtuous in many respects, they were incapable, due to "inconstancy," of keeping their vows of chastity. Indeed, argued one Alexandro Romano, indias had enough trouble keeping their marriage vows; they could not be expected to maintain the more rigorous demands of the religious estate.[81] According to this view, then, the same moral flaw that had undermined early Franciscan attempts to train a native clergy in the sixteenth century—the inability of indios to maintain a celibate lifestyle—still characterized the region's indigenous peoples, limiting their religious potential.[82]

In response to this position, supporters of Corpus Christi affirmed the full potential of New Spain's Indians for Christian maturation. To strengthen their case, they translated and published the hagiographic Life of Katherine Tekakwitha, an Iroquois woman whose reputation for sanctity had prompted French Jesuits to publish her hagiography in Paris in 1717.[83] In a recent study of this episode, Canadian historian Allan Greer raises a question that sheds light on the case of Catarina de San Juan: "Why select the Life of a northern Iroquois woman when the annals of Mexico and the rest of Spanish America offered several profiles, much closer to home, of Indian women of exemplary piety?" To answer this question, Greer contrasts the narrative of the Iroquois woman's life with the hagiographic profiles of five devout indigenous women that appear in Carlos Sigüenza y Góngora's *Paraíso occidental* of 1683. Whereas the Life of Catharina Tekakwitha, like Alonso Ramos's Life of Catarina de San Juan, contains rich details of her early life and conversion, the life stories of Sigüenza y Góngora's novohispano indias "remain sketchy, fragmentary and, in two cases out of five, literally anonymous." Indeed, one Petronila de la Concepción "simply materializes out of the shadowy suburban world of hispanized Indians who catered to the needs of New Spain's elites." By contrast, it was safe in New Spain to grant a full personal identity to an Iroquois woman; "[she] was not the intimate other, but the exotic other."[84]

In the case of the Corpus Christi debate, proponents won the day and the new convent opened in 1724. Of course, not all indias were welcome to join. Aspirants to membership had to prove the nobility of their lineage, the legitimacy of their birth, and the purity (albeit Indian) of their blood. Only then could they join the female spiritual elite of New Spain, its perpetual virgins.

Conclusion

During the 1690s, Alonso Ramos and other avid devotees of Catarina de San Juan must have experienced great disappointment at official measures taken to suppress this popular devotion. In 1691, the Holy Office of New Spain issued a prohibition against the circulation of portraits of Catarina de San Juan and Juan de Palafox, former bishop of Puebla.[85] In 1692, Spain's Holy Office banned Ramos's *Primera parte*. Four years later, the Holy Office of New Spain followed suit, thus prohibiting the volume from being owned or read within the territories of the viceroyalty. That same year (1696), the novohispano Holy Office ordered the closure of an oratory (shrine) dedicated to Catarina de San Juan.[86] In the wake of this institutionalized assault against the popular veneration of an illiterate holy woman, any potential cause for canonization died of stillbirth; the Sacred Congregation of Rites never opened hearings into Catarina's sanctity.

Scholars have offered several viable explanations for why inquisitors banned Ramos's *Primera parte*, including the marginal social status of its protagonist, the nature of the mystical experiences it describes, and the lack of hagiographic restraint on the part of its author.[87] For my purposes, the precise reason for the ban—which is impossible to determine at any rate—is less important than the fact that Ramos anticipated his readers' skepticism. Thus, to present pious poblanos and ecclesiastical officials with a desirable saint, he took great care to demonstrate the impeccability of Catarina's origins, portraying her as one whose social status and ethnicity conformed more closely to the profile of the typical New World holy person. While Ramos's protagonist was unique in terms of social type and geographic origins, the challenge he faced was not all that uncommon. Indeed, those who promoted the reputations and cults of white saints were often compelled to grapple with questions of origins and moral character. As criollo political grievances intensified after 1750, such concerns came to dominate the hagiographic treatments of Mexico City's criollo saint, Felipe de Jesús.

7

ʼBirth Pangs of a Criollo Saint

Defending the Mexican Origins of St. Felipe de Jesús

One of the more dramatic episodes in the early modern encounter between the Western and non-Western worlds occurred in 1597, when Japanese shogun Toyotomi Hideyoshi (1537–98) ordered the execution of twenty-six Roman Catholics, including seventeen local converts. Among the victims was a Franciscan friar named Felipe de las Casas Martínez, or Felipe de Jesús, a criollo of Mexico City. His beatification by Pope Urban VIII in 1627 made Felipe de Jesús the first American-born Spaniard to be so honored by Rome; Rosa de Santa María would not receive this honor until forty-one years later. In recognition of this milestone, civic and ecclesiastical authorities of Mexico City proclaimed him patron saint of their city in 1629.

In the wake of this auspicious beginning, the cult of Blessed Felipe de Jesús flourished in the central regions of New Spain, where Franciscan influence was particularly strong. Literary and artistic traditions soon developed around "el santo criollo," as Felipe came to be called long before his official canonization in 1862.[1] Even so, the cult of Felipe de Jesús seems to have been in decline by the last decades of the eighteenth century, the period of the so-called Bourbon Reforms instituted by the Spanish crown. Furthermore, as royal policies and peninsular attitudes became increasingly anti-criollo, Mexican-born devotees of Felipe de Jesús began attributing the neglect of his cult—manifested most grievously by the failures to build him a church or to properly honor the house of his birth—to "enemies" of New Spain. These unnamed enemies, whom criollo apologists frequently accused of conspiracy and cover-up, had raised questions about Felipe's moral character and his origins. On the one hand, they intimated that his life prior to 1597 showed little evidence of heroic virtue. On the other hand, they suggested that he might not have been born in Mexico City, since there was no record of his baptism in parish registries. Given the tenor of criollo-peninsular relations in the decades between 1750 and 1821, it is easy to understand the criollo reaction. Both sets of allegations—that Felipe was no saint and that he may not have been criollo—ultimately implied that nothing sublime could originate in New Spain.

This chapter highlights the criollo defense of San Felipe de Jesús through sermon and hagiography proper. Following a narrative overview of Felipe's life and martyrdom, I examine his evolving hagiographic tradition, giving particular attention to the period from 1750 to 1821, which witnessed a general souring of relations between novohispano criollos and their peninsular rivals.

Felipe de Jesús: Biographical Sketch

According to tradition, Felipe de las Casas Martínez was born to the Spanish-born merchant Alonso de las Casas and his wife Antonia Martínez on May 1, 1572, in Mexico City. The absence of any baptismal record, however, would prove highly problematic for Felipe's criollo devotees in later generations as they attempted to prove beyond a shadow of a doubt that he was indeed their fellow mexicano. As a young boy he studied Latin at the local Jesuit colegio of San Pedro y San Pablo under Pedro Gutiérrez; he may also have been a student of the colegio of San Ildefonso.[2] One tradition holds that Felipe learned the silversmithing trade as a youth, but there is little evidence to confirm the claim, which may have been a pious invention of the Platería de México, an artisan guild that later chose the mexicano martyr as its patron saint.

At about fifteen years of age, Felipe entered the Franciscan convent of Santa Bárbara (Puebla) as a novice, but left the novitiate after a short time and returned to Mexico City. Felipe's abandonment of the religious path may have embarrassed his family; it certainly became a problem for his hagiographers, who would feel compelled over the next two centuries to explain his apparent lapse in judgment.[3] By 1591, young Felipe was in Manila, probably sent there by his merchant father to look after the family's commercial interests. The elder de las Casas, who had worked as a commercial agent at the port of Acapulco, must have had firsthand knowledge of the Asian trade, as well as useful personal connections.[4]

Within a few years of his arrival in Manila, Felipe de las Casas once again turned to a religious career, entering the local discalced Franciscan Convento de Santa María. This time he persisted, making his religious vows around 1594.[5] His hagiographers are careful to explain that following his religious vows, Felipe underwent a profound religious conversion, marked by all the outward signs of heroic sanctity. Two years later, he decided to return to New Spain in order to receive ordination and say his first mass in the presence of his parents.[6] From Manila he embarked on a ship named the *San Felipe*—a providential sign, his hagiographers would later claim—in order to make his way home.

The voyage to Acapulco did not go according to plan, however, for a storm forced the ship aground on the Japanese coast near the city of Miyaco (modern Kyoto). The shipwrecked group of Spanish and Portuguese mendicants and merchants arrived in Japan in a moment of political crisis.[7] Toyotomi Hideyoshi was in the process of centralizing his political control at the expense of his rivals, both Japanese and foreign. Increasingly distrustful of the motives of Roman Catholic missionaries, he suddenly decided in 1596–97 to enforce his anti-Christian ban of ten years earlier. Thus, he ordered the execution by crucifixion of six Franciscans, three Jesuits, and seventeen Japanese converts, a sentence that was carried out near the port city of Nagasaki on February 5, 1597. In the aftermath of the crucifixions, Catholic witnesses described steps taken by the Japanese authorities to prevent the victims from becoming a cause célèbre. Although authorities left the victims' bodies on the crosses as a warning to other potential converts, they also constructed a retaining wall around the crosses and assigned guards in order to prevent sympathizers from stealing the bodies. During the months that followed, Catholic witnesses saw numerous miraculous signs, including columns of fire in the night sky, fresh emissions of blood from the martyrs' bodies, and carrion birds that refused to attack the sacred relics. Eventually, a group of Franciscans who escaped martyrdom removed the bodies of Felipe de Jesús and his fellow martyr Pedro Bautista to Manila, whence relics were later sent to Mexico.[8]

When Mexico City celebrated the beatification of its native son in 1629, Felipe's widowed mother was present at the festivities. On January 26 of that year, she gave sworn testimony before the city council that Felipe de Jesús was her son and a "criollo of this city."[9] She requested, moreover, that the "illustrious, noble and loyal City" properly honor its patron saint by providing financial assistance to his impoverished mother and sisters. The cabildo members agreed to her request, granting her a monthly income of thirty pesos.[10] In the years that followed, several religious institutions and social groups in New Spain developed traditions linking their histories to the person and cult of Felipe de Jesús.[11]

Felipe de Jesús: Hagiographic Traditions to 1750

Less than two years after the dramatic events of February 1597, Fray Marcello de Ribadeneyra passed through New Spain en route from Manila to Rome, carrying with him a manuscript history of sixteenth-century Roman Catholic missionary activity in Asia. Fray Juan Bautista, O.F.M., examined the manuscript and communicated his approval to authorities in Mexico City in December 1598. Following a second evaluation by officials in Rome, Ribadeneyra's *Historia de las islas del archipielago, y reynos de la gran China, Tartaria, Cuchinchina, Malaca, Sian, Camboxa y Iappon* was published in Barcelona in 1601. This early historical account disseminated knowledge of the Nagasaki martyrs throughout the Roman Catholic world and shaped later hagiographic accounts of the life of Felipe de Jesús. Estrada de Gerlero suggests that Ribadeneyra's narrative probably informed the earliest artistic renderings of these events in churches and convents of New Spain.[12]

In Ribadeneyra's *Historia,* as in the ecclesiastical art that commemorated the Nagasaki martyrs for several decades after the events, the story of Felipe de Jesús remained submerged in the broader histories of the Spanish Philippines and Roman Catholicism in Asia. Following his beatification and election as patron saint of Mexico City, however, the novohispano faithful began to honor Felipe de Jesús by providing patronage for his cult. In January 1636, Luis de Herrera, a Mexico City native and member of the cathedral chapter, urged the municipal cabildo to patronize Felipe's feast day more generously and to designate the house in which he was born for use as a parish church. A few years later, Herrera himself received praise for promoting Felipe's cult and providing material aid to his widowed mother and siblings.[13] During the same years, local writers and book printers gave greater prominence to Felipe de Jesús through the publication of select feast-day sermons. In 1638, Fray Luis Vaca Salazar, provincial of the Mercedarian province of Mexico and confessor to the wife of New Spain's viceroy, published a sermon he had preached in the cathedral on February 5, Felipe's feast day. In 1640, an Oratorian priest named Miguel Sánchez, known today for his 1648 account of the apparition of Our Lady of Guadalupe to Juan Diego, published a sermon acknowledging Felipe de Jesús as the "blessed one *(venturoso)* of Mexico" and "the most accomplished of all her criollos." On February 5, 1652, Jacinto de la Serna used the occasion of a feast-day sermon to honor the land of his own birth: "O, Imperial Mexico City, my Patria, . . . City and patria of the Illustrious Protomartyr of Japan San Felipe de Jesús."[14] The publication of sermons and novenas treating Felipe de Jesús as criollo, indiano, americano, and *compatriota* continued well into the nineteenth century.[15]

Despite this birth of a literary tradition, however, there was still no published work of hagiography proper memorializing Felipe de Jesús by 1673, when an anonymous writer began work on a text entitled *Vida de San Felipe de Jesús*. The impetus for this work of hagiography may have been the foundation of a convent of Capuchin nuns in 1666 under the spiritual patronage of Blessed Felipe de Jesús.[16] For some reason, the unidentified hagiographer failed to complete the Life, which consequently remained unknown for more than a century. Nevertheless, the manuscript prologue provides valuable insights into how criollos, especially those born in Mexico City, were beginning to interpret their saint's significance by the last decades of the seventeenth century. Describing Felipe de Jesús as "a criollo of Mexico City" and the pride of his patria, the would-be hagiographer laments that, despite the passage of almost a century, "no one, whether out of love for a countryman or for a Martyr of Christ, has written down [these things] for posterity." In a telling statement, he attributes this absence of a fitting literary tribute to Felipe's "poor fate of *being criollo*."[17] In these decades criollos of New Spain had begun to project their own anxieties onto the person of San Felipe de Jesús and to equate his fate with their own.

The anonymous author of the never-completed 1673 manuscript was alone neither in his assessment of the potential significance of Felipe de Jesús for the faithful of Mexico City nor in his exasperation that a proper hagiographic tribute had been so long in coming. Less than a decade later, the discalced Franciscan chronicler Baltasar de Medina published the first bona fide Life of Felipe de Jesús. Medina was an appropriate candidate for the task, for he was a native of Mexico City and a former visitor for the Franciscan province of San Gregorio de Filipinas. The publication of his *Vida, martyrio y beatificación* coincided with a general proliferation of printed criollo histories, religious and otherwise, in the second half of the seventeenth century[18] and served as a primary source for later writers and preachers. Dedicating his literary project "To the Illustrious Protomartyr of Japan, San Felipe de Jesús, Patron Saint of Mexico his Patria," Medina requests the assistance of his saint: "Guide me . . . as your younger brother by adoption and by grace, [O] new light to this New World your patria. . . . You are my countryman, Felipe, prove yourself my muse as well."[19] Francisco Romero y Quevedo, another native of Mexico City whose "Sentir" (Reflection) appears as a preface to Medina's published Life, describes the martyred saint as "our Felipe, a beautiful rose rising out of the Mexican lake."[20] Finally, the book's publisher, Juan de Ribera, reinforces this portrayal of Felipe as mexicano compatriot and advocate with an ink sketch of the criollo saint. The depiction, which is quite amateurish in artistic terms, shows the criollo protomartyr pierced with lances and hanging on a cross, rising above the ancient Aztec symbol of the nopal cactus, eagle, and serpent, which even in Spanish colonial art was coming to represent the viceregal capital. In the background are buildings representing Mexico City. Inscribed in Latin at the bottom of the page is the following phrase: "Your name, O Felipe, is invoked on behalf of your city and people."[21]

While a prolonged treatment of Medina's 1683 Life is not necessary at this point, two elements of his text merit brief attention. First, this native of Mexico City describes the criollo saint as unique among the twenty-six martyrs of 1597, one whose manner of death set him apart from the others.[22] Iconographers in New Spain had also began to spotlight Felipe de Jesús in the middle decades of the seventeenth century. Prior to public celebration of his beatification in Mexico City in 1629, Felipe had appeared in pious art as one martyr among many. Subsequently, he "began to appear alone on the cross in agony, without any allusion to his fellow martyrs" (see figure 7.1).[23] This characterization of Felipe de Jesús as superior to his fellow martyrs, a theme that eighteenth-century writers would further elaborate, was part of a larger campaign on the part of criollo clerics to claim for New Spain a special place in the history of the church universal.[24]

In the second place, hagiographer Medina seeks to reconcile certain contradictions in the hagiographic record. In this regard, he responds to questions about Felipe's place of birth and his moral qualities. Was Felipe de Jesús a criollo of Mexico City, or had he been born elsewhere? Moreover, had he merited the title of "martyr," and thus the prospect of canonization, or had he simply been an average religious who got caught in the wrong place at the wrong time? In his response to such crucial questions, Medina is neither defensive nor argumentative in tone. After 1750, however, criollo apologists who engaged these persisting doubts would become more combative.

Criollo Self-Consciousness in the Lives of Felipe de Jesús, 1750–1810

As late as 1750, pious elites of New Spain still had no equivalent to St. Rosa of Peru, for although the cult of Our Lady of Guadalupe had made great strides, neither a novohispano criollo nor a peninsular transplant like Sebastián de Aparicio had been canonized. For the region's clerical and civic leaders who were promoting numerous causes for canonization during the eighteenth century, this situation was untenable. If the proliferation of printed devotional literature is any indication, criollo devotees of Felipe de Jesús—particularly Franciscans and Oratorians—were more resolved than ever to promote his cult in New Spain and his causa in Rome. In an era of administrative, fiscal, and ideological changes that favored the metropolis at the expense of her colonies, their literary products reflected a growing criollo resentment.

In 1751, Fray Miguel Alcaráz published a second edition of Med-

FIGURE 7.1. "B. Felipe de Jesús. Mártir de el Japón y Patrón de la Ciudad de México, su Patria." (Blessed Felipe de Jesús, Martyr of Japan and Patron Saint of Mexico City, his homeland.) Illustration from Baltasar de Medina, *Vida, martyrio y beatificación del invicto proto-mártir de el Japón, San Felipe de Jesús, patrón de México, su patria, imperial corte de Nueva España en el nuevo mundo* (Madrid, 1751). (Courtesy of the Sutro Library, a branch of the California State Library)

ina's *Vida, martyrio y beatificación* with the financial support of the Mexico City silversmiths guild (Platería de México), to which he dedicated the work.[25] Alcaráz, who represented the discalced province of San Diego de la Nueva España at the courts of Madrid and Rome, set the tone for a more combative criollo defense of the Mexican saint and his homeland:

> San Felipe is my Countryman. [Alcaráz here lists the twenty-six martyrs of 1597, arranged according to religious order.] But since among all of them San Felipe is from my patria, his life requires special attention on my part. Although fruits from foreign lands have a more exotic taste, they are not as sweet or piquant as those from one's native soil. One's taste buds are more accustomed and suited to homegrown foods. . . . Felipe is bud, flower, and fruit of Mexico. By presenting to my patria the flower that is his life, and the fruit that is his Martyrdom, I demonstrate the fertility of the soil that nurtured such a plant and tree of life.[26]

Observing that it is usual for the panegyrist to laud the merits of his subject's patria, however, Alcaráz claims to follow St. Basil in rejecting this approach. "Am I somehow better," he asks, "simply because Mexico, Imperial Court of the New World, rests on crystalline soil, as does Venice? Or simply because Winter and Summer never usurp the special rights *(fueros)* of Spring?" Alcaráz continues with similar rhetorical questions regarding his patria's "famous breeds of cattle" and "rich mineral veins," as well as its "religion," "letters," and "outstanding political life." Once again emphasizing that such matters have no place in a saint's life, Alcaráz concludes, "Do such things make us more virtuous?"[27]

With this statement, the criollo author cleverly achieves two important goals. First, he strikes at the doctrine of climatic determinism, a then-fashionable ideology that linked the potential of human beings and human societies to climatic or celestial conditions. This theory, which would gain even more credibility in Europe following the publication of Corneille de Pauw's *Recherches philosophiques sur les Américains* (1768) provided Iberian policymakers with ideological justification for their anti-criollo policies.[28] By promising to "forget the greatness of Mexico" in order to "write the virtuous memories of San Felipe," Alcaráz appears to deny that physical or social environment affects human merit. On the other hand, of course, this mexicano patriot takes full advantage of the opportunity to praise the merits of his patria. Far from forgetting "the greatness of Mexico," he lauds his homeland for its superior soil and climate, its ranching and mineral wealth, and its religious, intellectual, and political maturity. Clearly, despite his protestations to the contrary, the criollo patriot connects the virtues of Felipe de Jesús to the merits of New Spain.

In the decades following Alcaráz's republication of the Medina Life, criollo apologists for the merits of San Felipe de Jesús would repeatedly deny allegations that their "protomártir mexicano," as they called him, had not been born in New Spain. In a generation that placed emphasis on scientific and historical rigor, Felipe's defenders found it more necessary than before to explain why there was no record of his baptism in either the cathedral or parish archives of Mexico City. In New Spain, as throughout the Roman Catholic world, baptismal registries *(libros de partida)* provided documentary verification of an individual's reception of the sacrament of regeneration as well as proof of his or her legitimacy, lineage, and place of birth. Thus, the absence of a baptismal record for Felipe de las Casas Martínez gave rise to questions about his origins, leading to speculation that he had been born in Spain. Lacking evidence from local registries, apologists of his Mexican origins could offer no proof of their claims. For eighteenth-century Spaniards, whether americanos or peninsulares, this matter was of paramount importance. In their value system, a person's merit depended to a very high degree on social origins. Moreover, the glory and honor of Felipe de Jesús would ultimately belong to whichever community could claim him as its native son. Clearly, the criollo quest to prove Felipe's mexicano origins was motivated by much more than historical curiosity.

In 1683, Baltasar de Medina had offered two theories about the absence of a baptismal record for Felipe de Jesús: either the priest who baptized him failed to properly record the act, or the written record was destroyed during one of Mexico City's frequent inundations.[29] After the 1750s pro-Felipe writers, who were quite familiar with Medina's twice-published Life of Felipe de Jesús, disseminated and elaborated on his theories. A reference to Felipe's missing baptismal record appeared in Antonio de Robles's Life of Don Alonso de Cuevas Dávalos, former archbishop of Mexico City. Attempting to account for the absence of a baptismal record for Cuevas Dávalos, Robles lamented how frequently baptisms had been improperly registered in Mexico City, citing as one example the case of "our illustrious martyr San Felipe de Jesús."[30]

In marked contrast to Medina and Robles, criollo writers from the 1760s forward tended to explain Felipe's missing baptismal records as the product of an anti-criollo conspiracy. This should not be surprising since the Bourbon reforms, which were both anti-criollo and mildly anticlerical in nature, were gaining intensity during the same years under King Charles III (1759–88). Iberian-born royal officials, led by visitor and later viceroy José de Gálvez, weakened the americano presence in the imperial administration by replacing outgoing New World–born bishops, judges, and corregidores with Europeans. The concurrent implementation of the French-inspired intendancy system enabled the metropolis to undermine existing Habsburg structures through which criollos had exercised a great deal of local control. The crown increased the tax burden on transatlantic and intercolonial trade while attacking the traditional privileges of merchant guilds. Moreover, persistent royal efforts to erode clerical privilege, especially the *fuero eclesiástico,* alienated a large portion of the criollo clergy. Worst of all, the crown's shocking expulsion of the Jesuits from Spain's Iberian and overseas territories in 1767 forced many of New Spain's native sons into exile in Italy. Americano whites, especially those in the clergy, perceived themselves to have been abandoned, even betrayed, by European masters jealous of their achievements. In the context of this broader process, criollo promoters of the cult of San Felipe de Jesús attributed his relative obscurity and lack of popular esteem to a plot by enemies of New Spain to rob their land of its rightful honor.

In 1760, for example, Patricio Alexandro de Chavaria Buitron blamed his unsuccessful attempts to locate Felipe's baptismal record on "the exaggerated malice [of] those who expurgated the Partida de la Fé de Bautismo and Regeneración of San Felipe de Jesús from the page on which it was written." Chavaria Buitron offers his own conspiracy theory; namely, that such an act of malice may have been carried out by "some foreigner or one of the many false Christians who came to this kingdom" around the time of Felipe's birth. While Chavaria Buitron is unable to identify the conspirators, he seems convinced that their motive was "to dishonor this noble and Loyal City and the whole realm [i.e., New Spain]."[31]

Another noteworthy reference to the enigma of San Felipe's missing baptismal record appears in the dedicatoria to José Manuel Rodríguez's celebrated Guadalupan sermon of 1768 entitled *El país afortunado*. The Cuban-born Franciscan, who was also chronicler of the
Franciscan province of Santo Evangelio (New Spain), cites "a certain
rumor" casting "doubts on the status *(calidad)* of Felipe de Jesús qua
mexicano," a rumor based solely on the saint's missing baptismal
record. Rodríguez challenges the validity of the rumor, noting that
although Baltasar de Medina had lacked baptismal records for many
of "the Venerable . . . criollos of Mexico" described in his *Chrónica de la
santa prouincia de San Diego de México*, no one had called into question
their "criollismo mexicano." In the case of Felipe de Jesús, Rodríguez
theorizes, the baptismal record had been recorded on one of the pages
that later went missing from the cathedral's third Libro de Bautismos.
Alleging to have discovered a lacuna in the records for a fifteen-month
period extending from May 1575 to August 1576, Rodríguez even hints
at bribery and cover-up.[32]

At the close of the eighteenth century, Father José Pichardo
brought together priestly piety, patriotic fervor, and a historian's attention to detail in writing *Vida y martirio del protomártir mexicano San Felipe
de Jesús de las Casas*. Pichardo, who also wrote a meticulously researched
treatise on the Texas-Louisiana boundary between 1808 and 1812, was
born in Cuernavaca, New Spain, around 1748.[33] He served for more
than twenty years as a presbyter of the religious congregation known
as the Oratorio de San Felipe de Neri.[34] The fathers of the Oratorio
in Mexico City believed that Felipe de Jesús had communicated miraculously with their congregation through a painted image and were convinced he had been born in the house that later became their church.
Pichardo's membership in this religious congregation gave him a natural affinity for Felipe de Jesús. Furthermore, his role as an occasional
confessor of the Capuchin nuns whose convent was under the spiritual patronage of Felipe de Jesús reinforced his tie to the criollo saint.
By the time of his death in 1812, Pichardo had completed a narrative
of Felipe's life through his years in Manila. He had also collected
numerous documents pertaining to the events of 1597 in Japan, and
clearly planned to write a second part. The unpublished narrative, along
with several of Pichardo's documents relating to the life of Felipe de
Jesús, is housed in the Nettie Lee Benson Latin American Collection at

the University of Texas at Austin.[35] In 1934, Archbishop Francisco Orozco y Jiménez of Guadalajara published Pichardo's *Vida y martirio* with the help of Dr. Carlos E. Castañeda.

It is unclear why Pichardo failed to complete the manuscript. It may be that he set it aside in order to begin work on the Texas-Louisiana treatise, a project of some urgency that offered a greater potential for remuneration. Letters written between 1794 and 1797 indicate that Pichardo was at work on the Felipe Life during those years, but it is not clear when he abandoned work on it. At any rate, since Pichardo never completed his manuscript, he never wrote the prologue or dedication that would have accompanied a published version. Thus, one is left to speculate as to his greater authorial vision and motivation. Two things, however, are quite clear. First, Pichardo considered his task to be more that of historian than panegyrist: he exercises great scholarly care in researching and documenting his work. Second, Pichardo writes with the intention of bringing honor to his patria. He may be a historian, but he is not a disinterested one.

Castañeda—who placed Pichardo in a league with great Mexican scholars like Andrés Cavo, Mariano Fernández Echeverría y Veytia, Félix Osores, and Antonio León y Gama—praised "his vast erudition, his untiring dedication to research, his profound knowledge of the sciences and humanities, and his continual enthusiasm for collecting and preserving the primordial sources for [Mexico's] history."[36] Indeed, Pichardo the historian left no stone (nor page) unturned. Through exhaustive archival searches, personal interviews, and a review of a vast literature in both Spanish and Italian, he sought to reconcile competing accounts of his protagonist's life, often by refuting one version or another. There were two clear explanations for the development of contradictory traditions surrounding Felipe's life. First, early chroniclers and panegyrists, more concerned with biblical topoi and moral lessons than with historical accuracy, made Felipe's early life conform to the biblical parable of the prodigal son, and his crucifixion to that of Jesus Christ. Second, various religious and social sodalities (such as the Platería de México) developed oral and written traditions linking Felipe's life narrative to their own histories. In the *Vida y martirio,* Pichardo systematically evaluated these poorly documented, moralized accounts, concerned that their continued existence allowed doubt and speculation to cloud the truth, ultimately weakening Felipe's causa at

Rome and undermining the status of Mexico City as birthplace of "el santo criollo." Convinced that the historical facts would support his case, Pichardo showed his patriotic zeal by seeking to lift Felipe de Jesús from the plane of myth to that of history.

In keeping with this objective, Pichardo presents a painfully detailed examination of his protagonist's origins. He opens his narrative with an in-depth treatment of Felipe's illustrious family lineage. Noting the antiquity, nobility, and heroic service of Felipe's ancestors, Pichardo traces the lineage of the Casas clan of Seville to a French nobleman named Guillén Bec who helped King Ferdinand III of Castile seize that city from the Moors in 1236. The criollo author describes the Bec line as "easily . . . one of the greatest families in Spain," and presents a long list of illustrious forebears of Felipe de Jesús, noting their service to Castilian monarchs in the conquest of Granada and suppression of the Comunero revolt. In order to establish the family's very early ties to New Spain, Pichardo identifies one Francisco de las Casas as a companion of Hernán Cortés's in the conquest of New Spain and as a member of the first municipal council of Mexico City in 1524.[37]

Pichardo devotes his most detailed attention—fully half of book 1—to the question of Felipe's birthplace. His purpose is to refute once and for all the speculation that Felipe de Jesús had been born somewhere other than Mexico City. From Pichardo's treatment of this controversy, we learn more about the possible sources of these rumors and gain a fuller picture of the resentment they aroused in criollo clerics of his day. Pichardo notes, for example, José Sicardo's intimation in *Christiandad del Japón* that Antonia Martínez may have given birth to the future saint in Spain, at sea, or in Chilapa (New Spain). But rather than dismiss these notions as the harmless speculations of early chroniclers, Pichardo directs his ire at those who continued to disseminate such rumors.

Pichardo reveals his criollo colors through his criticism of a 1778 work entitled *Tardes americanas*. The work's author, an Iberian-born bishop of Sonora (New Spain) named José Joaquin Granados y Gálvez, narrates an imaginary dialogue between a Spaniard and an Indian. In the course of their conversation, the Indian reveals that "numerous [people] believe and give assurances behind closed doors that [Felipe] was born and baptized in the Parish of San Miguel of Sevilla and brought as a very young child to these parts." Pichardo takes great offense at these lines from *Tardes americanas,* which he quotes in full, and he alleges that Bishop Granados y Gálvez did not include this passage as a harmless example of private speculation. Rather, Pichardo accuses the bishop of libel, noting that "through the laments of his Indian, he shows very well his [own] passion . . . and reveals to us his [own] opinion." The proliferation of this error, concludes Pichardo, greatly offends Mexico, "which counts among its greatest glories that of being the Patria of San Felipe."[38]

Pichardo's negative reaction to this passage from *Tardes americanas* undoubtedly must have been influenced by the fact that Granados y Gálvez dedicates his book to a cousin, José de Gálvez, the Andalusian-born administrator of the crown's major reform program in New Spain between 1765 and 1771. José de Gálvez had angered many criollos and injured relations between the colonies and the metropolis during his years in New Spain, especially through his ruthless suppression of pro-Jesuit manifestations following the 1767 expulsion. Pichardo and his fellow criollo patriots must have found especially galling a passage from Bishop Granados y Gálvez's *dedicatoria* in which he praises José de Gálvez for his "pleasant disposition *(carácter dulce)*" and "inclination to agreement rather than severity."[39] For José Pichardo, the bishop's willingness to praise his infamous cousin's political virtues and to spread doubts about St. Felipe's Mexican birth was implicitly anti-criollo.

As I have already noted, however, Pichardo himself possessed no concrete proof that Mexico City was Felipe's birthplace. His attempt to make such a case, therefore, consisted of discrediting all other possibilities while attempting to uncover evidence supporting a Mexico City birth. It is here that Pichardo's historical rigor is evident, for he orders searches of archives in Salamanca and Sevilla and makes his own investigations in Mexico City.

In order to discredit the theory of a birth in Spain or at sea, Pichardo attempted to piece together a time line for the lives of Antonia Martínez and Alonso de las Casas prior to their departure from Spain. His a priori agenda was to prove that Felipe's mother could not have given birth to him in the brief period between her marriage to Alonso de las Casas and their emigration to the New World.[40] Estimating her date of birth to have been between 1557 and 1560, he set out to find confirmatory evidence. In 1794, he commissioned a thorough search of parish baptismal registries for the city of Salamanca, Spain, hoping to find a record of Antonia's birth. This investigation of local registries brought him negative responses from eighteen parish priests (see figure 7.2). In a letter dated March 30, 1796, his agent in Madrid, who had coordinated the search and gathered the resulting letters, informed him in a brief note that no *partida de bautismo* had been found for Antonia Ruiz Martínez.[41]

Although disappointed with this outcome, Pichardo remained undaunted, requesting that searches be made of the parish and cathedral marriage registries in the diocese of Sevilla. His motives for paying for this second search were twofold. First of all, evidence of a Sevilla wedding would increase the likelihood that the couple had embarked for New Spain very shortly after exchanging vows. Second, such proof would undermine rumors that Felipe de Jesús might have been born out of wedlock. With regard to this matter, Pichardo admits having read in a chronicle of the discalced province of San Gregorio de Filipinas that Antonia Ruiz Martínez and Alonso de las Casas had fallen in love in Salamanca and fled together to Sevilla in order to marry.[42] Such a tale, which smacked of passion and spontaneity, opened the door for rumors of prenuptial relations between the two, thus casting doubt on the legitimacy of Felipe's birth. To Pichardo's relief, the second archival investigation paid off; his agents found a record in Sevilla registries of a marriage between one Alonso de las Casas and Antonia Martínez on November 5, 1570.[43]

With evidence of the couple's marriage date, Pichardo attempts through a series of logical deductions to establish the date of their departure for New Spain as August 1571, only seven or eight months after their wedding. Once content that his theory is sound, he suggests that common sense itself dictates that Felipe was born in New Spain. After all, Antonia Martínez could not have given birth to a child of legitimate union between the dates of the couple's marriage and their embarkation for New Spain. Furthermore, he argues, it would have been imprudent and unnecessary for the couple to set out on their transatlantic journey if Antonia had recently given birth. Nor would they have done so if she were expecting to give birth soon.[44] By combining documentary and circumstantial evidence with common sense, Pichardo hopes to convince his readers that Felipe de Jesús was born neither in Spain nor at sea. As for Sicardo's reference to a theory that

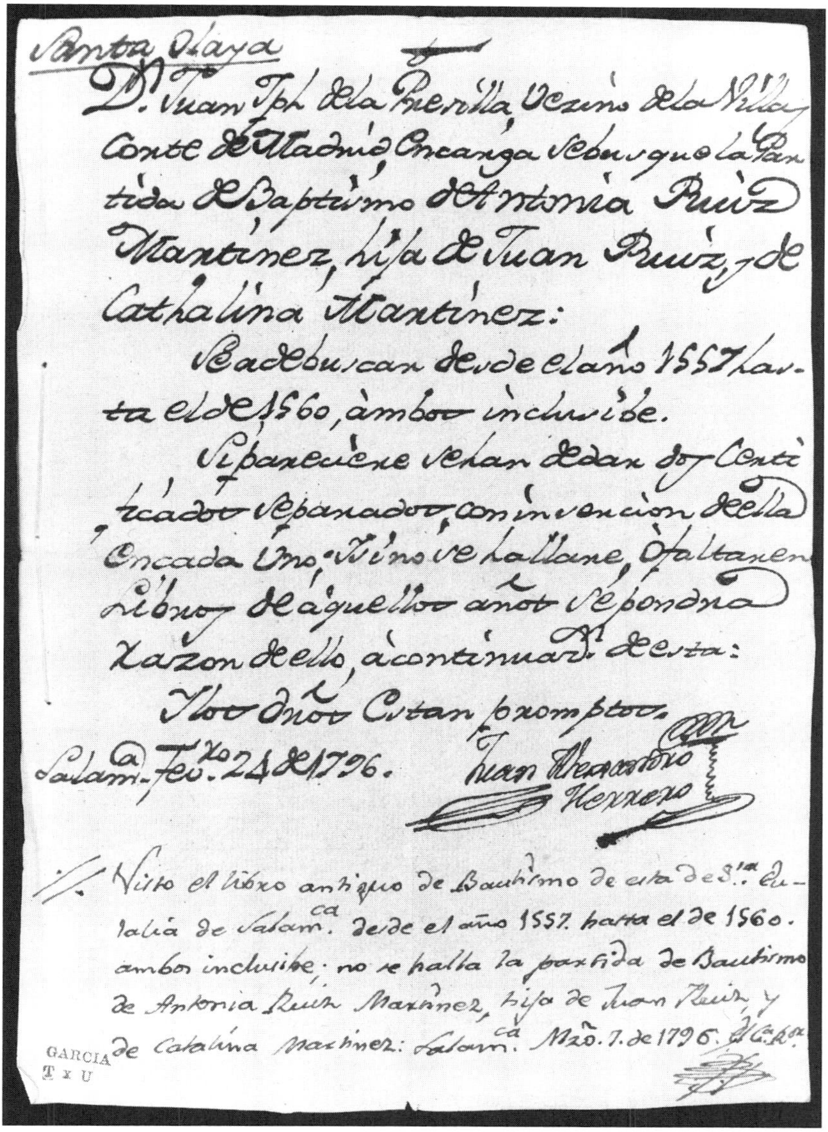

Santa Olaya

D.n Juan Jph de la Presilla, Vezino de la Villa y Corte de Madrid, encarga se busque la Partida de Baptismo de Antonia Ruiz Martinez, hija de Juan Ruiz, y de Cathalina Martinez:

Se ha de buscar desde el año 1557 hasta el de 1560, ambos inclusive.

Si pareciere se han de dar dos Certificados separados, con insercion de ella en cada uno; y si no se hallare, ó faltaren Libros de aquellos años se pondrá razon de ello, á continuacion de esta:

Los drños estan promptos.

Salam.ca Feb.ro 24 de 1796. Juan Bernardino Herrero

V.to el libro antiguo de Bautismo de esta de S.ta Eulalia de Salam.ca desde el año 1557. hasta el de 1560. ambos inclusive: no se halla la partida de Bautismo de Antonia Ruiz Martinez, hija de Juan Ruiz, y de Catalina Martinez: Salam.ca Mzo. 7. de 1796.

FIGURE 7.2. A parish priest of the church of Santa Eulalia, Salamanca (Spain), responds to Juan Joseph de la Presilla's inquiry (larger hand) about a baptismal record (partida de bautismo) for Antonia Ruiz Martínez, mother of San Felipe de Jesús. His reply, in the smaller hand at the bottom of the page, translates as follows: "Having examined the old book of baptisms of this [church] of Santa Eulalia de Salamanca, from the year 1557 to 1560, inclusive, I find no baptismal record for Antonia Ruiz Martínez, daughter of Juan Ruiz and Catalina Martínez. Salamanca, March 7, 1796." On March 30, 1796, Presilla sent this letter, along with seventeen others like it, to Father José Pichardo in Mexico City, informing him that, unfortunately, no baptismal record could be found. (Courtesy of the Benson Latin American Collection, University of Texas at Austin)

Felipe had been born in Chilapa, New Spain, during his father's tenure there as corregidor, Pichardo dismisses this unsubstantiated rumor as "pure fable" *(pura fábula).*[45]

Yet Pichardo is not content simply to disprove rumors of a non-Mexican birth. This Oratorian priest, who is by this point a man on a mission, describes his own quest for positive proof that his saint was born in the viceregal capital. Pichardo's quest, which required him to account for Felipe's missing baptismal record, sent him to the Mexico City cathedral archives. There he uncovered evidence confirming Antonio de Robles's published statement about improperly registered baptisms. In a letter of May 1794 to José Francisco Valdés, Pichardo excitedly reported his findings:

> I have discovered a great secret; that is, that in the Life of Señor Cuevas, Archbishop of Mexico, it says on page 5 that when he was baptized in the year 1590, it was the practice of the time for infants to be baptized in the parish church of their parents' choosing, and to this end water was carried from the baptismal font of the Parish. [The author] says that for this reason many baptismal records were lost, including that of San Felipe, because they were not careful to register them properly. This was indeed the practice, for yesterday afternoon I went through the cathedral books, in which I saw numerous baptismal records that say, "baptized in the church of the Jesuits, of San Domingo, of San Agustín, etc."[46]

As he explains in the *Vida y martirio,* Pichardo finds the Robles statement to be consistent with the explanations that Baltasar de Medina had offered in 1683; namely, that Felipe's missing baptismal record was the result of either the great floods of 1580 or the inattention of the baptizing curate. Felipe's parents may have baptized him in a parish church rather than in the cathedral, and those records could have been destroyed during a time of flooding.

At the same time, what Pichardo found in the cathedral records disproved José Manuel Rodríguez's allegation of 1768 that pages were missing from the cathedral's third Libro de Bautismos.[47] In the aforementioned letter to Valdés, Pichardo explains that "in these same sacristy books I also discovered to be false what Father Rodríguez says in the sermon entitled 'El Pais Afortunado,' for nothing is missing, a fact that is apparent to anyone who sees it." In the end, Pichardo blames the error on the Chavaria Buitron manuscript of 1760, which he concludes Rodríguez must have seen.[48]

In the end, although Pichardo can offer no conclusive proof that Felipe de Jesús was born and baptized in Mexico City, he contents himself with having demonstrated why such proof is unattainable. He strengthens his case by presenting testimony from literary and archival sources between 1599 and 1782 to the effect that San Felipe de Jesús was indeed a criollo, born in Mexico City. "According to all this [evidence] and to credible witnesses, it is time for those who say [St. Felipe de Jesús] was born in Spain or at sea to shut their mouths and stop speaking against [the facts], for this Saint was born and baptized in Mexico City."[49] For Pichardo, the time had arrived for a definitive shift in the Felipe discourse.

One final aspect of Pichardo's investigation merits mention in light of my attention to the criollo consciousness that pervades his text. In a chapter entitled "The House in This Mexico City in Which San Felipe de Jesús Was Born," Pichardo laments the numerous, mutually exclusive oral traditions regarding the saint's actual place of birth: "If one asks every inhabitant of Mexico City about which house is the fortunate one, one will find that all are in disagreement, and worse yet, that none of them is right."[50] For his part, Pichardo offers the Calle de San Agustín, a street "inhabited by the weavers *(texedores)* and those who trade in fine silks,"[51] as the likely location of Felipe's birth house. To strengthen his case, Pichardo explains that the Calle de San Agustín was a useful street of residence for a merchant due to its proximity to a market *(tianguis)* called San Juan, or Portales de Texada. Curiously, Pichardo digresses at this juncture from his discussion of Felipe's place of birth in order to entertain or impress his readers with an episode from Francisco de Cervantes Salazar's 1554 *Diálogos* that is set in the San Juan marketplace. In the scene, three European visitors to New Spain named Zuazo, Zamora, and Alfaro alternately disparage or defend the native people, their customs, or their products. One theme that emerges from this seven-page dialogue further elucidates Pichardo's intent as hagiographer; namely, that in a world marked by diverse peoples and customs, the novelty of something does not suggest its inferiority. In the words of one of Cervantes Salazar's European interlocutors, neither the waterways of Venice nor the medical knowledge of Galen, Hippocrates, and Avicenna are superior to their counterparts in New Spain.

Rather, from the *nopal tuna* (cactus) to the cotton *huipil* (loose shirt), all "are products of a new world."[52]

At first glance, this excerpt from Cervantes Salazar's *Diálogos* seems of little relevance to Pichardo's discussion of the birthplace of St. Felipe de Jesús. In fact, the only obvious conjunction lies in the fact that the dialogue between Zuazo, Zamora, and Alfaro takes place in the San Juan marketplace, near the Calle de San Agustín, where Pichardo believes Felipe was born. This excursus very clearly suits the purposes of a Mexican-born priest writing in defense of his saint and patria, however. Pichardo utilizes these fictional Iberian-born mouthpieces to express his own passion, namely that things American, including holy persons, are not inferior to things European.

Although Pichardo's manuscript Life of Felipe de Jesús remained incomplete and unpublished, writers and book printers continued to show interest in "el santo criollo" after the turn of the nineteenth century. In 1801, José María Montes de Oca published a devotional book of thirty engravings entitled *Vida de San Felipe de Jesús: protomártir de Japón y patrón de su patria México.*[53] Through his artistic representations of key episodes from Felipe's life, Montes de Oca disseminated elements of the hagiographic narratives in a more popular and economical form.[54] Among the thirty engravings, each of which bears a brief written description, are depictions of key episodes from Felipe's life and death, including several representations of his crucifixion in Japan. Montes de Oca engages the controversy surrounding his subject's birth and baptism in a picture that shows Felipe being baptized by churchmen while family members and a young acolyte bear witness (see figure 7.3). The engraver narrates the scene with the following phrase: "It is conjectured based on the available proofs that Blessed Felipe de Jesús was baptized on the first day of May in the year 1575." Montes de Oca also includes the now-familiar image of Felipe de Jesús hovering over the nopal cactus, eagle, and serpent, just as Baltasar de Medina had done in his 1683 Life. To this nineteenth-century version, Montes de Oca adds two female devotees, one a Spanish noblewoman and the other an elite indigenous woman, and a patriotic caption identifying "fortunate Mexico City" as the birthplace of San Felipe de Jesús (see figure 7.4).

In 1802, José María Munibe published in Mexico City *Breve resumen de la vida y martyrio del Beato Felipe de Jesús.* As Munibe explicitly

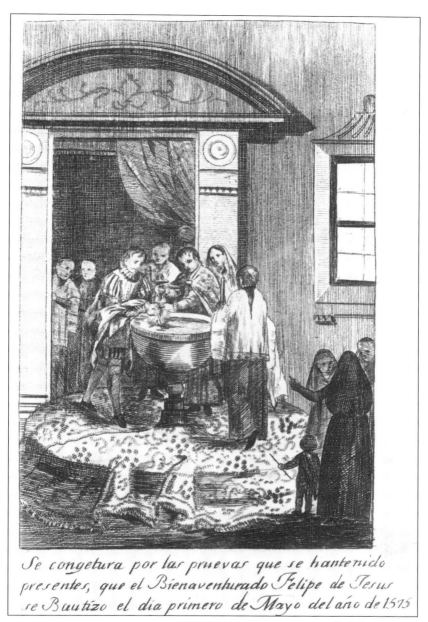

Se congetura por las pruevas que se hantenido presentes, que el Bienaventurado Felipe de Jesus se Bautizo el dia primero de Mayo del año de 1575

FIGURE 7.3. Baptism of St. Felipe de Jesús. "Se conjetura por las pruebas que se han tenido presentes, que el Bienaventurado Felipe de Jesús se Bautizó el día primero de Mayo del año de 1575." (It is conjectured based on the available proofs that Blessed Felipe de Jesús was baptized on the first day of May in the year 1575.) Illustration from José Maria Montes de Oca, *Vida de San Felipe de Jesús: protomártir de Japón y patrón de su patria México* (México, 1801). (Courtesy of the Sutro Library, a branch of the California State Library)

Nombra la afortunada México por Patron principal al Biena.^{do} Felipe de Jesus, á quien le dió la Cuna

FIGURE 7.4. "Nombra la afortunada México por patrón principal al Bien.º Felipe de Jesús á quien le dió la Cuna" (Fortunate Mexico City names as its primary patron saint the Blessed Felipe de Jesús, to whom it provided a birthplace.) Illustration from José María Montes de Oca, *Vida de San Felipe de Jesús: protomártir de Japón y patrón de su patria México* (México, 1801). (Courtesy of the Sutro Library, a branch of the California State Library)

states, his aim is to rekindle the flames of devotion to San Felipe and to generate enthusiasm and financial support for the construction of the saint's own church "in [order that] he might be worshipped *(adorado)* in his own house."⁵⁵ A strongly self-conscious criollismo permeates the various letters that preface Munibe's hagiographic text. In one carta, a native of Mexico City named José Manuel Sartorio explains that if a spirit of patriotism moved criollos in the past to foment the cult of their "much beloved compatriot," it was because their saint's virtues "have brought much glory to the Mexican soil."⁵⁶ However, he notes, the *Breve resumen* will show things that past devotional works failed to make clear, including "the glories with which [Felipe's] illustrious blood . . . has embellished his Patria Mexico." Sartorio's carta, along with a sonnet he offers in praise of Munibe, describe Felipe de Jesús as "Mexican Martyr," "Paisano Saint," "beloved American," and "Indiano youth."⁵⁷

In the actual text of the *Breve resumen,* Munibe introduces little that is new. In fact, he essentially distills the details of Medina's 1683 vida into an abbreviated version that can be distributed more widely. However, he deviates from the Medina original when it comes to a discussion of Felipe's allegedly obscure origins and impious beginnings; on these matters, Munibe takes a strongly defensive tone. For example, he opens his chronological narrative by criticizing attempts by other cities and Franciscan provinces to usurp from Mexico City and the discalced province of San Diego the honor of being Felipe's patria. In a statement reflecting generations of pent-up frustration over peninsular anti-americano prejudices, Munibe compares the relationship between Felipe and his Mexican patria to that of a fruitful seed and the soil in which it germinates and thrives. The "blooming" of virtue in Felipe's life, he argues, confounds those "impassioned ones [who] deny criollos *(Indianos)* have any aptitude for the cultivation of the sciences [or] anything pertaining to society, [as well as] others who . . . suggest that Indians *(indios)* are incapable of the imprint of grace." In the same vein, Munibe seeks to correct the wrong impressions that many hold of Felipe as having been, prior to his martyrdom, an "unbridled youth [who was] prostituted to every disorder." In his view, such conjectures are aimed at diminishing the glory of Felipe and his nation by gainsaying his martyrdom "as a mere accident." Munibe counters this notion by portraying Felipe as singular among the twenty-six martyrs, "as if he were the principal one, the Captain of that venerable and glorious company."[58] As his rhetoric makes clear, Munibe's *Breve resumen* continues the eighteenth-century tradition of blaming the retarded condition of Felipe's cult on the slanderous rumors of unnamed enemies of Mexico and its criollos.

Roughly a decade following the publication of Montes de Oca's devotional book of engravings and Munibe's *Breve resumen,* José Joaquin Fernández de Lizardi's *El glorioso protomártir mexicano* appeared in print in Mexico City. Rather than tiptoe around the polemical elements of the Felipe tradition, Fernández takes them up in his opening octets:

> *Of valiant generals let them sing*
> *The exploits, feats and conquests,*
> *Battles by land and by sea*
> *Of heroic deeds never before seen.*
> *Let panegyrists in timely fashion*
> *fill the annals with their praise,*
> *as the boastful lip sings the glory of the*
> *FAMOUS AMERICANO CHAMPION.*
>
> *Mexico [City], despite [the claims of our] emulators,*
> *gave this illustrious youth his cradle,*
> *in order to ennoble these regions*
> *or increase our fortune.*
> Here *he trampled the Devil's banner:*
> *Prior to* here, *he did not see light:*
> Here *his father first kissed him,*
> *And his blessed mother gave him that sweet nectar.*
>
> *To noble, rich, and virtuous parents*
> *was born this Mexican, this prodigy.*
> *What happy days! The street called Tiburcio,*
> *And the houses of San Eligio*
> *Witnessed his birth, O jealous fellows.*
> *Of this there is neither doubt nor dispute.*
> *But is, perchance, his happy house a Temple?*
> *["No,"], she says, "I am criollo, I am ashamed."*[59]

As his rhetoric suggests, Fernández de Lizardi was among the criollo devotees who attributed doubts about Felipe de Jesús's origins to the envy of Mexico City's rivals and the neglected condition of his cult to a lack of criollo pride. In an explanatory footnote to the opening line of the second octet, he makes his view most explicit:

> The statement of [Felipe's mother] does not allow for interpretation, for she literally declares, "I married the aforementioned Alonso de las Casas and we had as our children, first of all, the Glorious Martyr Saint San Felipe de Jesús and de las Casas, criollo of this city, etc." The font *(pila)* in which he was baptized is a witness, as is an unbroken tradition. If on account of floods his baptismal record cannot be found, those who are envious doubt that he is mexicano. On this pretext, they might as well question whether he was a Christian.[60]

Like the criollo eulogizers of Blessed Felipe de Jesús who preceded him, including José Antonio Pichardo, Fernández de Lizardi must resort to local tradition. Lacking a baptismal record that might verify their saint's local birth, mexicano and novohispano writers ultimately base their case on testimony attributed to Felipe's mother and on the traditional claim that he received the sacrament of regeneration in the baptismal font of the Mexico City cathedral. In an era when historical proof was much more valued and essential than in earlier centuries, such would not have been their preference. However, it was all they had by way of evidence. And, of course, they supplemented their limited evidence with their own conspiracy theories; certainly the enemies of Mexico and its native children had done all they could to deny it a saint of its own.

Conclusion

It might appear from this discussion that the criollo devotees of Felipe de Jesús, particularly after 1750, were haters of all things Iberian. In their references to New Spain's "emulators" and "enemies," as well as in their intimations of ill motives and foul play, these mexicano writers seem on the surface to have been likely candidates for an independence movement. In fact, like the novohispano establishment in general, most remained loyal to the Spanish crown during the decade of civil unrest that followed Father Miguel Hidalgo's rebellion of 1810. One may recall that during the early stages of that movement, Hidalgo called for the expulsion of all gachupines from New Spain, suggesting that only the criollo Spaniard should dwell and rule in the americano homeland. His lower-caste followers, however, made little distinction between Iberian-born and criollo whites. In their assault on Guanajuato, for instance, they attacked and killed social elites with no regard for place of origin. The impoverished workers from the haciendas and mines of the Bajío region identified the "other" as those whose land tenure, labor practices, and taxation policies had come to threaten their physical existence. In the face of this threat to their property and very lives, criollo and peninsular elites patched up their differences in rapid, if temporary, fashion.

José Munibe, author of the 1802 *Breve resumen,* recognized the rift that was developing between criollos and peninsulares in the years prior to the Hidalgo rebellion. He also was astute enough to discern that this rivalry and distrust had taken the form of competing devotional allegiances to the various "Virgins" of New Spain. The best-known rivalry of this sort is the one that developed between devotees of "La Criolla" (Our Lady of Guadalupe) and "La Conquistadora" (Our Lady of Remedios).[61] With such divisions clearly in mind, and perhaps conscious that devotion to the Marian advocations diminished patronage for "el santo criollo," Munibe attempts to endear Felipe de Jesús to potential veneraters and financial donors among the region's Spaniards, criollo or otherwise, appealing explicitly in his prologue to the "very generous Europeans" as well as the "most noble Mexicans." To both parties, "beneficent Gentlemen united by [your] adhesion to [Mexico's] lands," he offers Felipe de Jesús as their common spiritual protector.[62] After all, he explains, while the protection of the church's canonized saints extends to all places, God destines certain saints to be special protectors of specific places. Thus, he continues, whether the Europeans and criollos *(mexicanos)* of New Spain recognize it or not, all the benefits they receive originate from Felipe de Jesús, "[who is] the first and principal Patron, the Tutelary of Mexico, after the Most Holy Mary of Guadalupe." Although it may be true that the Virgin Mary in her various advocations—including Balvanera, La Paz, and Aranzazú—showers the faithful with spiritual riches and temporal goods, she does so through the mediation of Felipe de Jesús. This occurs, explains Munibe, because "Felipe is always at the foot of her Royal bridal bed *(tálamo),* reminding her of his Mexican blood, persuading her to aid not only mexicanos, but any other national group *(nación)* that resides in their land."[63]

With this argument, the criollo hagiographer Munibe urges American-born and European-born elites to recognize their mutual link to the Mexican patria by investing spiritually and financially in a saint who will unite them and protect their vested material interests. In one sense, Munibe was a prophet, for when Hidalgo's rebellion broke out in 1810, "the long-standing rivalry between the Virgin of Guadalupe (La Criolla) and the Virgin of Remedios (La Conquistadora) became clearly marked along nationalist and political lines."[64] In a different sense, however, Munibe's optimistic predictions fell short. Neither in 1810 nor in 1821, the year of Mexican independence from Spain, did criollos and peninsulares rally around St. Felipe de Jesús as their unifying symbol.

8

Conclusion

S tudents of sacred biography frequently note the gap that exists in such literature between biography and hagiography; that is, between writers' efforts to recover the individual subject and their willingness to exchange that person for a symbolic persona who embodies a society's spiritual, social, or political needs.[1] In a study entitled *Islam Observed,* anthropologist Clifford Geertz makes such a distinction. Comparing two great Muslim figures, he observes: "These men are metaphors. Whatever they originally were or did as actual persons has long since been dissolved into an image of what Indonesians or Moroccans regard to be true spirituality."[2]

Given the propensity of human societies to transform historical figures over time into metaphors, it is hardly surprising that the writers of Spanish American hagiography did the same. These hagiographers, who celebrated their New World saints and holy persons in the context of emerging societies, were constructing sacred Christian histories for formerly non-Christian spaces. The literary or artistic promotion of autochthonous saints allowed criollo devotees to articulate what it meant to be americano, mexicano, or quiteño, thereby fueling the civic pride of their compatriots, whether inchoate or militant.

The colonial-era hagiographies examined in this study provide wonderful insights into Spanish American identity formation because their authors invite their readers, as members of identifiable social groups or entities (e.g., municipality, religious order or confraternity, etc.), to interpret the lives of their protagonists in public, communal terms. Similarly, they direct each pious audience to view the spiritual attainments of its local or regional saint as a reflection of its own merit. Through the creative imagination of each criollo hagiographer, the holy protagonist takes on an identity that transcends his or her historical individuality.

The identity of each New World saint, like the identities of the diverse social types and groups from which he or she arose, was multilayered and ambiguous. As I noted in the case of Sebastián de Aparicio, both American-born criollos and Iberian-born immigrants belonged to two worlds. Although born in Spain, Aparicio's reputation for sanctity grew up in the hills and haciendas surrounding the city of Puebla. When he witnessed apparitions, he saw not only figures commonly reported in similar cases back in Spain, but also Indians dressed in white tilmas. Moreover, he rubbed shoulders with Indians and castas, as well as peninsulares and criollos, and it was this heterogeneous novohispano populace that first recognized his heroic sanctity and directly benefited from his healing power. Yet Sebastián de Aparicio would never fully belong to the criollo community, nor could his glory be construed as theirs. Even criollo hagiographer Diego de Leyba, in order to appeal to potential patrons back in Spain, highlighted Aparicio's Old World roots by placing him within the pantheon of gallego saints. Such reminders of their Old World origins, made necessary at times because of americano dependence on the decisions of the metropolis, constantly suggested to criollos that their own identities and glory were derivative.

A desire to reproduce the best of European civilization in Spain's New World colonies shaped the hagiographic representations of both Sebastián de Aparicio and Rosa de Santa María. For example, in accommodating the Rosa narrative to a traditional format, her European and americano hagiographers portrayed her as a replica of Raymond of Capua's Catherine of Siena, "an American variation of a European theme."[3] A similar tendency appears in early-seventeenth-century limeño histories and chronicles, whose authors portray their city as a faithful copy of Old World, especially Italian, prototypes.[4]

George Kubler once characterized pre-independence Spanish America as a "cultural colony," that is, "a society in which no major discoveries or inventions occur, where the principal initiative comes from the outside rather than from within."[5] In response to Kubler, D. A. Brading counters that "no matter how much Spanish America depended on Europe for its art forms, literature, and general culture, its chroniclers and patriots succeeded in creating an intellectual tradition that . . . was original, idiosyncratic, complex, and quite distinct from the European model."[6] Such creative idiosyncrasy, avers Rubial García, characterized the writing of the saint's Life in colonial New Spain. Prior to the nineteenth century, he reminds his readers, every type of historical writing concerned itself with "the paradigmatic *(lo modélico)*, the general," a factor that encouraged the replication of traditional literary forms and motifs. This was especially true for hagiographic literature, which tended to privilege the exemplarity of the saintly protagonist over his or her individuality. However, New World hagiography emerged just as intellectual and ecclesiastical forces in Europe moved Catholic theologians and papal bureaucrats to require that hagiography be historically accurate. This increasing valorization of verifiable facts and witnesses—real persons, places, and events—allowed the unique social and environmental realities of New Spain to "impose distinctive characteristics on the European [hagiographic] model." Moreover, this adaptation of an Old World cultural form to a New World context was affected by the so-called "baroque," the prevailing seventeenth-century cultural language "that exalted opposites." Thus, suggests Rubial García, "with elements from the European and indigenous traditions, the Mexicans created for the first time their own space, a language teeming with puns and double meanings, . . . a literature and art full of originality."[7]

Thus, while the early vidas of St. Rosa de Lima may have "lacked any specifically Peruvian content," the later memorials of Juan Meléndez, O.P., and Luis Antonio Oviedo y Herrera displayed the sort of originality to which Rubial García alludes. While imperial ideology might portray St. Rosa as a sort of universal defender of Spanish imperialism, she appeared in the pious literature of late seventeenth-century Peru as the saint who put Dutch pirates to flight and moved Andean idolaters to genuflect. As the first criollo saint, Rosa held Old World and New World Spaniards together in a pact of orthodox Roman Catholic survival. As I have shown, however, the indigenous peoples of Peru viewed her through a very different lens.

Criollo identity, like the processes through which it came to be experienced and articulated, was full of complexity and nuance. In Jacinto Morán de Butrón's *La Azucena de Quito* one discovers the precursor of what Benedict Anderson describes as "a well-known doubleness in early Spanish-American nationalism, its alternating grand stretch and particularistic nationalism."[8] After nearly three decades of frustrated attempts to publish Mariana's Life, Morán de Butrón concluded that his saint's permanent position in the shadow of St. Rosa de Lima was but one more manifestation of the unfair administrative, economic, and cultural hegemony of the viceregal capital. His rhetoric illustrates the fact that criollos defined themselves not only in reference to Indians, Protestant heretics, or Iberian-born rivals, but also in reference to each other. The traditional Iberian love for and identification with the patria chica persisted in the New World, as natives of Puebla favorably compared their patria with Mexico City, and quiteños evaluated their own status and achievement in reference to Lima. Yet such dividing lines were hardly impermeable. For example, limeños and quiteños referred to themselves alternately as *indianos, americanos,* or *peruanos,* labels that Morán applies to both Mariana de Jesús and Rosa de Lima, and by extension, to himself.

Throughout the colonial period, the fomenting of ethnic rivalry between criollo and peninsular was of limited value to either group. As noted in the introduction, the criollo Meléndez rejected the use of ethnic designators such as indiano and criollo on the grounds that Europeans too readily misused them, lumping Peru's pure-blooded hijos de españoles into the same social category as mestizos, mulattoes, and Indians. In his view, St. Rosa and the Peruvian criollos shared a common homeland with the Indians, but not a common identity.

Despite criollo assertions to the contrary, however, the line separating American-born Spaniard from nonwhite casta was not a thick one. For American-born criollos seeking to enjoy the benefits of pure Spanish lineage, the indigenous peoples of highland Peru posed an ominous threat; they might simply absorb them. *Mestizaje,* a reality since the earliest encounters between Spanish men and indigenous women, presented social, legal, and religious challenges in colonial society. Descendants of Spaniards defended their exclusive social status vis-à-vis the castas by appealing to the ideology of limpieza de sangre. As a corollary to this practice, people of mixed blood improved their social rank by obscuring their nonwhite origins.[9] By the close of the eighteenth century, the sale and purchase of certificates of pure blood *(cédula de gracias a sacar)* had become quite common in Spanish colonies, particularly in New Spain.

In general, individuals and groups in search of status and privilege in the hispanized population centers did so through assimilation of Spanish values and identities, a strategy that is evident in Alonso Ramos's three-part Life of Catarina de San Juan. In an urban novohispano world that exalted its Spanish heritage at the expense of its prehispanic and non-Christian roots, the manifestation of divine favor and charismatic power in the person of a dark-skinned, illiterate domestic servant woman required a special explanation. The Catarina narratives reveal an attempt on the part of the beata and her confessors to construct for her a noble, Christian, and light-skinned lineage. Like criollo chroniclers of the seventeenth century and politicians of the early republics, Ramos explores an exotic non-Spanish past without reshuffling the multiracial order of colonial society.[10]

Beginning in the seventeenth century, "the historical arguments and the religious myths which figured so largely in the [criollo] patriotic tradition were always liable to acquire a political resonance";[11] the tendency grew stronger after 1750, reflecting the increased tension between criollo and peninsular interests. Following the royal expulsion of the Jesuits from Spanish America in 1767, criollo priests became more restless, especially in New Spain.[12] In this ideological climate, criollo priests and lay patriots like José Joaquin Fernández de Lizardi adamantly and resentfully rebuffed questions about the origins and virtues of St. Felipe de Jesús. For these patriots of the late colonial years, the question of Felipe's origins was not one of mere semantics. On the contrary, the debate over Felipe's birthplace and spiritual merits was a defense of the criollo character. This very real concern motivated Father José Pichardo to search far and near for the baptismal record of Mexico City's "santo criollo."

My focus on sacred biography as a reflection of Spanish American identities may obscure the fact that New World saints were not primarily political symbols. In general, those who memorialized these holy persons' lives through printed sermons and hagiographies were more interested in disseminating spiritual ideals than with fomenting civic pride or fueling criollo-peninsular polemics. The saints and the ritual activities surrounding their cults reflected a worldview that exalted obedience, humility, and historical continuity over individualism, arrogance, and progress. The saints recognized the ephemeral, illusory nature of human life and invested accordingly. They considered prayer to be more productive than action, self-abnegation more fulfilling than the pursuit of personal pleasure.

Clerical promoters of these pious cults reinforced a religious system that touched virtually every aspect of life. Priests and their institutions were at the center of this world, "forging popular piety and religiosity through their writings, [religious] confraternities, feast days, sermons, confession, and spiritual direction."[13] On behalf of their saints, they recruited potential patrons, solicited pious donations, and built churches and chapels. But as I have noted throughout this study, their sermons and hagiographies instructed Roman Catholics from New Mexico to the Río de la Plata to understand society as a community united in its devotion to a spiritual patron or patroness and living under that saint's protection. In theory at least, the new Spanish American states that arose following the wars for independence could have constructed national identities around devotion to regional saints.

Such, of course, did not occur, for in Spain's colonies as elsewhere, powerful challenges to the saint-filled, providential worldview had emerged and taken root. In 1857, Mexican Liberals under the leadership of Benito Juárez convened in the city of Querétaro to draft a new constitution. The resulting document institutionalized the anticlericalism of "La Reforma."[14] But this was more than an attack on ecclesiastical privilege and property; it challenged the metaphysical, economic, and social assumptions of a traditional Catholic world in which the saints had played a central role. Such Liberal efforts to weaken the socioeconomic, educational, and legal roles of the church in Spanish American society would have a profound impact on the place of the saints in society, especially as public symbols. By challenging the religious institutions within which saints arose and were recognized, Liberals throughout the Spanish American republics attacked the saints themselves. Not surprisingly, New World saints played a crucial symbolic role during these transition years. When Mexican Liberals offended Conservative sensibilities by proclaiming their anticlerical constitution on February 5, 1857—the feast day of Blessed Felipe de Jesús—Pope Pius IX countered by canonizing Mexico City's native son in 1862, just as French forces were poised to restore the Mexican Empire and place a Habsburg on the throne.

Since the late nineteenth century, the public role of Roman Catholic institutions, clergy, and spiritual symbols has varied from country to country in Spanish and Portuguese America, and within each country, has shifted in response to the vagaries of national life. In general, however, diverse political forces have constructed national identities around non-Catholic symbols, be they sociopolitical ("progress" or "revolution"), ethnic (Europeanization, *indigenismo,* etc.), or cultural (tango, samba, etc.). Meanwhile, diverse religious movements have challenged the hegemonic place of Roman Catholicism in Latin America, while certain progressive elements within Roman Catholicism have abandoned the patience and strict otherworldliness associated with traditional saints. As their priorities have shifted from the idealization of voluntary poverty to crusades for social justice, these Roman Catholic voices have proposed new models of heroic sanctity, including activist bishops like Bartolomé de las Casas and Oscar Romero.

Notes

Chapter 1. Introduction

1. Peter Brown presents one of the more enlightening discussions of this topic in *Cult of the Saints*. See also Kieckhefer, "Imitators of Christ," 29–34.

2. Michel de Certeau discusses hagiography as historical writing in *Writing of History*, 269–83.

3. Kieckhefer, "Imitators of Christ," 29. Throughout this study, I refer to this "hagiography proper" by several virtually synonymous terms, including *hagiography, sacred biography, Life*, and *vida*.

4. For related discussions, see Boureau, "Franciscan Piety and Voracity;" Kleinberg, *Prophets in Their Own Country;* and Vauchez, *La Sainteté*.

5. Jacques Fontaine, introduction to Sulpice Sévère, *Vie de Saint Martin*, quoted in Certeau, *Writing of History*, 270.

6. For the best discussions of this phenomenon, see Brading, *First America;* and Pagden, "Identity Formation."

7. Rubial García, "Los santos milagreros," 77.

8. The original publication of *Quetzalcoatl and Guadalupe* (1974) was a French-language edition. In Mexico, the Fondo de Cultura Económica has published two editions in Spanish (1977, 1985), and the English edition was published in 1976. In *Our Lady of Guadalupe*, Poole challenges the conclusions of Lafaye and others regarding the origins of Mexico's Guadalupe legends, while clarifying the role that inchoate Mexican nationalism played in their elaboration and growth over time. For further historical perspectives on Our Lady of Guadalupe in Mexico, see Anaya, *La milagrosa aparición;* O'Gorman, *Destierro de sombras;* and Taylor, "Virgin of Guadalupe." In *Mary* and *La Morenita*, Virgil Elizondo emphasizes the theological and pastoral. For a sociological treatment, see Jeanette Rodriguez, *Our Lady of Guadalupe*.

9. In a recent study on Mexican saints, Antonio Rubial García observes, "Until now, the study of these persons had been restricted to the realm of religion, and their lives were described in hagiographic treatises [alone]; scientific history did not consider it worthwhile to spend time on these quasi-mythical Lives." Rubial credits Michel de Certeau for pointing to hagiography as a branch of "the writing of history" (*La santidad controvertida*, 11).

10. Stone, *Past and Present*, 87. Primary examples of the renewed interest in narrative and story are Davis, *Fiction in the Archives* and Hunt, *Family Romance*. On the revival of narrative, see Hunt, ed., *New Cultural History*, and Stone, *Past and the Present*, 74–96. For a discussion of the implications for Mexican studies of these new methodologies, see various articles in the May 1999 special edition of *Hispanic American Historical Review*.

11. Brading, *First America*, 4, 337–40.

12. Josefina Muriel and Asunción Lavrin have pioneered the study of colonial convents,

especially those of New Spain. See Lavrin, "Female Religious," "La vida femenina," "Unlike Sor Juana?" and "Women and Convents"; and Muriel, *Conventos de monjas*. See also Burns, *Colonial Habits;* García Ayluardo and Ramos Medina, eds., *Manifestaciones religiosas* (vol. 2); and Ramos Medina, *Imagen de santidad* and *Místicas y descalzas*. Many of these studies treat not only the social and economic life of the convent, but also the pious literature that nuns produced.

13. Rubial García, *La santidad controvertida;* García Ayluardo and Ramos Medina, eds., *Manifestaciones religiosas* (2 vols.); Hampe Martínez, *Santidad e identidad criolla;* and Iwasaki Cauti, "Mujeres al borde de la perfección," "Santos y alumbrados"; and "Vidas de santos." Further studies of saints' cults and hagiographic traditions in colonial Spanish America include Cussen, "Fray Martín de Porres"; Graziano, "Una verdad ficticia"; and Millones, *Una partecita del cielo.*

14. These were Gregorio López, Bartolomé Gutiérrez, María de Jesús, Juan de Palafox, and Antonio de Margil.

15. Rubial García, *La santidad controvertida,* 12.

16. Brading, *First America,* 2.

17. Pagden, "Identity Formation," 51.

18. In colonial New Spain in particular, the ethnic label "casta" referred to a person of mixed racial ancestry. Well into the seventeenth century, however, most persons of mixed blood were not categorized as such, tending instead to be absorbed into the Spanish, Indian, or black groups. In the eighteenth century, however, the number of so-called castas multiplied, due both to the numerical growth of their group and to a heightened race consciousness that led to the proliferation of new racial categories (Tenenbaum, *Encyclopedia of Latin American History,* 2:8).

19. See the discussion of antigüedad in Lockhart and Schwartz, *Early Latin America,* 61.

20. See, for example, the *Parecer* (Opinion) of the Audiencia de México, dated May 1598, quoted in Pagden, "Identity Formation," 54.

21. Bakewell, "La maduración," 41–70.

22. Dorantes de Carranza, *Sumaria relación,* 234, quoted in Pagden, "Identity Formation," 58.

23. Pagden, "Identity Formation," 60–61.

24. Regarding the rivalry within the mendicant orders, see Morales, *Ethnic and Social Background,* 54–75 (especially 67–71).

25. Burkholder and Chandler, *From Impotence to Authority,* 70–80; Pagden, "Identity Formation."

26. Lavallé, *Las promesas ambiguas,* 18.

27. J. Arrom, *Certidumbre de América,* 11–26; the Sahagún quotation is on p. 18.

28. Francisco de Viedma, intendant for Upper Peru, to José de Gálvez, November 3, 1784, quoted in Lynch, *Bourbon Spain,* 337.

29. Pagden, "Identity Formation," 57.

30. One of the more famous members of a converso family was Teresa de Ahumada y Cepeda, better known as St. Teresa of Avila. For a discussion of her Jewish roots, see Bilinkoff, *Avila of St. Teresa.*

31. Lockhart and Schwartz, *Early Latin America,* 10.

32. J. Arrom, *Certidumbre de América,* 14.

33. Mier, *Memoirs,* xxvi.

34. Meléndez, *Tesoros verdaderos,* vol. 1, bk. 4, ch. 4; quoted in Lavallé, *Las promesas ambiguas,* 60–61.

35. J. Arrom, *Certidumbre de América,* 13; for a discussion of the origins and uses of the term "criollo" in Spain's New World colonies, see pp. 11–26.

36. Garcilaso de la Vega, *Royal Commentaries,* 1: 607; emphasis mine.

37. J. Arrom, *Certidumbre de América,* 13.

38. My work differs in this respect from *La santidad controvertida;* Rubial García highlights five holy persons who represent five distinct hagiographic models or saint types: Gregorio López (hermit), Bartolomé Gutiérrez (martyr), María de Jesús (female religious), Juan de Palafox (bishop-reformer), and Antonio de Margil (missionary).

However, although I have not overly concerned myself with the diversity of the saints themselves in terms of social type (race, gender, social status), religious order, or region, I have been able to achieve a relatively diverse sampling. For example, my case studies include three women and two men. The five holy persons and their hagiographers had connections with the three most influential male religious orders in Spanish America (Franciscans, Dominicans, and Jesuits). In terms of regional representation, there are three cases from New Spain, one from Lima, and one from the northern Andean province of Quito. Three of five holy persons had life experiences outside the Americas (one in Spain, two in Asia). Finally, the fact that only one of the five individuals was a *casta* (nonwhite) does not suggest an imbalance in terms of ethnicity, for the individuals whose spiritual lives were preserved in hagiographies were overwhelmingly Spanish-born or criollo whites.

Finally, my decision to highlight narrative strategies rather than saints per se made the question of each individual's canonical status (i.e., whether the holy person received official recognition as "blessed" or "saint") a secondary matter. This is somewhat of an advantage, since post-Tridentine reforms turned the canonization of saints into a long, bureaucratic, and often arbitrary affair (see Burke, "How to Be a Counter-Reformation Saint.") On the other hand, there is a clear correlation between a saint's potential canonical success and the willingness of his or her devotees to fund the writing and publication of religious biographies. Thus, it is no accident that one finds more published Lives of those holy persons whose devotees believed canonization was likely, a factor that explains why my sampling is weighted in favor of individuals who finally attained such official recognition. (There is one exception among my case studies. The Roman Catholic Church never even opened official investigations into the sanctity of Catarina de San Juan, whose hagiographies I examine in chapter 6.) See chapter 2 for a discussion of post-Tridentine changes in the saint-making process and how these affected the hagiographic process.

39. Chartier continues:

> The choice of the single object permits "relocating" objects too hastily considered the common legacy of an immobile, generalized, and supposedly popular culture. Indeed, many widely distributed printed pieces were used, at least at first, in the service of a party or a power, of a religious order or a particular shrine, of a community or an institution. This means that underlying the letter of the tale, be it hagiographic or extraordinary, and behind the evident purpose of glorification of the monarch, lies a hidden or explicit polemical intent to justify, persuade, and rally support (*Culture of Print,* 3, 5).

See also Sarah Maza's analysis of historians and narrative studies in "Stories in History," 1509.

40. Kleinberg, *Prophets in Their Own Country,* 3.

41. Baron and Pletsch, eds., *Introspection in Biography;* Williams, "*Life of Antony* and the Domestication of Charismatic Wisdom."

42. Maza, "Stories in History," 1513. For discussions of the polemical function of the saint's Life, see Boureau, "Franciscan Piety and Voracity"; Brennan, "Athanasius' *Vita Antonii*"; and Rubial García, *La santidad controvertida*.

43. Kieckhefer views the hagiographic text both as imitation of existing models and idiosyncratic product: "The precise nature of the composite—the way the biographer built upon available models—would inevitably vary according to the facts of the saint's life and according to the special interest of the biographer" ("Imitators of Christ," 31).

Chapter 2. A New World of Piety

1. Jiménez, "Vida de Fr. Martín de Valencia," 51–52. It is unclear whether Jiménez wrote his Life of Fray Martín with hagiographic intentions or not. On the one hand, he intimates in the opening paragraphs that he is making a tentative case for his subject's heroic sanctity. On the other hand, Jiménez's portrayal of the missionary friar is not exactly an idealized one. For example, Jiménez discusses at length Fray Martín's desire to abandon evangelistic work in New Spain in order to find elsewhere a people more suitable for spiritual conversion and maturation. Furthermore, despite the fact that by the 1530s claims of heroic sanctity had to include evidence of miracles, Jiménez makes reference to none. It is impossible to discern the author's intent regarding this last matter, however, since the only extant manuscript copy of his 1536 Life is missing its last pages. See López's discussion of the problem of the incomplete manuscript in Jiménez, "Vida de Fr. Martín de Valencia," 80–83. One may also find a copy of the Jiménez manuscript, as well as an introductory study by Pedro Ángeles Jiménez, in Rubial García, *La hermana pobreza*, 211–61.

2. For excellent discussions of the transference of medieval Iberian piety and religious institutions to New Spain, see Weckmann, *Medieval Heritage of Mexico*, 157–325, and Rubial García, *La hermana pobreza*.

3. A novena (from the Latin, *novem*) is "a public or private devotion repeated nine successive times," often preceding or following the mass. Such devotions are often associated with adoration of the saints. See McBrien, ed., *HarperCollins Encyclopedia of Catholicism*, 922.

4. Burkholder and Chandler, *From Impotence to Authority*, 225–26; and Chocano Mena, "Colonial Printing," 71. A press began to function in Lima in 1583.

5. Chocano Mena, "Colonial Printing." During the same period, works in the native languages of New Spain comprised 31 percent of all publications in Mexico City, while texts in Latin accounted for 29 percent.

6. Ibid., 72.

7. The publication of hagiography and religious biographies peaked in the period from 1650 to 1770 (DeStefano, "Miracles and Monasticism," 28).

8. See Vauchez, *La Sainteté* and *Les laïcs;* and Weinstein and Bell, *Saints and Society*.

9. Francisco Solano, O.F.M. (1549–1610), who attained a reputation for sanctity for his missionary work among the Indians of the northern Argentine and for his preaching in Lima, was beatified in 1675 and canonized in 1726. Luis Beltrán, O.P., sometimes spelled "Bertrán" or "Bertrand" (d. 1581), was beatified in 1608 and canonized in 1671. Pedro Claver, S.J. (1580–1654) attained renown for his catechetical ministry among African slaves who arrived to the Caribbean port of Cartagena (in modern Colombia). Because of the numerous controversies surrounding the Jesuit order in the late seventeenth and the eighteenth centuries, he did not receive papal recognition as blessed until 1851. Eight years after Claver's canonization in 1888, Pope Leo XIII declared him patron saint of the church's missions to black peoples.

10. Of the three prelates, only Mogrovejo was canonized (1727). For the careers of Moya and Mogrovejo, see Poole, *Pedro Moya de Contreras;* and Rodríguez Valencia, *Santo Toribio de Mogrovejo.* In "Blessed Connections," Cummins discusses the canonization processes for Moya and Mogrovejo. Rubial García treats the career of Palafox, the polemical nature of his hagiographies, and the unsuccessful attempts by his devotees to gain official recognition for a cult (*La santidad controvertida,* 203–50).

11. The martyr type included missionaries who died on the frontiers of Spanish America and in Japan (see chapter 7), as well as the sixteenth-century "niños de Tlaxcala," indigenous children of New Spain who were allegedly martyred for their Christian faith. Motolinía recorded the story of the niños de Tlaxcala in his *Memoriales.*

Rubial García treats the careers and posthumous fame of hermits Gregorio López and Bartolomé de Jesús María in *La santidad controvertida,* 129–60. Francisco Losa authored a Life of Gregorio López, the most famous hermit in sixteenth-century New Spain, which was published in Spain in 1613. Hagiographic portrayals of Bartolomé de Jesús María can be found in Francisco de Florencia, S.J., *Descripción;* and José Sicardo, *Interrogatoria.*

Dominican lay brothers Martín de Porres (or Porras) and Juan Macías (or Massías) fit the pious layman category. Juan Meléndez included hagiographic sketches of both men's lives in his *Tesoros verdaderos* (3:201–346 and 3:451–677, respectively). For a recent treatment of the posthumous reputation of Porres, see Cussen, "Fray Martín de Porres."

12. Félix de Jesús María, Francisco Pardo, and Diego de Lemus published vidas of Sor María de Jesús, Pedro Salmerón authored a Life of the Carmelite Isabel de la Encarnación, and José Bellido memorialized the mystic María Agueda de San Ignacio. For modern treatments of these poblana nuns and their local fame, see Ramos Medina, "Isabel de la Encarnación"; and Rubial García, *La santidad controvertida,* 161–201.

13. St. Teresa's *Libro de su vida* (published in English as *Life of St. Teresa de Jesús*), along with her more mystical writings, greatly influenced nuns in Spanish America. See, for example, Sor María Anna Agueda's *Marabillas* and *Meditaciones,* as well as María Josefa del Castillo y Guevara, *Obras completas.*

14. For an example of a female-authored vida in limited hagiographic style, see Zavaleta, *Copia de la carta.*

15. Scholars of Spanish American literature and history have recently rediscovered and published numerous rare, often unpublished texts by talented colonial-era women. As these scholars frequently point out, ecclesiastical restrictions and the widespread misogyny of the era kept the vast majority of female-authored manuscripts from ever being widely circulated or published. Moreover, women writers of spiritual biography or autobiography stressed themes and priorities distinct from those of male authors. For example, while male biographers gave much attention to the relationship between male confessor and female penitent, female writers often ignored this relationship altogether. On women as writers, see Arenal and Schlau, *Untold Sisters;* Ibsen, *Women's Spiritual Autobiography;* Jaramillo, Robledo, and Rodríguez-Arenas, eds., *¿Y las mujeres?;* Merrim, ed., *Feminist Perspectives;* and Sampson Vera Tudela, *Colonial Angels.* The last two decades have witnessed the publication of the autobiographies of several seventeenth- and eighteenth-century nuns. Among those previously unpublished works are Jerónima Nava y Saavedra, *Autobiografía;* Ursula Suárez, *Relación autobiográfica;* and the writings of María de San José, published first as *Word from New Spain* (ed. Kathleen Myers) and more recently as *A Wild Country* (ed. Kathleen Myers and Amanda Powell). Regarding the divergent priorities of male and female writers of spiritual biography, see

Donahue, "Writing Lives"; and Franco, *Plotting Women*. On the spirituality of women, both actual and prescribed, a good place to begin is the extensive work of Asunción Lavrin, particularly "La normatividad" and "Unlike Sor Juana?"; see also Vallarta, "Voces sin sonido."

16. Throughout this study, I employ the term "beata" to denote women who practiced exemplary devotion and piety outside the context of the female convent. Although the term had a number of uses in the Spanish world of the sixteenth and seventeenth centuries, it generally referred to "a woman who had made a simple (that is, temporary) vow of chastity, wore a habit, and observed a religious rule of some kind, whether temporarily or permanently, cloistered or in society, or alone or in company of others" (Christian, *Local Religion,* 16).

17. Members of religious orders or communities that lived according to a religious rule were referred to as "regular clergy" (Latin, *regula*). For example, Franciscans, Dominicans, Augustinians, and Jesuits were all members of the regular clergy. Although most members of these orders were ordained priests, a significant minority never took holy orders. Such was the case with Fray Sebastián de Aparicio, the Franciscan lay brother whose biographies form the subject of chapter 3.

18. One such work was José de Lezamis's Life of Francisco de Aguiar y Seixas, archbishop of Mexico City. The secular clergy consisted of ordained priests who did not take communal religious vows. These tonsured clerics lived not in cloistered monasteries but in "the world" (Latin, *seculum*). Although many members of the secular clergy made their living as parish priests, bishops, or officers in cathedral chapters, most were unable to obtain benefices and had to seek alternate career paths (Schwaller, *Church and Clergy*).

19. Palou, *Relación histórica*.

20. Ponce de León, *La abeja* and *La azuzena;* and Gómez, *Vida*.

21. Exceptions are the Lives of Catarina de San Juan by Alonso Ramos and José del Castillo Grajeda, and Pedro de Loayza's Life of St. Rosa de Lima.

22. Kieckhefer explains:

> The Gospels center on the death of Christ: he foretells his dying and goes deliberately toward it; he consoles and instructs his disciples just before the event; his passion is recounted in detail; and after death he is exalted in glory. Echoes of this theme occur frequently in the saints' vitae. The saints too predict their demise, gather disciples about their deathbeds for comfort and instruction, and after death are seen gloriously rising toward heaven. Whether the authors of these vitae were conscious of the influence or not, their Christian culture would inevitably condition them to see life's termination as the culminating display of life's merit. ("Imitators of Christ," 30–31)

23. Ibid.

24. Hagiographers tended to insert such discussions in book 1 (early life) or book 2 (religious life and virtues).

25. For my discussion of changes in the process of canonization and the writing of saints' Lives, I have relied on the following sources: "Saints, Devotion to the," *New Catholic Encyclopedia* (hereafter NCE) 12:962–63; "Canonization of Saints (History and Procedure)," NCE 3:55–59; "Hagiography," NCE 6:894–97; and Burke, "How to Be a Counter-Reformation Saint."

26. For the Council of Trent decrees on the mass, purgatory, and the veneration of saints, see Schroeder, *Canons and Decrees of the Council of Trent* 150–51, 214–17.

27. Christian, *Local Religion,* 162. Christian adds that Roman authorities, along with royal

and ecclesiastical elites in Spain, attempted through various measures to prevent those abuses attributed to "the common people" (*vulgo*). They mandated that only images of genuine saints be venerated, and that the images be properly adorned. They also tried to regulate activities associated with shrines and holy places, including *veladas* (vigils), processions, and pilgrimages.

28. For example, Urban VIII decreed that canonization proceedings were not to be initiated until fifty years after the death of the would-be saint (Burke, "How to Be a Counter-Reformation Saint," 46–47).

29. Regarding the relationship between causa and hagiographic text, see also chapter 3.

30. Literary scholar Cynthia Brown defines the paratext as "the book-related material physically surrounding the literary text." In her view the diverse elements of the paratext—"title pages and colophons, author images in miniatures and woodcuts, privilege advertisements and prefatory material, authorial signatures and devices"—enhanced the authority of the author vis-à-vis the central text (*Poets, Patrons, and Printers*, 61).

31. This particular statement appears in the censura that prefaces Diego de Leyba's *Virtudes y milagros*.

32. Chartier, "Texts, Printing, Readings," 157.

33. See Bilinkoff, "Confessors," 94–95. As Bilinkoff notes, writers of saints' Lives used this scholarly venue to discuss sensitive matters that they might otherwise fear broaching directly. One example of this practice is evident in the Lives of Bishop Juan de Palafox of Puebla, whose hagiographers broached church-state relations and controversies surrounding the Jesuit order (Rubial García, *La santidad controvertida*, 203–50).

34. An example of this point of view can be found in Macklin and Margolies, "Two Faces of Sainthood," 67: "I shall assume that because of the saints' relationship with the supernatural, they participate—perforce—in hagiography, their lives constructed and reconstructed, written to edify the populace: the history of Catholicism 'from above'."

35. Peter Burke acknowledges this sort of limitation in his study of Counter-Reformation sanctity: "Historians and sociologists have not always been sufficiently conscious of a central problem of method, of the need to decide whether to treat the saints as witnesses to the values of the age in which they lived or the age in which they were canonised" ("How to Be a Counter-Reformation Saint," 48). Burke opts to follow the second criterion, including in his study those saints who were formally canonized between 1588 and 1767. Such an approach, however, would require me to exclude a figure like Mariana de Jesús, who did not attain official status (beatification) until 1850.

36. Ahlgren, *Teresa of Avila*, ch. 5.

37. In this vein, see William Taylor's discussion about the shared piety of priests and rural Mexican parishioners in *Magistrates of the Sacred*, 1–8.

38. Chocano Mena, "Colonial Printing," 84.

39. Pierre Ragon points out that Sebastián de Aparicio conformed very poorly to official post-Tridentine models of Christian virtue and sanctity. Even so, he argues, popular veneration of Aparicio as a worker of miracles (both in his lifetime and posthumously) eventually paved the way for his beatification, suggesting that he may have been as much a "popular" saint as an "official" one ("Sebastián de Aparicio, un santo mediterráneo," 17–19).

40. Chocano Mena, "Colonial Printing," 70.

41. Loreto López, "La fiesta de la Concepción," 96. Loreto López notes that this fiesta, by incorporating participants from diverse religious confraternities and other types of corpora-

tions, served to strengthen the sense of community identity while at the same time rein-forcing values of hierarchy and exclusion. For related discussions on public spectacle in New Spain, see Cañeque, "Theater of Power"; and Curcio-Nagy, "Introduction" and "Native Icon."

42. Gonzalbo Aizpuru, "Las devociones marianas."

43. Publishers favored sermons because they were economical to produce and marketable to a wide readership. As a result, the sermon was the most commonly published type of reli-gious literature in New Spain. The greater likelihood of publication, notes Chocano Mena, heightened the interest of colonial scholars in producing such works: "The limited entre-preneurial capacity of Mexican printing shops affected the options available to authors, com-pelling them to print summaries or extracts of longer works, which frequently remained in manuscript form. Torn between publishing a long treatise on an esoteric or complex topic or a sermon which had been attended by the viceroy and other powerful bureaucrats, the scholar struggling with limited resources would probably choose the latter, as it could secure a more immediate return in terms of public recognition, favor, and patronage" (*Colonial Print-ing,* 77–78). Ragon discusses the popularity and affordability of devotional literature in "Libros de devoción."

44. On Sánchez as criollo patriot, see Poole, *Our Lady of Guadalupe.*

45. The small book of engravings was a popular medium for disseminating the saint's life narrative in the form of pictures and explanatory captions. In chapters 3 and 7, respectively, I present images from Mateo Ximénez's *Colección de estampas* (1789) and Montes de Oca's *Vida de San Felipe de Jesús* (1801). For additional discussions of the relationship between icono-graphic traditions and printed texts (whether hagiographies or religious chronicles), see Curiel, "San Felipe de Jesús"; Estrada de Gerlero, "Los protomártires del Japón"; Flores Araoz et al., *Santa Rosa de Lima y su tiempo;* and Vargas Lugo, "Proceso iconológico."

46. Loreto López, "Familial Religiosity."

47. For enlightening treatments of sanctity as performance, see Caciola, "Through a Glass, Darkly"; and Kleinberg, *Prophets in Their Own Country,* 1–9.

48. Iwasaki Cauti, "Vidas de santos"; and Romero de Valle, *El indio santo del Perú.*

49. Cussen, "Fray Martín de Porres"; García-Rivera, *St. Martin de Porres;* and Hampe Martínez, "Los testigos." For a discussion of how individuals of marginal social status employed the traditional language of mysticism and sanctity as a means of upward social mobility, see Bilinkoff, "Confessors"; Kagan, *Lucrecia's Dreams;* and Perry, "Beatas and the Inquisition."

50. For excellent studies of the process of acculturation among the native peoples of cen-tral New Spain, see Cline, *Colonial Culhuacan;* and Lockhart, *Nahuas.*

51. Gallagher, "Indian Nuns."

Chapter 3. Holy Immigrant

1. Details for this biographical sketch have been taken from three vidas: Fray Bartolomé Letona, "Relación auténtica sumaria"; Fray Diego de Leyba, *Virtudes y milagros;* and Bartolomé Sánchez Parejo, *Vida y milagros.* For a concise outline of the life of Sebastián de Aparicio, consult NCE 1:652–53.

2. Sánchez Parejo, *Vida y milagros,* 16–18.

3. As a lay brother, Sebastián de Aparicio performed manual and domestic service for his community as a servant, much like his renowned contemporary in Lima's Convento de Santo Domingo, Martín de Porres (d. 1639, canonized 1960). He passed through a novitiate, wore a habit, and took vows. In contrast to Franciscan priests, he did not take holy orders.

4. For a catalog of these witnesses' names, see Letona, "Relación auténtica sumaria," 91–108.

5. Torquemada's *Vida y milagros del sancto confesor de Christo Fr. Sebastián de Aparicio* was published in New Spain in 1602 and reprinted in Valladolid, Spain, in 1615. Today the work is exceedingly rare; I have not located an extant copy. Despite its rarity, the Torquemada Life is important due to its influence on subsequent hagiographers, most of whom were aware of its existence and some of whom actually had access to it as they wrote their own versions of Aparicio's life (Ángeles Jiménez, "Fray Sebastián de Aparicio: hagiografía e historia," 248–49. Had I access to Torquemada's Life, I would be able to judge more accurately the originality of the subsequent works. Fidel Chauvet, O.F.M., twentieth-century editor of Sánchez Parejo's *Vida y milagros,* frequently compares the two versions in his editorial notes (e.g., Sánchez Parejo, *Vida y milagros,* 19, 36, 41).

6. According to Chauvet, the Universidad de México granted Sánchez Parejo the title of doctor at some later date (Sánchez Parejo, *Vida y milagros,* vii–x).

7. The hagiographers' references to Fray Aparicio as "father" (*padre*) are honorific, for the lay brother was never ordained as a priest. Diego de Leyba justifies the usage, however, noting that although St. Francis of Assisi was never ordained, Pope Gregory IX called him "father."

8. Sánchez Parejo published an antiphon (*antífona*) and a prayer to Aparicio, and distributed them among the poblano faithful (*Vida y milagros,* vii). An antiphon is a devotional verse sung responsively by two choirs as part of the liturgy, especially during the saint's feast-day celebrations.

9. Sánchez Parejo, *Vida y milagros,* ix–x. For an eighteenth-century discussion of the medicinal efficacy of mineral waters in the region of Puebla, see Fernández de Echeverría y Veytia, *Historia de la fundación de Puebla,* 1:274–77.

10. Editor Fidel Chauvet cites Letona ("Relación auténtica sumaria," 88) as his source for this information (Sánchez Parejo, *Vida y milagros,* ii).

11. For Chauvet's discussion of the original manuscript, see Sánchez Parejo, *Vida y milagros,* i–vii. Prior to its rediscovery and publication, the *Vida y milagros* was known to have existed through references to it by subsequent hagiographers. There are three references to it in Letona's 1662 "Relación auténtica sumaria," although this text was also unpublished prior to this century. Diego de Leyba acknowledged the existence of Sánchez Parejo's manuscript in the "Protesta" (Disclaimer) to his *Virtudes y milagros.* In fact, he justifies his own hagiographic project by explaining that neither Sánchez Parejo nor Letona had published their vidas of Fray Aparicio.

12. In this regard, the Sánchez Parejo and Letona Lives present us with an interesting study in contrasts. Sánchez Parejo's work, which is unrelentingly polemical in tone, criticizes the cold juridical process that subjects his beloved saint's reputation to the opinions of "learned men." While conceding in his final chapter that ultimately the pope will decide whether to recognize Sebastián de Aparicio as a saint, he argues in advance against any reluctance to do so. Even as he wrote, however, Pope Urban VIII was issuing the aforementioned decrees of non cultu (see chapter 2). Writing a few decades after these reforms, Letona expresses his deference to "Our Mother the Holy Roman Apostolic See," acknowledging its prerogative to decide whether his use of such terms as "sanctity, virtue, miracle, revelation, or prophecy" are appropriate in Aparicio's case ("Relación auténtica sumaria," 29).

13. Leyba, *Virtudes y milagros,* pt. 2, fol. 155r–56v, 160v. Rubial García notes a parallel example in Francisco Pardo's Life of Sor María de Jesús of Puebla (*La santidad controvertida,* 185–86).

Pardo, a contemporary of Leyba's, defends devotees of María de Jesús who had begun to venerate her relics, arguing that since the decrees of non cultu had not yet been published in New Spain, these devotees had not acted disobediently. Moreover, notes Pardo, once those decrees were published in New Spain, devotees of María de Jesús had turned in the reputed relics to papal commissaries.

14. Leyba, *Virtudes y milagros,* pt. 2 fol. 34r–34v. Fray Paschal Baylon (1540–92) was a Franciscan lay brother of Aragon (eastern Spain) who was beatified in 1618 and canonized in 1690, not long after Leyba published his vida (Farmer, *Oxford Dictionary of Saints,* 42).

15. Leyba, "Protesta," in *Virtudes y milagros,* unnumbered. Leyba continues this theme in his hagiographic narrative, which begins in pt. 1, bk. 1, ch. 1.

16. Leyba, *Virtudes y milagros,* pt. 1, fol. 135v–38r; Sánchez Parejo, *Vida y milagros,* 167–68. Indeed, notes Leyba, whenever the Devil wished to tempt Aparicio with food, he offered him nothing but tortillas and chilies, for he knew the abstemious lay brother would eat nothing else (138r).

17. God frequently preserved Aparicio's cartload of grain from ruin during rainstorms (Sánchez Parejo, *Vida y milagros,* 102). Similarly, when a sudden hailstorm threatened to destroy the fruit-laden trees of a benefactor, Aparicio's prayers saved the harvest (102). Aparicio's cart and oxen fell into a raging river during a flash flood, but God saved them (104). In a departure from these examples, Sánchez Parejo describes how a penitent Aparicio often exposed himself to the rain and cold in order to deny his bodily needs or punish his flesh (160–71). See related discussion in Ragon, "Sebastián de Aparicio: un santo mediterráneo."

18. Leyba, *Virtudes y milagros,* pt. 1, fol. 31v–33r; Sánchez Parejo, *Vida y milagros,* 128–34. Sánchez Parejo recounts an occasion when the Devil appeared to Aparicio in the form of an Indian (p. 129). Aware of Aparicio's resolve to rely on God for his physical sustenance, his spiritual enemy spoke to him "in the Mexican tongue [i.e., Nahuatl]," inviting him to eat "some tortillas or bread of the Indies and chilies." But Aparicio, aware of his enemy's strategies, replied defiantly: "Bellaco, depart from me! I don't need this food, for God cares for worms and for men!"

19. Leyba, *Virtudes y milagros,* pt. 1, fol. 66v–67r; Sánchez Parejo, *Vida y milagros,* 96–97.

20. Reports of similar theophanies are rather commonplace in colonial religious chronicles and hagiographies. At least in the case of New Spain, angelic apparitions often take the form of Indians dressed in white, while demonic forces find personification as black or mulatto males. The Jesuit hagiographer of Catarina de San Juan (see chapter 6) reports a vision in which Catarina's guardian angel appears to her as a young Indian man dressed in a tilma, "like those who work in the kitchens wear" (Ramos, *Primera parte,* 50v).

21. Bilinkoff, "Francisco Losa and Gregorio López." See Francisco Losa, *La vida que hizo el siervo de Dios Gregorio López.*

22. This contrast is particularly clear in Sánchez Parejo's unpublished *Vida y milagros,* which was written much sooner after the actual events than the later vidas.

23. See discussion in Chevalier, "La signification sociale."

24. On the early Franciscan evangelizers of New Spain, see Brading, *First America,* 102–27; Morales, *Ethnic and Social Background;* and Ricard, *Spiritual Conquest.*

25. On the founding of Puebla, see Brading, *First America,* 108; Chevalier, "La signification sociale"; and Motolinía, *Memoriales,* 138–39, 262–67.

26. Motolinía, *Memoriales,* 263.

27. See Morgan, "New Laws of 1542," in Werner, *Encyclopedia of Mexico* 2:1020–21.

28. Motolinía, *Memoriales,* 264. Motolinía does not credit himself with having said Puebla's first mass, but Fray Juan de Torquemada later added this detail (*Monarquía indiana,* bk. 3, ch. 30). Historian Edmundo O'Gorman suggests that Torquemada's account is probably accurate in this regard (Torquemada, *Memoriales,* 264, n. 8).

29. There are numerous scholarly treatments of this process in New Spain. See Padden, "Ordenanza del Patronazgo of 1574"; Ricard, *Spiritual Conquest;* Schwaller, "Ordenanza del Patronazgo in New Spain"; and Van Oss, *Catholic Colonialism.*

30. In the carta preface to Leyba's Life, Fray Isidro Alfonso Castaneyra describes Aparicio as one whose life offers examples for all persons: "orphans, youths, servants, masters, single men, married men, farmers, carters, rich persons, poor persons, . . . virgins, and members of religious orders" (Leyba, *Virtudes y milagros,* unnumbered).

31. Sánchez Parejo, *Vida y milagros,* 14, 19, 17. Whereas Sánchez Parejo depicts Aparicio's career shifts as evidence of his work ethic, some of his other eulogizers interpret his decisions to domesticate cattle or to run the carting route between Mexico City and Zacatecas as conscious responses to public need. See for example, Ximénez, *Compendio,* 10–22.

32. Sánchez Parejo, *Vida y milagros,* 22–25.

33. Leyba, *Virtudes y milagros,* pt. 1, fol. 36v–37r.

34. Sánchez Parejo, *Vida y milagros,* 18, 22–25.

35. Aguilera Castro y Sotomayor, *Elogio christiano,* 12–13.

36. Letona states that Aparicio was sixty years old when he married for the first time ("Relación auténtica sumaria," 39). Sánchez Parejo places the bachelor's age at fifty-eight or sixty (*Virtudes y milagros,* 34, n. 20). These pious, chaste marriages are so central to Sánchez Parejo's narrative that he devotes all of book 2 to a discussion of the matter.

37. Sánchez Parejo, *Vida y milagros,* 33ff.

38. Ibid., 24.

39. For a discussion of women and marriage in colonial New Spain, see S. Arrom, *Women of Mexico City;* Lavrin, ed., *Sexuality and Marriage;* and Seed, *To Love, Honor, and Obey.* There are good discussions of urbanization, prostitution, and municipal attempts to regulate the "world's oldest profession" in Perry, "Magdalens and Jezebels"; Van Duesen, "Instituciones religiosas y seglares"; and Viforcos Marinas, "Los recogimientos."

40. Sánchez Parejo, *Vida y milagros,* 26–28. Historian Pierre Ragon suggests that Aparicio "was probably a greedy and profit-hungry man" who rejected the father's various dowry offers because they were insufficient (Ragon, "Sebastián de Aparicio, un santo mediterráneo," 22).

41. Sánchez Parejo, *Vida y milagros,* 36n. 22.

42. Ibid., 33, 34–35. Regarding the medieval practice of spiritual marriage among pious laypersons, see Elliott, *Spiritual Marriage,* 202–4.

43. Sánchez Parejo, *Vida y milagros,* 36.

44. In recounting Aparicio's family problems, his first two hagiographers defend very different points of view. Torquemada argues that the poverty of the second wife's parents justified their anxious desire for descendants, while Sánchez Parejo attributes the conflict to the greed of the in-laws rather than to any error on Aparicio's part. See Chauvet's discussion of the two hagiographers' diverging interpretations in Sánchez Parejo, *Vida y milagros,* 41 (n. 26).

45. Doubts about the propriety of Aparicio's marital relations placed a major stumbling block in his path to beatification. It was only after university theologians at Salamanca, the Sorbonne, and Padua cleared his name in this matter (1720–22) that beatification proceed-

ings were allowed to continue (*Bibliotheca Sanctorum*, 11:773–76; Ximénez, *Compendio*, vi–vii, 225). Hagiographer Sánchez Parejo responded to these doubts in his *Vida y milagros*, devoting all of book 2 to a defense of "the virginal marriages and the chastity of Fray Sebastián." His aim was to re-establish his protagonist's reputation among local believers, a reputation that had been damaged by the bureaucratic caution of "non-devotees" (44).

46. Motolinía, *Memoriales*, 263.

47. Sánchez Parejo, *Vida y milagros*, 16–18.

48. The introduction of large mammals was not wholly beneficial. See Melville, *Plague of Sheep*.

49. Leyba, *Virtudes y milagros*, pt. 1, fol. 71r–93r; Sánchez Parejo, *Vida y milagros*, 98–114.

50. Leyba, *Virtudes y milagros*, pt. 1, fol. 66r–66v; Sánchez Parejo, *Vida y milagros*, 100.

51. García-Rivera, *St. Martin de Porres*, 58–67.

52. Poole, *Pedro Moya de Contreras*, 163–76; Powell, *Soldiers, Indians, and Silver*.

53. For a discussion of later artistic representations of this episode, see Ángeles Jiménez, "Fray Sebastián de Aparicio: hagiografía e historia," 253–58.

54. Sánchez Parejo, *Vida y milagros*, 18.

55. Noting the similarities between Aparicio and St. Francis, Leyba cites several parallel episodes from St. Bonaventure's *Life of St. Francis* (*Virtudes y milagros*, pt. 1, fol. 53r–55r).

56. Sánchez Parejo, *Vida y milagros*, 22–23. See also Agustín Quintela's 1791 sermon, *La sencillez hermanada con la sabiduría*, 14–55, where the preacher-author rhetorically invites "the destitute (*miserables*), poor Indians, farmers, travelers, naked ones, the desperate widow, and the poor debtor" to step to his pulpit and testify about Aparicio's charity toward them. He says, for example, "You, poor Indians, make known that he was your refuge, causing your masters to treat you more gently, whenever you turned to him as to a sweet intercessor."

57. Sánchez Parejo, *Vida y milagros*, 175.

58. It is important to note that Aparicio's heroic virtue, like that of the Jesuit Pedro Claver who was canonized for his ministry to black slaves in seventeenth-century Cartagena, found expression in a lifetime of charity toward the socially oppressed, especially nonwhites. Yet while these two future Roman Catholic saints provided the oppressed with material, spiritual, and mediative aid, they did not engage in the sort of ideological protest for structural change championed by Fray Bartolomé de las Casas in the sixteenth century.

59. Sánchez Parejo, *Vida y milagros*, 83–86.

60. Letona, "Relación auténtica sumaria," 28.

61. Ibid., 30.

62. Leyba, "Censura" and "Aprobación," in *Virtudes y milagros*, unnumbered.

63. Brading, *Miners and Merchants*.

64. See dedicatory letter "Al Illmo. Señor D. Manuel Ventura Figueroa," unnumbered, in Rodríguez, *Vida prodigiosa*. We learn from the dedicatoria that Ventura Figueroa was also a key negotiator of the 1737 concord between King Ferdinand VI and Pope Clement XII that had given the Bourbon monarchs greater rights of patronage over the Spanish church.

65. See Fernando Ocaranza, *La beatificación*.

66. Carmona, *Panegírico sagrado*, 2.

67. Aguilera Castro y Sotomayor, *Elogio christiano*, 8–9.

68. Aguilera employs the phrase "our own particular interests." Ibid., 2.

69. "Al Illmo. Señor Doctor Don Salvador Biempica y Sotomayor," unnumbered, in Aguilera Castro y Sotomayor, *Elogio christiano*.

70. Quintela also published in 1769 a sermon in honor of Santiago entitled *Oración gratulatoria en la primera función, que celebró en México la Congregación de Naturales y Originarios del Reino de Galicia a su patrono el apóstol Santiago* (Berstáin de Souza, *Biblioteca hispano-americana septentrional,* 4:179).

71. "A Santiago el Mayor, Apóstol de Jesús, Patrón de las Españas," in Agustín Quintela, *La sencillez hermanada con la sabiduría,* unnumbered.

72. Quintela, *La sencillez hermanada con la sabiduría,* 2–3.

Chapter 4. Heretics by Sea, Pagans by Land

1. In 1862, Rome canonized San Felipe de Jesús, a Mexican-born Franciscan who was among the Spanish missionaries and Japanese converts who died martyrs' deaths near the site of modern Nagasaki in 1597. For a discussion of the hagiographic traditions surrounding Felipe de Jesús (beatified 1627), see chapter 7.

2. Polvorosa López, "La canonización de Santa Rosa." See also Bruno, "Rosa de Santa María. Muerte y glorificación"; and Hampe Martínez, "El proceso de canonización."

3. Polvorosa López, "La canonización de Santa Rosa," 638, 636–37.

4. Hampe Martínez, "Los testigos de Santa Rosa," 170. Hampe Martínez bases this conclusion in part on demographics; i.e., that among those who testified before ecclesiastical officials investigating Rosa's life and miracles in 1617–18 and 1630–32, two-thirds were Spanish criollos. This fact may not have much significance, however, given the ethnic demographics of early-seventeenth-century Lima.

5. Brading, *First America,* 338–39. Although Brading directs this remark at Pedro de Loayza's *Vida de Santa Rosa de Lima* (1619) and Leonardo Hansen's *Vita mirabilis et mors pretiosa* (1664), this characterization also applies to Andrés Ferrer de Valdecebro's *Historia de la vida* (1669). In this chapter, I cite the first published edition of the Loayza Life (1965) and an 1895 Spanish translation of the Hansen work, entitled *Vida Admirable de Santa Rosa.*

6. Brading, *First America,* 338.

7. Meléndez, *Tesoros verdaderos;* Oviedo y Herrera, *Vida de la esclarecida virgen.*

8. Bakewell, "La maduración."

9. Loayza, *Vida de Santa Rosa de Lima,* i. According to Gonzalo de la Maza, Gaspar de Flores began serving as an harquebusier in 1557 (Millones, *Una partecita del cielo,* 147). Elvira claims that Gaspar de Flores was born in Spain (Elvira, *Compendio histórico,* 8–9). See also Lohmann Villena, "De Santa Rosa, su padre y su hermano."

10. In a deposition before ecclesiastical officials in 1618, Gaspar de Flores claimed to be ninety-three years old (Hampe Martínez, "Los testigos de Santa Rosa," 157).

11. Hansen, *Vida admirable de Santa Rosa,* 176.

12. Hansen, *Vida admirable de Santa Rosa,* 4; Millones, *Una partecita del cielo,* 149. Flores Araoz doubts the authenticity of this story linking Rosa's name change to Bishop Mogrovejo, citing archival sources that seem to weaken its credibility (*Santa Rosa de Lima y su tiempo,* 263–64). There is certainly no reference to the episode in Pedro de Loayza's Life of St. Rosa. According to Loayza, young Isabel had mixed feelings about being called Rosa until the Virgin of the Rosary revealed her own pleasure with the epithet. From that point forward, explains Loayza, Isabel was called Rosa de Santa María in honor of the Virgin (*Vida de Santa Rosa de Lima,* 2).

13. Loayza, *Vida de Santa Rosa de Lima,* 5–12, 84–87. Compare Loayza's narrative with Raymond of Capua, *Life of St. Catherine of Siena,* 30–59. For a related discussion, see Coakley, "Representation of Sanctity."

14. Hansen, *Vida admirable de Santa Rosa,* 10–12; Loayza, *Vida de Santa Rosa de Lima,* 3; Millones, *Una partecita del cielo,* 150.

15. Loayza, *Vida de Santa Rosa de Lima,* 73–74.

16. Hansen, *Vida admirable de Santa Rosa,* 14. In the late-sixteenth-century work entitled *La perfecta casada,* Luis de León urged women to exercise such skills as a means of decreasing household expenses and generating income. See related discussion in Seed, "Social Dimensions of Race," 585–87.

17. Hansen, *Vida admirable de Santa Rosa,* 21.

18. Elvira, *Compendio histórico,* 73–89.

19. Elvira, *Compendio histórico,* 73–79; Loayza, *Vida de Santa Rosa de Lima,* 23–25; and Vargas Ugarte, *Vida de Santa Rosa de Lima,* 43–47.

20. Loayza, *Vida de Santa Rosa de Lima,* 23.

21. Phelan, *Kingdom of Quito,* 193–94. Lavrin discusses episcopal efforts in Spanish America to reform lax religious observance in "Female Religious."

22. For a detailed discussion of the persecution of *alumbrados* in sixteenth-century Spain, see Bataillon, *Erasme et l'Espagne.*

23. On official mistrust in Spain of popular female visionaries, see Imirizaldu, *Monjas y beatas embaucadoras;* Perry, "Beatas and the Inquisition"; Sánchez Ortega, "Woman as Source of 'Evil'"; and Weber, "Saint Teresa, Demonologist."

24. See Iwasaki Cauti, "Mujeres al borde de la perfección," for a discussion of restrictions on female beatas in Lima during St. Rosa's lifetime.

25. Hansen, *Vida admirable de Santa Rosa,* xv–xvi, 177.

26. Hansen, *Vida admirable de Santa Rosa;* see also Iwasaki Cauti, "Mujeres al borde de la perfección," 590–96.

27. See Rodríguez Cruz, "Juan de Lorenzana."

28. Hansen, *Vida admirable de Santa Rosa,* 75–76, 137–52.

29. Graziano, "Una verdad ficticia," 303–6.

30. Iwasaki Cauti, "Mujeres al borde de la perfección."

31. Hansen, *Vida admirable de Santa Rosa,* 420–21; Loayza, *Vida de Santa Rosa de Lima,* 4, 21.

32. Loayza, *Vida de Santa Rosa de Lima,* 21–25, 43–44.

33. On this couple's role in the life and posthumous career of Rosa de Lima, see Iwasaki Cauti, "Mujeres al borde de la perfección" and "Santos y alumbrados." See the text of Maza's 1617 testimony before ecclesiastical investigators in Luis Millones, *Una partecita del cielo,* 145–209.

34. Millones, *Una partecita del cielo,* 149–50.

35. Loayza, *Vida de Santa Rosa de Lima,* 5; Millones, *Una partecita del cielo,* 149–53.

36. Loayza, *Vida de Santa Rosa de Lima,* 112–20. Juan del Castillo, along with the laywomen Luisa de Melgarejo and María Antonia, saw visions in which Rosa appeared in heaven (117–20).

37. Hampe Martínez, "Los testigos de Santa Rosa."

38. See Flores Araoz et al., *Santa Rosa de Lima y su tiempo;* Getino, *Santa Rosa de Lima,* 64–136; Iwasaki Cauti, "Mujeres al borde de la perfección"; and Zevallos Ortega, *Rosa de Lima.*

39. Loayza, *Vida de Santa Rosa de Lima,* 7–11. See also Bynum, *Holy Feast, Holy Fast;* and Ibsen, *Women's Spiritual Autobiography,* 81–83, 90–92.

40. Ibid., 12–20; Millones, *Una partecita del cielo,* 156–59.

41. Francisco Solano, a peninsular Spaniard, achieved fame as a missionary and preacher

during twenty years in Peru. Clement X declared Solano blessed in 1675 and Benedict XIII canonized him in 1726 (*Bibliotheca sanctorum* 5:1241–44).

42. Loayza, *Vida de Santa Rosa de Lima,* 13.

43. Vargas Ugarte, *Vida de Santa Rosa de Lima,* 103–4.

44. Loayza, *Vida de Santa Rosa de Lima,* 26.

45. Ibid., 55–56; see also Millones, *Una partecita del cielo,* 169–71. Not all of Rosa's mystical experiences were enjoyable ones. She told her confessors about periods of great affliction in which she sensed that her soul was "in exile." When God finally delivered her from these sensations of hell and purgatory, her sense of relief was characterized by "a most pleasant, supernatural warmth" (Loayza, *Vida de Santa Rosa de Lima,* 33).

46. Loayza, *Vida de Santa Rosa de Lima,* 54. See artistic renderings of such scenes, both on canvas and in stone sculpture known as *piedra de Huamanga,* in Flores Araoz, *Santa Rosa de Lima y su tiempo,* 152, 236, 269, 316, 321. The story of Mary and Martha, from John 11, came to represent the holy person's struggle between contemplation of the Lord (Mary) and activity in the world (Martha).

47. Loayza, *Vida de Santa Rosa de Lima,* 42–43, 54, 62–63.

48. Raymond of Capua, *Life of St. Catherine of Siena,* 99–101.

49. Zealous clerics in Spain and her colonies during this period often voiced concern not only over the theological integrity of the female mystic's visions, but also over the purity, or lack thereof, of her body (Perry, "Beatas and the Inquisition"). The episode of the spiritual marriage, at least as narrated by her Dominican hagiographers, highlights two additional elements of Rosa's spirituality that made her a desirable religious role model for the post-Tridentine church. The first is the central place of religious images in her devotional life. The key moments in Rosa's spiritual life occur in the presence of images of Our Lady of the Rosary and the Niño Jesús, Medoro's painting of the *Ecce Homo,* and the consecrated Host. This fact reminded Roman Catholics that divine power was still at work through the saints and the sacraments, despite Protestant assertions to the contrary. Second, by submitting her desire for spiritual marriage to the discretion and mediation of her priest-confessor Velázquez, Rosa recognized the intercessory authority of the clergy. In fact, throughout her life Rosa sought direction and regulation of her spiritual life from clerical advisors, allowing them veto power over her penitential practices and interpretive authority over her diverse mystical experiences (Loayza, *Vida de Santa Rosa de Lima,* 28, 31, 40, 48–49, 68–71). Whereas independent-minded mystics posed a threat to Catholic discipline and orthodoxy, the cooperative, submissive penitent who obeyed her male pastors was a useful religious model for the seventeenth-century church.

50. Hansen, *Vida admirable de Santa Rosa,* 14; Loayza, *Vida de Santa Rosa de Lima,* 28–29. For example, Loayza notes that Rosa began to imitate López' refusal to communicate to his body the things he experienced mystically in his soul (Loayza, *Vida de Santa Rosa de Lima,* 28–29). For the effect of these various influences on Rosa's spiritual life, see Flores Araoz, *Santa Rosa de Lima y su tiempo,* 74–88, 115–36; Iwasaki Cauti, "Mujeres al borde de la perfección," and Rubial García, "Los santos milagreros."

51. Flores Araoz, *Santa Rosa de Lima y su tiempo,* 79.

52. Ferrer de Valdecebro, *Historia de la vida,* 79.

53. Flores Araoz, *Santa Rosa de Lima y su tiempo,* 82. Rosa's actual birthdate was April 20, 1586.

54. Isturizaga, *Sermón,* 5; also quoted in Flores Araoz, *Santa Rosa de Lima y su tiempo,* 79.

55. Loayza, *Vida de Santa Rosa de Lima*, 73. For Raymond of Capua's defense of St. Catherine, see *Life of St. Catherine of Siena*, 301–14.

56. See Carol A. Smith's discussion of the social restriction of women as a guarantee of racial purity in "Race-Class-Gender Ideology in Guatemala."

57. Loayza, *Vida de Santa Rosa de Lima*, 121–26.

58. Millones, *Una partecito del cielo*, 203–4.

59. Mugaburu, *Chronicle of Colonial Lima*, 137–39, 149, 152, 164. For biographical information on Josephe Mugaburu, see the editor's introduction (1–10). Following Mugaburu's death in 1686, his son Francisco continued the diary entries until 1697.

60. Hampe Martínez, "Los testigos de Santa Rosa," 151–53.

61. Loayza's manuscript remained unpublished until 1965; nevertheless, it was a valuable resource for papal officials and subsequent hagiographers (including Hansen), who frequently consulted it.

62. Hampe Martínez, "El proceso de canonización" and "Los testigos de Santa Rosa."

63. All references are to Fr. Jacinto Parra's Spanish translation of Hansen's *Vita mirabilis*, published in 1895 as *Vida admirable de Santa Rosa*.

64. Vargas Lugo, "Proceso iconológico," 70–78.

65. Meléndez, *Tesoros verdaderos*, vol. 2, books 2 and 3.

66. Specifically, Meléndez challenges the printed histories of postconquest evangelization by Fr. Antonio de la Calancha, O.S.A. (*Crónica moralizada del orden*), and Fr. Alonso Remon, O.M. (*Historia general de la orden*), which in his view give undue credit to their respective orders. Thus, the insertion into his chronicle of the Lives of Rosa de Lima, Martín de Porres, Juan Massías, and other Dominican heroes both reflects and contributes to this polemic. Consider, for instance, the statement that prefaces his vida of Martín de Porres, a mulatto Dominican lay brother from Lima who would eventually be beatified and canonized by Rome:

> And although in all Religious Orders . . . there have always stood out very holy men, who serving as living examples of good works, stirred the people to imitation; it appears that the divine light has shone more than anywhere else on . . . . the great athlete of the Church, Domingo. . . . Since . . . the first workers and diligent ministers of the Gospel, who like heavenly farmers carefully sowed the seed of the word of God in the unplowed fields of Peru, were the religious of our illustrious Patriarch Saint Dominic; it was providential that God should pay this great Father in heavenly coinage for the untiring labor of his sons, in bringing souls to the faith; for common sense and divine precept would dictate that the fruit would be of the Preachers [i.e., Dominicans], since the seed was theirs. (*Tesoros verdaderos*, vol. 3, bk. 2, p. 202)

Meléndez's defense of the earliest conquerors of Peru and the Dominican friars who accompanied them is also evident in one of the book's prefaces, a letter from a Spanish friar named Antonio Francisco de Montalvo. Montalvo claims to have evidence that the *Brevísima relación*, theretofore attributed to the famous (or infamous) Dominican Bartolomé de las Casas, was a forgery perpetrated by enemies of the Spanish crown and people. French interests hostile to Spain had composed the work in the French language, translated it into Castilian, and published it in the French city of Lyon under the misleading subtitle, "Printed in Seville, by D. Fr. Bartholome de las Casas, Bishop of Chiapa" (*Tesoros verdaderos*, vol. 1, unnumbered). The Montalvo letter, placed just prior to Meléndez's own introduction "To the Reader," reinforces the pro-Dominican content of the entire polemic.

67. See "A n. Rev. Padre F. Antonio de Monroy," in Meléndez, *Tesoros verdaderos*, vol 1,

unnumbered (emphasis mine). Here Meléndez refers to his order's founder, St. Dominic Guzmán (d. 1221).

68. Meléndez continues this exaltation of the achievements of the "sons of the Indies" throughout the work. In a chapter on the male and female religious foundations in the city of Lima, Meléndez makes explicit his reasons for enumerating such achievements: "From these brief notes . . . one can infer the political and religious improvements enjoyed by those very regions which the misinformed *vulgo*, confused by the tales (*fábulas*) of certain writers, number among such barbarous peoples as the Citas and the Chichimecos. Here [such misinformed readers] will learn that the first Spaniards who brought that New World under the mild rule of their Prince, did not depopulate the region by their cruelty and tyranny, but rather ennobled it with Religion, piety and justice" (*Tesoros verdaderos*, 2:172).

69. Oviedo y Herrera's poem in octet verse was published first in Madrid (1711), and subsequently in Mexico City (1729). I have consulted the 1895 reprint of the 1729 edition.

70. Miguel Núñez de Roxas, whose "Censura" is among several prefatory documents to the 1729 edition, extols the manner in which Oviedo y Herrera "interweaves history with fiction" so as to "make the truth more delightful" ["*sin desviarse un punto de la obligación de Historiador, ni de los preceptos de Poeta, pues si entretexió la Historia de la Ficción, fue, no confundiendo, sino haciendo mas deleytable la verdad, hermoseandola vistosamente*"] (in Oviedo y Herrera, *Vida de la esclarecida virgen*, unnumbered).

71. *No permite el que dá ley á las leyes,*
Y dominar exércitos blasona,
que á la Ciudad destruyan de los Reyes
de quien la Rosa, Estrella es, y corona"
(Oviedo y Herrera, *Vida de la esclarecida virgen*, canto décimo, LXI)

72. Polvorosa López, "La canonización de Santa Rosa," 638.

73. Secret Vatican Archives, Riti, 1573, unnumbered folio; quoted in Hampe Martínez, "El proceso de canonización," 724–25.

74. See Duviols, *La destrucción de las religiones andinas*; Mills, *Evil Lost to View?* and *Idolatry and Its Enemies*; Spalding, *Huarochirí*; and Stern, *Peru's Indian Peoples*.

75. Hansen, *Vida admirable de Santa Rosa*, 243.

76. For a more complete discussion of Quives today and in the past, see Millones, *Una partecita del cielo*, 56ff.

77. The editor of the 1895 edition of Hansen's Life of St. Rosa included this vignette among the notes he appended to the text but failed to acknowledge his source (see pp. 493–94).

78. Luis Millones attributes the story of Archbishop Mogrovejo's curse to Ricardo Palma's nineteenth-century "literary reconstruction" (*Una partecita del cielo*, 44). Like Oviedo y Herrera, Palma may have drawn upon popular oral legend in constructing this episode. For a discussion of the career and canonization of Mogrovejo, see Cummins, "Blessed Connections."

79. Loayza, *Vida de Santa Rosa de Lima*, 93.

80. Hansen, *Vida admirable de Santa Rosa*, 246.

81. Túpac Amaru ruled briefly as the final Incan ruler in the last Inca capital (Vilcabamba), but was publicly executed by the Spanish Viceroy Francisco de Toledo in 1572. Two centuries later (1780), his descendant José Gabriel Condorcanqui led a revolt against the abuses of colonial rule, taking the name Túpac Amaru. Like his ancestor, the second Túpac Amaru

was captured and put to death by royalist forces (Tenenbaum, *Encyclopedia of Latin American History*, 5:279–80).

82. Glave Testino, "El virreinato peruano."

83. Bradley, *Lure of Peru* and "Maritime Defense."

84. Mugaburu, *Chronicle of Colonial Lima*, 168–69.

85. Ibid., 171.

86. Ibid., 300–3.

87. See Bradley, "Maritime Defense," 160–62.

88. Salinas y Córdoba, *Memorial de las historias*, 134.

89. Córdoba Salinas, *Crónica de la religiosísima provincia*, 376. Josephe Mugaburu also refers to the recruitment of priests to the military defense of Lima in 1686 (*Chronicle of Colonial Lima*, 303).

90. Millones, *Una partecita del cielo*, 171–72. According to María de Oliva, Rosa feared these enemies would assault the temples and profane the sacred vessels (Vargas Ugarte, *Vida de Santa Rosa de Lima*, 101).

91. Loayza, *Vida de Santa Rosa de Lima*, 59. It is probable, since Loayza refers here to Rosa's mother, that he took this information from the testimony of María de Oliva in the proceso ordinario of 1617–18.

92. Hansen, *Vida admirable de Santa Rosa*, 238–42; Meléndez, *Tesoros verdaderos*, 2:370–73.

93. Hansen, *Vida admirable de Santa Rosa*, 242. The limeña Francisca Hurtado de Bustamante testified in the proceso apostólico of 1630–32 (Hampe Martínez, "Los testigos de Santa Rosa," 163).

94. "Censura," in Oviedo y Herrera, *Vida de la esclarecida virgen*, unnumbered.

95. Bradley, "Maritime Defense," 174.

96. Altman, "Family and Region," 262–63.

97. Córdoba Salinas, *Crónica de la religiosísima provincia*, 944.

98. López, "Identity and Alterity," 265.

99. For example, in his narration of the frequent maritime conflicts around Callao and Lima, the criollo Córdoba Salinas blurs the line between peninsular and americano, describing the opposing parties as "the heretics" and "the Spaniards" (*Teatro de la Santa Iglesia*, 380).

100. Lorea, *Santa Rosa, religiosa de la tercera orden de S. Domingo*, 332–33, quoted in Flores Araoz et al., *Santa Rosa de Lima y su tiempo*, 137. Lorea also wrote a vida of the aforementioned Archbishop Toribio de Mogrovejo (published in Madrid, 1679).

101. Flores Araoz, *Santa Rosa de Lima y su tiempo*, 182–83. Figure 4.2 depicts a similar painting from the Monastery of Santa Teresa de Jesús of Cuzco (*Santa Rosa de Lima*, 178–79).

102. Ibid., 138–39.

103. Ibid., 135, 141.

104. "El ancla de Santa Rosa de Lima," in Flores Araoz et al., *Santa Rosa de Lima y su tiempo*, 186.

105. Ibid., 187–88.

106. Cahill, "After the Fall," 66–69.

107. Durand Flórez, *Colección documental*, 2:241–44; Szeminski, "Why Kill the Spaniard?," 179–83.

108. Flores Araoz et al., *Santa Rosa de Lima y su tiempo*, 190–95. Following the royalist defeat of insurgents from Buenos Aires in Upper Peru in 1811, Rosa's devotees offered prayers of thanksgiving for God's preservation of Lima in the midst of "the infernal *furias* . . . and the darkness that surround us on all sides." One royalist preacher declared confidently that "in

the middle of the battlefield, Rosa guides the impetuous bullet, and [our] soldier remains intact" (p. 190). Royalists, however, were not the only ones to claim Rosa's patronage. The Congreso Independentista de Tucumán that gathered in 1816 placed a statue of St. Rosa in its meeting place, declaring that "the campaign of liberation was under the Patronage of St. Rosa de Lima." During the War of the Pacific, Peruvian naval captain Miguel Grau kept an image of St. Rosa in his chamber aboard the ship *Huascar*. During that conflagration, which allies Peru and Bolivia eventually lost to Chile, combatants attributed victories to the intercession of St. Rosa (p. 190–92).

Chapter 5. Hagiography in Service of the Patria Chica

1. Polvorosa López, "La canonización de Santa Rosa," 638.

2. Diego Antonio Bermudez de Castro, *Theatro angelopolitano,* 85, quoted in Vargas Lugo, "Proceso iconológico," 82. Such patriotic language also characterizes Fr. Pedro del Castillo's *La estrella del occidente,* published in Mexico City in 1670.

3. Letter of October 8, 1715 (Archivo General de las Indias, Indiferente 3032), quoted in Rubial García, *La santidad controvertida,* 190. See also Jesús María, *Vida, virtudes y dones sobrenaturales;* Martínez de Adame, *Sermón de San Felipe de Jesús;* and Valdés, *Sermón del glorioso martyr mexicano San Felipe de Jesús,* 15.

4. All references in this chapter are to the 1955 edition of Morán de Butrón's *La Azucena de Quito,* published in Quito under the title *Vida de Santa Mariana de Jesús* and edited by Bishop Aurelio Espinosa Pólit. This edition is based on Morán de Butrón's original and previously unpublished manuscript, which was lost around 1703 and rediscovered in 1949, just months before Mariana's canonization. For the publication history of *La Azucena de Quito,* see Espinosa Pólit's introduction (*Vida de Santa Mariana de Jesús,* 1–12) and Larrea, *Las biografías,* 55–62, 67–73. For twentieth-century Roman Catholic interpretations of Mariana's life, see Espinosa Pólit, *Santa Mariana de Jesús, hija de la Compañía de Jesús* and Moncayo de Monge, *Mariana de Jesús, Señora de Indias.*

5. Morán de Butrón, *Vida de Santa Mariana de Jesús,* 60.

6. Ibid., 132–41.

7. Morán de Butrón, *Vida de Santa Mariana de Jesús,* 65–108, 132–41. Morán explains that Cosme de Caso and the mother superior of the convent of Santa Clara made arrangements for Mariana to enter this prestigious religious community with an ostentatious ceremony, as was customary. Mariana resisted their plans, however, "praying to her Husband very ardently that He show her His will, for such was the only religious rule she desired to follow." In response, God revealed to Mariana his desire that she remain "secluded in her own house, with a more rigorous enclosure than [exists] in the most sheltered convent" (136). Thus, just as God intervened to prevent St. Rosa from taking the veil, so also with Mariana. This theme appears frequently in late Medieval and early modern Roman Catholic vidas, whose authors treat the holy woman's entrance into the cloister, or her failure to do so, as the work of Providence not the outcome of family strategies or economic factors. As these texts often reveal, however, social and economic factors often played a determinative role in the outcomes. In the case of Mariana, Morán narrates how Cosme de Caso and Jerónima de Paredes eventually lost their fortune and were unable to provide their daughters Juana and Sebastiana with dowries for marriage. If we allow that such misfortune may have befallen them earlier, we conclude that they may have been financially unable to place Mariana in the Convento de Santa Clara. For a discussion of convents as economic institutions, see Lavrin "Female Reli-

gious" and "Women and Convents." Luz del Carmen Vallarta discusses the hagiographic theme of circumstance and divine providence in "Voces sin sonido," 39–42.

8. Morán de Butrón, *Vida de Santa Mariana de Jesús,* 188–91. Bleeding was a common medical procedure of the era that may well have contributed to Mariana's death. Nonetheless, self-flagellation and the spilling of blood in imitation of the suffering of Christ were also long-standing penitential practices with roots in the Middle Ages.

9. Ibid., 173–80.

10. Regarding the Association of the Holy Christ of Consolation, see Appendix 4: "Las congregaciones y cofradías establecidas en la iglesia de la Compañía de Jesús en Quito," in Jouanen, *El modelo de las jóvenes cristianas,* 305–6. For a discussion of the Marian devotions established and promoted by the Jesuits in New Spain, see Gonzalbo Aizpuru, "Las devociones marianas."

Jouanen notes that in the years following Mariana's death, there was a significant increase in the number and size of pious donations toward the adornment of the chapel of Our Lady of Loreto in the Jesuit church. One Doña Catalina de Angulo, for example, donated pearls and gold worth 1,300 pesos (*Historia de la Compañía de Jesús,* 264–65).

11. Jouanen, *Historia de la Compañía de Jesús,* 259–60. Jouanen explains that Mariana's first resting place was in the vault near the altar of San José. Later, her remains were placed near the altar of Our Lady of Loreto, to whom Mariana had been an ardent devotee during her lifetime. Later, some of Mariana's relatives arranged to have her remains transferred to a niche near the main altar.

12. Rojas, *Sermón* (published 1646), reprinted in Jouanen, *El modelo de las jóvenes cristianas,* 310–23. Aurelio Espinosa Pólit called the Rojas *Sermón* "the most immediate document . . . that preserves the living palpitation of the popular enthusiasm encircling the glorious coffin" (*Santa Mariana de Jesús,* 3). For a fuller treatment of the Rojas sermon and its influence upon the hagiographic traditions surrounding the life of Santa Mariana, see Larrea, *Las biografías,* 67–70.

13. Jouanen, *El modelo de las jóvenes cristianas,* 315, 317, 318.

14. Simons, "Reading a Saint's Body," 11.

15. Bilinkoff, "Confessors,"; Coakley, "Friars as Confidants" and "Gender and the Authority of Friars."

16. Simons, "Reading a Saint's Body," 12.

17. For a discussion of the inquests and the resulting documents (procesos), see Larrea, *Las biografías,* 55–65.

18. Morán de Butrón, *Vida de Santa Mariana de Jesús,* 24–25.

19. For background information on Morán de Butrón and the circumstances surrounding his writing of *La Azucena de Quito,* see Espinosa Pólit, "Prólogo del editor," in Morán de Butrón, *Vida de Santa Mariana de Jesús,* 1–12; Jouanen, *Historia de la Compañía de Jesús,* 263–64; Páez, "El biógrafo de la Azucena de Quito"; and Pérez Pimentel, *Diccionario biográfico del Ecuador,* 2:193–96.

20. The quotation is from Juan Francisco Marcos Aguirre of the Centro de Investigaciones Históricas de Guayaquil, who in 1930 published Morán's *Compendio histórico de la provincia y puerto de Guayaquil,* along with a corresponding *Plano* (Pérez Pimentel, *Diccionario biográfico del Ecuador,* 2:196–97). Morán's unpublished manuscripts entitled "Lógica, física, y matemática" and "Comentario sobre los ocho libros de la física de Aristoteles" evidently remain in the Archivo Nacional de Historia del Ecuador (Pérez Pimentel, *Diccionario biográfico del Ecuador,* 2:194).

21. Despite their failure to compose and publish the Lily's Life, the Jesuits had generated and collected a number of documents that were essential for Morán's literary project. In a statement made prior to his death in 1746, Morán swore that he had seen these original documents, which included Mariana's own writings, letters from her spiritual directors, and a set of notebooks that Father Pedro de Alcocer, S.J., made before his premature death. (See Morán's declaration in *Vida de Santa Mariana de Jesús,* 14–20, or in Jouanen, *El modelo de las jóvenes cristianas,* 327–29.)

22. See the brief chapter entitled "Sor Mariana de Jesús, professed in the Third Order of Our Father Saint Francis," in Córdoba Salinas, *Crónica de la religiosísima provincia,* 525–39. The text of the Cazco letter is found in Compte, *Varones ilustres de la orden seráfica.*

23. A twentieth-century Jesuit viewpoint from Aurelio Espinosa Pólit can be found in *Santa Mariana de Jesús, hija de la Compañía de Jesús,* 184–211. Rather than dispute whether or not Mariana wore the habit of a Franciscan tertiary, Espinosa Pólit follows Morán de Butrón by challenging Franciscan interpretations of the event. In taking the habit of a Franciscan tertiary, he argues, the Lily of Quito established a merely canonical relationship with that order; her principal affective and spiritual relationship continued to be with the Jesuits and their devotions.

24. Morán de Butrón, *Vida de Santa Mariana de Jesús,* 502, 106, 108–16, 327–40.

25. Ibid., 122.

26. From Morán de Butrón's original 1697 "Prólogo al lector" (unpublished before 1955), in *Vida de Santa Mariana de Jesús,* 38.

27. Morán de Butrón, *Vida de Santa Mariana de Jesús,* 221–22.

28. Ibid., 22, 42–43, 62–63.

29. Ibid., 42.

30. Ibid., 60–63, see also 209.

31. Ibid., 42, 336, 42, 60–61, 106, see also 172. Morán quotes a letter from the former archbishop of Charcas to Queen Mariana of Austria. Having learned of the Lily's reputation for sanctity while visiting the region of Quito, the bishop asserted that "the tenor of her life . . . was very much like that of the illustrious virgin Santa Rosa, Patroness of these Kingdoms" (p. 61).

32. Zealous to identify the circumstances of Mariana's life as closely as possible with the life of Rosa, Morán errs in his assertion that "not seventy days passed between the transplanting of [Rosa] in heaven and the birth of she who was born for the glory of our land" (Morán de Butrón, *Vida de Santa Mariana de Jesús,* 42). Editor Espinosa Pólit explains the problems with Morán's chronology (p. 60, n. 2).

33. Morán de Butrón, *Vida de Santa Mariana de Jesús,* 135.

34. Ibid., 456, 405–6, 249.

35. Ibid., 504, 192. The Rose/Lily metaphor also informs a group of ten-line poems (*décimas*) by Moravian-born Marcus Zaurek, S.J. (d. 1702), first published in the 1724 Madrid edition of *La Azucena de Quito* (Morán de Butrón, *Vida de Santa Mariana de Jesús,* 27–33). Among this collection of Latin verse is a poem bearing the title "To the Venerable Virgin Mariana de Jesús, Otherwise Known as Flores, in Death a Rose" ("Venerabilis virgo Mariana de Jesu, seu de Flores, in morte Rosa"). In these lines, Zaurek reaffirms a key theme from the Morán vida; by dying for her patria, Quito, Mariana becomes that city's Rose.

36. Morán de Butrón, *Vida de Santa Mariana de Jesús,* 501. Phelan puts the death toll at 2,000 Spaniards and 10,000 Indians (*Kingdom of Quito,* 191).

37. See Herrera and Enriquez, *Apunte cronológico.*

38. Morán de Butrón, *Vida de Santa Mariana de Jesús,* 191.

39. Ibid., 502–3.

40. In an attempt to curb the growing power of the northern encomendero class, Pizarro appointed his younger brother Gonzalo as governor in 1540. See Tenenbaum, *Encyclopedia of Latin American History,* 4:517.

41. Vargas, *Historia de la iglesia en el Ecuador,* 52.

42. Burkholder and Chandler, *From Impotence to Authority,* 1–80; see also Tenenbaum, *Encyclopedia of Latin American History,* 4:517–18; Phelan, *Kingdom of Quito,* xv.

43. For an explanation of the privileges and responsibilities that accrued to the Spanish crown under the *patronato real,* see Shiels, *King and Church;* and Tenenbaum, *Encyclopedia of Latin American History,* 4:323–24.

44. The Jesuits established themselves in Lima (1568) before moving on to Tucumán (1585), Quito (1586), and Santiago (1593) (Tenenbaum, *Encyclopedia of Latin American History,* 3:317).

45. See discussion in Vargas Lugo, "Proceso iconológico." Following Rosa's beatification and canonization, there emerged in New Spain a considerable market for pious literature devoted to her. For example, a second edition of Don Luis Antonio Oviedo y Herrera's *Poema heroyco,* the work considered in the previous chapter, was printed in Mexico City in 1729.

46. For a discussion of European theories about how climate affected human character and potential, as well as criollo efforts to counter such notions, see Brading, *First America,* 422–46.

47. Morán de Butrón, *Vida de Santa Mariana de Jesús,* 65–67 (quotation on pp. 66–67). Here Morán implies that when the Catholic faithful in a certain locality give attention to the cult of their saints, those saints intercede on behalf of their devotees to ward off spiritual and physical danger. As noted, Morán attributed the survival of Quito in the face of the earthquakes and pestilence of 1645 to Mariana's protection. Thus, he here asserts that the people of Quito had guaranteed their continued good fortune by devoting themselves to numerous pious cults. This would presumably have included the cult of Our Lady of Loreto, one of Mariana's favorite devotions during her lifetime and one that the Jesuits promoted.

48. "Atendió juntamente la omnipotencia divina al cultivo de sus naturales con el riego de su gracia, produciendo fecundas plantas de virtudes y fragantes [sic] flores de santidad, así en los retiros de la monástica disciplina como en el tráfago y bullicio de ciudad tan populosa; de modo que en grande volumen no cupieran las vidas de los que en ellas se granjearon créditos de virtudes muy heroicas y públicas aclamaciones de santos. Y el no haber dado a la estampa ejemplares tan divinos, no ha sido tanto descuido, como la falta que padece este país de una prensa en que pueda dar a la pública luz sus honores" (Morán de Butrón, *Vida de Santa Mariana de Jesús,* 68).

49. Tenenbaum, *Encyclopedia of Latin American History,* 5:305–6. The Universidad de San Marcos predated the universities of Charcas (1614) and Córdoba (1621). For a discussion of the founding of the Dominican Colegio de San Luis and Universidad de Santo Tomás, see Vargas, *Historia de la iglesia en el Ecuador,* 295–310.

50. Lavallé, *Las promesas ambiguas,* 105–41.

51. This prologue remained unpublished for two and a half centuries, appearing for the first time in 1955 (Morán de Butrón, *Vida de Santa Mariana de Jesús,* 34–38). According to editor Espinosa Pólit (p. 35, n. 1), the potential hagiographers Morán refers to are his fellow Jesuits Pedro de Alcocer, Diego Abad de Cepeda, and (probably) Sebastián Luis Abad.

52. Morán de Butrón, *Vida de Santa Mariana de Jesús,* 24–25.

53. Larrea, *Las biografías,* 78. The *Compendio* was reprinted in Mexico City in 1732 (see figure 2.1).

54. See this prologue in *Vida de Santa Mariana de Jesús,* 56–58. From Morán's reference to a period of seventy-six years, one can surmise that he wrote his "Prólogo al lector" in 1721. In his original, unpublished prologue of 1697, Morán also apologized for his order's long delay in writing Mariana's Life (*Vida de Santa Mariana de Jesús,* 34–38).

55. Ibid., 57.

56. Ibid.

57. Ibid., 40–51.

58. Jouanen, *Historia de la Compañía de Jesús,* 257.

59. Morán de Butrón, *Vida de Santa Mariana de Jesús,* 23, 209, 56.

60. Ibid., 62.

61. Ibid., 42–43, 60–61, 209.

Chapter 6. "Very Good Blood"

1. Francisco de la Maza describes this three-volume vida as the lengthiest published work in the history of colonial New Spain (*Catarina de San Juan,* 26). The Bancroft Library at the University of California, Berkeley, owns original copies of the *Primera parte* and *Segunda parte,* and the John Hay Library at Brown University houses microfilm copies. I have not seen a copy of Ramos's *Tercera parte,* though one appears to exist in Mexico City.

2. See Maza, *Catarina de San Juan;* and Myers, "Testimony for Canonization."

3. According to Kathleen Myers, "all accounts [of Catarina's life] plot a compelling story that echoes elements from the most popular forms of baroque narrative, including captives' tales, picaresque novels, and, of course, hagiographic biography" ("Testimony for Canonization," 273). See Elisa Sampson Vera Tudela's argument for similarities between novohispano hagiography and travel narrative in *Colonial Angels,* 1–13.

4. Castillo Grajeda, *Compendio de la vida,* 115.

5. Soons, "Alonso Ramírez," 201, quoted in López, "Identity and Alterity," 259.

6. López, "Identity and Alterity," 258.

7. For two further discussions of authorial voice, see J. Arrom, "Carlos de Sigüenza y Góngora" and Myers, "Mystic Triad."

8. Although I refer occasionally to Castillo Grajeda's version of events, I have found his *Compendio de la vida* of relatively less value given my purposes. Castillo Grajeda, who prefers to emphasize the more historically verifiable aspects of Catarina's life, is very spare and matter-of-fact in his treatment of her origins. For a more detailed discussion of how and why Castillo Grajeda diverges from Ramos in his narrative approach, see Myers, "Testimony for Canonization," 282–95.

9. Ramos, *Primera parte,* 4v–6r.

10. Ibid., 4v–6r. The Mughals, a Turkic-speaking group from Central Asia, came to power in northern India under Zahir-ud-Din Muhammed Babur in 1526, ruling there for more than two centuries. See Neill, *Christianity in India,* 51, 99–108, 169–85, 363.

11. Ramos, *Primera parte,* 5v (also, 5r-6v, 20v–21v). Ramos claims to have consulted with missionaries who had been in Asia. In addition, he specifically cites an annual report (*carta annua*) of 1677 by Enrico Roth, Father Athanasius Kircher's *China ilustrada,* and other "reliable sources" (Chinese, Indian, Castilian, and Portuguese), as well as histories by Fathers Bartoli and "Zachino." Daniello Bartoli (d. 1685) authored *Missione al Gran Mogor* (1672), while

Francesco Sacchini, S.J. (d. 1625) published his *Historiae Societatis Iesu* between 1620 and 1661 under the latinized name Franciscus Sacchinus. For an in-depth treatment of Jesuit histories of India, see Correia Afonso, *Jesuit Letters and Indian History.*

12. Ramos, *Primera parte,* 10r, 19r, 21r–21v, 8r–9r.

13. Ibid., 8r–8v. Octavio Paz has noted the influence of the German Athanasius Kircher, S.J. (1602–80) on the intellectual life of late-seventeenth-century New Spain. In Kircher's published works, notes Paz, "Jesuit syncretism reaches a totality that embraces all times and all places" (*Sor Juana,* 166). Theorizing that ancient Egypt had prefigured Catholic Rome, Kircher pointed to similarities between the religious practices of ancient Egypt and those of pre-Christian China, India, and America. Kircher's postulation of such continuities, especially in regard to pre-Hispanic Aztec cults, fascinated creole intellectuals like Sor Juana Inés de la Cruz and Carlos Sigüenza y Góngora, both of whom were contemporaries of Alonso Ramos's. The most important implication of Kircher's thought for subsequent developments in European philosophy was the concept that all religions derive from one pure source. It is possible that these theories influenced Ramos's interpretation of the religious origins of Catarina's family. For the influence of Kircher's *Oedipus Aegyptiacus* (1652–54) on Sigüenza y Góngora, see Brading, *First America,* 364.

14. Ramos, *Primera parte,* 20r–21v.

15. Neill, *Christianity in India.*

16. Ibid.

17. Ramos, *Primera parte,* 12v–14r.

18. Piracy was constant on India's coasts during the sixteenth and seventeenth centuries; renegade Portuguese as well as Muslim adventurers were notorious for such activity, and East Indian slaves, mostly women and children, were sold regularly in markets from Manila to Mombasa. The city of Guhti, located on the Ganges delta far beyond the control of the Portuguese governors and judges in Goa and Cochin, became a center for such activity. The pirates of Guhti eventually drew the ire of Shah Jahan, grandson of Akbar, who ordered the town's destruction in 1632 (Neill, *Christianity in India,* 263). See also Boyajian, *Portuguese Trade in Asia.*

19. Ramos, *Primera parte,* 16r–16v.

20. Ibid., 16r–26v.

21. Ibid., 27r–29r.

22. Ibid., 23v–25r.

23. Ibid., 15r–15v; 25r–26v.

24. Ibid., 19r–19v.

25. Ibid., 31v–32r.

26. In *Las mujeres en la Nueva España,* Pilar Gonzalbo Aizpuru has pointed out that although the vast majority of Mexican women did not have access to formal education during the colonial period, women of all social levels learned in their homes the skills that society deemed acceptable and necessary for them to exercise.

27. See Patricia Seed, "Social Dimensions of Race," 585–87.

28. S. Arrom, *Women of Mexico City.* The term *ama de llaves,* which translates roughly as "head housekeeper," is from León, *Catarina de San Juan y la china poblana,* 22.

29. See Loreto López, "Familial Religiosity," for an examination of the connection between domestic religious space and the internalization of piety among household members (including servants) in eighteenth-century Puebla.

30. Maza, *Catarina de San Juan,* 43. See further discussion in Maza, *Arquitectura de los coros de monjas,* 64.

31. Ramos, *Primera parte,* 35r.

32. Ramos, *Primera parte,* 30v–31r, 65v–71r. For Catarina de San Juan and many other beatas of her era, the confessional relationship was much more than one merely of confession and absolution, becoming at times a very affective and emotionally supportive alliance. On the one hand, the female penitent might ask her spiritual guide for advice, intervention in family conflicts, or if she were white, for help in procuring dowry funds so that she might enter a convent. A female often submitted her interior life to the scrutiny and examination of her confessors in order to gain assurances that God, not the Devil, had been visiting her. At the same time, a beata reputed as a particularly holy woman might offer advice, spiritual counsel, and prophetic messages to her confessor. Each of these elements characterized the relationships between Catarina de San Juan and her confessors. For a treatment of the relationship of confessors and holy women in the Middle Ages, see Coakley, "Friars as Confidants" and "Gender and the Authority of Friars." Excellent studies of St. Teresa of Avila and her confessors include Ahlgren, *Teresa of Avila;* and Bilinkoff, *Avila of Saint Teresa.* On interactions between confessors and female penitents in early modern Spain and New Spain, see Bilinkoff, "Confessors"; Lavrin, "La vida femenina"; Myers, "Mystic Triad"; and Vallarta, "Voces sin sonido."

33. Gonzalbo Aizpuru, "Las devociones marianas."

34. "Convertida en confidente de cuitas domésticas y decidida defensora del mantenimiento de la honra familiar" (Gonzalbo Aizpuru, "Las devociones marianas"), 115.

35. Ramos, *Primera parte,* 26r, 5r–21v, passim; see also 65v–71r. Ramos emphasizes Catarina's self-effacing responses to the Virgin's words. He records a mystical conversation in which the Virgin Mary said, "Catarina, you know that I am your Mother, do you not?" In humility, Catarina replied, "No, Señora, I am not worthy to be your daughter but only your slave" (Ramos, *Primera parte,* 63v). For a brief analysis of Catarina's Marian visions, see Rubial García, "Mariofanías extravagantes."

36. Ramos, *Primera parte,* 25.

37. Castillo Grajeda, *Compendio de la vida,* 38.

38. Ramos, *Primera parte,* 124v–135v.

39. See Jesús Maria, *Vida, virtudes y dones sobrenaturales;* Lemus, *Vida, virtudes, trabajos, fabores y milagros;* and Pardo, *Vida y virtudes heroycas;* see also Rubial García, "Los santos milagreros," 90–100.

40. Castillo Grajeda, *Compendio de la vida,* 54–58.

41. I have already noted efforts by Rosa's hagiographers to link her story to that of Archbishop Toribio de Mogrovejo. In the case of Catarina, Ramos claims that Bishop Juan de Palafox heard her confessions for a time, a claim that would have been impossible to disprove since Palafox was long since dead. For a discussion of this controversial bishop's reputation for sanctity and the efforts to gain his beatification, see Brading, *First America,* 228–51; and Rubial García, *La santidad controvertida,* 203–50.

42. Ramos, *Primera parte,* 11.

43. Ramos, *Primera parte,* 125r. The purpose of such an institution was to protect its residents from sexual scandal, provide for their education in religion and domestic skills, and facilitate their integration into respectable Spanish colonial society by arranging suitable marriages for them. In order to avoid scandal, the constitution for such colegios usually required

that male overseers (mayordomos) be married. See, for example, the constitution (ca. 1550) for a Mexico City colegio called La Caridad in Gonzalbo Aizpuru, *El humanismo y la educación*, 125–36.

44. Ramos, *Primera parte*, 11.

45. "Despose, y Vele, a Domingo Suárez, etc., con Catarina de San Ioan [sic], *china, india, natural de la India, etc.*" . . . "En estas partes se llaman 'chinos' naturales de la India, todos los que vienen del Oriente, por via de Philipinas, conducidos de nuestros Portugueses" (Ramos, *Primera parte*, 11, emphasis mine).

46. Seed, "Social Dimensions of Race."

47. McCaa, "Calidad, Class, and Marriage," 477–78.

48. See García Sáiz, *Las castas mexicanas*.

49. For a discussion of the inexactness of racial language in the colonial period, see Jackson "Race/Caste and the Creation and Meaning of Identity." Jackson is interested in "questioning the subjectivity and imprecision of these sources as indicators of the realities of race based social status" (150).

50. Ramos, *Primera parte*, 125r–29v.

51. Aguilera Castro y Sotomayor, *Sermón*, 9r.

52. Ramos, *Primera parte*, 125–30.

53. Ramos, *Segunda parte*, 82. Francisco de la Maza asserts that this alliance began in 1644, but gives no basis for the date (*Catarina de San Juan*, 61). Ramos claims, on the other hand, that Castillo y Altra asked his advice as Catarina's confessor before extending the invitation. If this claim is indeed true, the offer must have been extended after 1658 (date of Ramos's arrival in New Spain), or more likely, after 1673. Ramos tells us he became Catarina's last confessor in that year, though it is possible that he did hear her confessions in a less formal way prior to that date.

54. In his description of the skillfulness and thrift that she demonstrated in the home of Miguel de Sosa and Margarita de Chaves, Alonso Ramos observes that she was able to support herself after she left their home. Ramos recounts an episode from very late in Catarina's life in which a community of nuns insisted that she continue to prepare their chocolates even after her eyesight had failed (Ramos, *Primera parte*, 29v).

55. Ramos, *Segunda parte*, 115v, 139r–40v.

56. Castillo Grajeda, *Compendio de la vida*, 191–202; Maza, *Catarina de San Juan*, 122–31.

57. *Práctica de la theología mystica*, 436, quoted in Rubial García, *La santidad controvertida*, 200–1. Godínez is the hispanized name of Michael Wadding (1591–1644), an Irishman from Waterford. After he joined the Jesuit order in 1609, he traveled to New Spain, where he spent the rest of his adult life. For a discussion of his treatise, see Rubial García, *La santidad controvertida*, 166–201, passim. On his origins and literary production, see Beristáin de Souza, *Biblioteca hispano-americana septentrional*, 2:360.

58. Ramos, *Primera parte*, 39–41. In Catarina's practice of frequent communion, she had "daily, if not continual" experiences in which the consecrated Host, having become Christ himself, moved about in her mouth and refused to be swallowed, "leaving impressed a seal, or image of himself, all over her body" (Ramos, *Primera parte*, 41–45). Whenever Catarina saw visions depicting the twelve stages of the cross, she would plead with Christ's tormenters to punish her instead of him. Seeing his blood spilt on the ground, she would lick it up "like a dog." She once awoke from ecstasy to discover her body marked by the stigmata "as [one

sees] in reference to *other santos and santas*," as well as by a life-sized image of the wounded Christ himself (Ramos, *Primera parte*, 36–39; emphasis mine).

59. Ramos, *Segunda parte*, 116v.

60. Ramos, *Primera parte*, 114v–115r. Like Rosa de Lima, Catarina saw visions of French and English corsairs lying in wait for Spanish vessels, and protected the ports of New Spain through her prayers (Ramos, *Primera parte*, 123–24). Catarina saw and predicted the safe arrival of viceroys in Veracruz, as well as the deaths of the marquesa de Mancera and the duque de Veraguas (Ramos, *Primera parte*, 127–30). In a chapter entitled "On the Value of Her Prayers for the Extension and Defense of Christianity and the Catholic Monarchy," Ramos describes two instances of particular significance given the climate of political anxiety in late-seventeenth-century Spain. In the first case, Catarina recognized a plot against King Felipe IV (r. 1621–65) and cried out to God on his behalf. Some time later, word came from Spain regarding the fall of three disloyal knights (Ramos, *Primera parte*, 117v). A second episode involved King Carlos II (r. 1665–1700), whose failure to sire a successor to the throne had become a cause for much concern by the 1680s. Catarina claimed to have been transported to the royal court on May 14, 1680, the day of the king's wedding to María Luisa of Bourbon. (According to *Webster's Biographical Dictionary*, p. 287, the couple actually married in 1679.) In her vision, Catarina discovered the Devil waiting to harm the couple's offspring and break the line of succession. She therefore prayed for a royal heir and prophesied that God would sustain the Habsburg house on the throne of Spain (Ramos, *Segunda parte*, 118–20).

61. Literary scholar Kathleen Myers notes that the length and polemic nature of its prefatory materials makes Ramos's *Primera parte* a unique item among colonial Mexican printed texts ("Testimony for Canonization," 284–85).

62. Ramos, *Primera parte*, unnumbered.

63. The decree of October 16, 1692, reads as follows:

> We order collected and prohibited . . . another book printed in folio, whose title is *Primera parte, de los prodigios de la omnipotencia de Dios, y milagros de la gracia, en la Venerable sierva de Dios, Catarina de San Juan, natural de el Gran Mogul*, etc. Written by Padre Alonso Ramos, a professed member of the Society of Jesus, printed in Puebla in the printing plant of Diego Fernández de León, 1689; for containing revelations, visions, and apparitions that are useless, untrue, full of contradictions and comparisons that are improper, indecent, and fearful, and that are almost blasphemies (*sapiunt blasphemiam*), abusive of the highest and ineffable ministry of the Incarnation of the Son of God, and of other parts of the holy scripture, and containing doctrines that are fearful, dangerous, and contrary to the sense of the doctors and practice of the Universal Church, without more basis than the vain credulity of the author. (DeStefano, "Miracles and Monasticism," 68)

For the decree in its original Spanish, see Nicolás León, *Catarina de San Juan*, 71–73.

64. Proverbs 30:24–28.

65. Vidal, "Parecer," in Ramos, *Primera parte*, unnumbered. Núñez de Miranda sounds a similar note in the "Carta y discurso preocupativo," where he seeks to impose a proscribed reading on the Ramos narrative by offering his readers "a few theological suppositions for reading the Life of Catarina de San Juan."

66. I Samuel 2:1–10; Luke 1:46–56, 16:19–31; I Corinthians 1:18–31.

67. Ramos, *Primera parte*, unnumbered. Fernando Iwasaki Cauti argues elsewhere that the clergy of Lima promoted the saintly reputations of individuals of marginal social status in

order to shame elites into greater morality and piety ("Vidas de santos," 55).

68. Castillo Grajeda, *Compendio de la vida*, 111–27; Maza, *Catarina de San Juan*, 84–86; and Ramos, *Primera parte*, 92v.

69. Aguilera, *Sermón*, 13v.

70. Myers discusses this feature of Castillo Grajeda's *Compendio* ("Testimony for Canonization," 288–89).

71. See García-Rivera, *St. Martin de Porres*, 61; and Weber, *Rhetoric of Femininity*, 35–41.

72. Ramos, *Primera parte*, 123.

73. Such was the case with Mariana de Jesús, who in response to frequent amorous approaches by male admirers, prayed to be made ugly (see chapter 5).

74. ". . . de rara hermosura; su color más blanco que trigueño, el cabello más plateado que rubio, la frente espaciosa, los ojos vivos" (Ramos, *Primera parte*, 111).

75. "En breve tiempo se fueron poco a poco secando, y consumiendo sus carnes: y se mudaron las faiciones de su rostro; enturbiose el cabello, y se achinó el color del rostro, desuerte, que más parecia vieja, que niña; más fea, que hermosa, más retostada China, que blanca y rubia Mogora; más India avellanada, de las más tostadas del Occidente, que blanca y hermosa Oriental de los confines de la felix Arabia" (Ramos, *Primera parte*, 122v–123r).

76. Aguilera, *Sermón*, 9v–10r. Both Aguilera and Ramos describe Catarina's transformation as being both spiritual and physical. Employing a common religious metaphor of his day, Ramos contrasts Catarina's priorities with those of the majority of people, who think more highly of themselves than they should because they gaze into the mirror of worldly things (beauty, intelligence, etc.). Catarina, on the other hand, looked upon Christ, the mirror of the soul (Ramos, *Primera parte*, 132–35). See also Ramos, *Primera parte*, 95v, where Christ speaks to Catarina in spiritualized terms about her skin color and physical appearance.

77. Castillo Grajeda, *Compendio de la vida*, 33. See also Ramos, *Primera parte*, 4v.

78. Ramos, *Segunda parte*, 73r–73v. Ramos inserts this statement in his rather lengthy discussion of Catarina's search for a capable, devoted confessor in the years before she settled upon him. When one confessor implied that she might be faking mystical experiences in order to receive alms from pious admirers, she replied, "I have very good blood in these veins, even though I look like a china and everyone views me as one."

79. On marriage and sexuality in New Spain, see S. Arrom, *Women of Mexico City;* Gonzalbo Aizpuru, *Historia de la educación;* Seed, *To Love, Honor, and Obey;* and Twinam, "Honor, Sexuality, and Illegitimacy."

80. Gallagher, "Indian Nuns"; Lavrin, "Indian Brides of Christ"; Muriel, *Las indias caciques;* Rubial García, *La santidad controvertida;* and Sarabia Viejo, "La Concepción y Corpus Christi."

81. For Romano's testimony before the audiencia of New Spain, see Archivo General de la Nación, historia, vol. 109. exp. 2, fol. 33r–33v, Alexandro Romano, May 20, 1723 (cited in Greer, "Iroquois Virgin").

82. For a discussion of sixteenth-century efforts to train a native clergy in New Spain, as well as the abandonment of that project after midcentury, see Ricard, *Spiritual Conquest*, 217–35.

83. Urtassum, *La gracia triunfante.*

84. Greer, "Iroquois Virgin."

85. DeStefano, "Miracles and Monasticism," 63–67; Myers, "Testimony for Canonization," 292.

86. DeStefano, "Miracles and Monasticism," 67–68. Why this four-year delay in the publication of the ban in New Spain? Francisco de la Maza theorizes the published ban may not have arrived in New Spain for several years and, therefore, that the Holy Office of New

Spain was unaware of it (*Catarina de San Juan,* 116). Kathleen Myers points to another possibility; namely, that inquisitors in Mexico City were aware of the document but "the case was too hot to handle in New Spain." Given the local popularity of Catarina de San Juan and the desire among the faithful of Puebla to venerate a local holy person, notes Myers, "the simultaneous prohibition of the oratory and biography came only under great pressure" ("Testimony for Canonization," 293).

87. DeStefano, "Miracles and Monasticism," 68; and Myers, "Testimony for Canonization," 292–93.

Chapter 7. Birth Pangs of a Criollo Saint

1. Curiel, "San Felipe de Jesús: figura y culto"; and Estrada de Gerlero, "Los protomártires del Japón."

2. Cuevas, *Historia de la iglesia,* 2:460; Villanueva, *Vida del protomártir mexicano,* 14.

3. Whereas earlier hagiographers interpreted this putting off of the Franciscan habit as the act of a restless teen who was not yet ready for the religious life, José Antonio Pichardo (ca. 1800) explained the decision as the product of instability in the governance of the local house. For one thing, he argued that the extreme poverty of the community made life there very hard. Moreover, he reasoned that the decision by Viceroy Alvaro Manrique de Zúñiga to exile the Franciscan commissary general (Fr. Alonso Ponze) and the founder of the poblano convent (Fr. Miguel de Talavera) would have left a young novice like Felipe feeling abandoned. Finally, Pichardo saw in these events divine providence, for God willed that Felipe de Jesús should die as a martyr in Japan (Pichardo, *Vida y martirio,* 274–99).

4. Ibid., 307–21.

5. Historians and hagiographers differ as to the date of Felipe's vows (Villanueva, *Vida del protomártir mexicano,* 19).

6. Medina, *Chrónica,* ch. 12. Quesada Brandi's commemorative work *San Felipe de Jesús* includes a facsimile of chapter 12 of the Medina *Chrónica,* an abbreviated hagiographic narrative of Felipe's life.

7. C. R. Boxer describes these events in *Christian Century in Japan.*

8. Estrada de Gerlero, "Los protomártires del Japón," 83. For an inventory of relics that ended up in New Spain, see Medina, *Vida, martyrio, y beatificación.*

9. Fernández de Lizardi, *El glorioso protomártir,* 1.

10. Villanueva, *Vida del protomártir mexicano,* 86.

11. Estrada de Gerlero, "Los protomártires del Japón."

12. Ibid., 73–78. Other influential published accounts of the early missionary presence in Japan, including the dramatic events of 1597, were Daza, *Quarta parte* (1611); Frois, *De rebus iaponicis* (1599); and Sicardo, *Christiandad del Japón* (1698). For a modern history of Christianity in sixteenth- and seventeenth-century Japan, see Neill, *History of Christian Missions.*

13. Pichardo, *Vida y martirio,* 146–47. Herrera paid for a retablo honoring Blessed Felipe de Jesús, which was installed in the Mexico City cathedral around 1638 (Estrada de Gerlero, "Los protomártires del Japón," 83).

14. Pichardo, *Vida y martirio,* 151 (both quotations). For a discussion of the role played by Sánchez in the growth of the Guadalupan tradition, see Poole, *Our Lady of Guadalupe.*

15. Baltasar de Medina provides an index of literary treatments of Felipe de Jesús up to the 1680s in his *Vida, martyrio y beatificación.* The list includes the sermons by Vaca Salazar, Sánchez, and de la Serna, as well as a fourth by Jacinto de Caxica (published 1639). Eigh-

teenth- and early-nineteenth-century works include (in chronological order) Río, *Separación y singularidad* (1715); Mateos Herrera, *Tierno recuerdo* (1774); Martínez de Adame, *Sermón de San Felipe de Jesús* (1781); Valdés, *Sermón del glorioso martyr mexicano San Felipe de Jesús* (1782) and *Novena consagrada* (1804); Fernández de Lizardi, *El glorioso protomártir* (1811); Sartorio, "Devoción para el día cinco" (1812); Fernández de Lizardi, *Memorial de la madre* (1821); and Antonio Gálvez, *Sermón* (1824). Post-independence religious and pastoral publications on San Felipe de Jesús include Riviere, *San Felipe de Jesús* (1853); Carrillo y Ancona, *Vigesimatercera carta pastoral* (1897); and Villanueva, *Vida del protomártir mexicano* (1912).

16. Pichardo, *Vida y martirio,* 155–56. Pichardo does not reveal where he found this manuscript. The events surrounding the dedication of the Capuchin nuns' church are related in Diego de Rivera, *Breve relación,* cited in Medina, *Vida, martyrio y beatificación,* 160.

17. Pichardo, *Vida y martirio,* 155–66; emphasis mine.

18. As Michael DeStefano has observed, the publication of hagiography and religious biographies peaked during the period between 1650 and 1770 ("Miracles and Monasticism," 28–29).

19. Dedication entitled "To the Illustrious Protomartyr of Japan, San Felipe de Jesús, Patron Saint of Mexico his Patria," in Medina, *Vida, martyrio, y beatificación,* unnumbered.

20. "Sentir," in Medina, *Vida, martyrio, y beatificación,* 1683, unnumbered. For biographical information on Medina and Romero y Quevedo, see Beristáin de Souza, *Biblioteca hispano-americana septentrional,* 3:210 and 4:256, respectively. Romero y Quevedo's allusion to "the Mexican lake" is a reference to Mexico City itself, built on the foundations of the ancient Aztec capital of Tenochtitlán which had rested on an island in Lake Texcoco. In the late seventeenth century, the Valley of Mexico contained much more lake area than it does today. Indeed, the flooding that plagued the capital in this period directly shaped hagiographic traditions regarding Felipe de Jesús.

21. "Nomen tuum (O Philippe) invocatum est super civitatem et super populum tuum" (Medina, *Vida, martyrio, y beatificación,* unnumbered). On the symbolism of the eagle, nopal, and serpent, see Florescano, *La bandera mexicana,* Estrada de Gerlero, "Los protomártires del Japón," 83, and Cuadriello, "La personificación de la Nueva España."

22. Medina, *Vida, martyrio, y beatificación,* 161.

23. Curiel, "San Felipe de Jesús: figura y culto," 80.

24. In *Separación y singularidad* (published 1715) Río described Felipe as singular among the twenty-six protomartyrs of Japan, for he received three lance thrusts instead of the one or two suffered by the others. Fray Joseph Francisco Valdés, O.F.M., also emphasizes the uniqueness of Felipe's martyrdom (*Sermón del glorioso martyr mexicano San Felipe de Jesús,* 3).

25. Alcaráz, "A la devota, noble, y generosa Platería mexicana." In this dedicatory letter, Alcaráz lent his own authority to an oral tradition that Felipe de Jesús had served an apprenticeship in the silversmiths guild in Mexico City following his abandonment of the Franciscan novitiate in Puebla. José Pichardo, whose hagiographic contribution (ca. 1800) I examine later in the chapter, found written reference to this effect in the aforementioned anonymous manuscript of 1673. Expecting to find some documentary proof for the claim, he visited the guild archive. Having found nothing of substance, he concluded that earlier writers had misconstrued certain references to Alonso de las Casas's involvement with *plateros,* who must have been not artisans but merchants who traded with and financed the ventures of silver miners. Pichardo attributes Miguel Alcaráz's confident assertions about Felipe's apprenticeship to a need to convince the Platería that its own interests were served by sponsoring pub-

lication of the second edition of the Medina vida. Pichardo bases his conclusion on a letter from Alcaráz to the Platería that he had seen in the guild archive. There Alcaráz, who refers explicitly to his own poverty, urges the guild to assume the costs of publication "since [Felipe] was your apprentice" (Pichardo, *Vida y martirio*, 307–12).

26. Alcaráz, "A la devota, noble, y generosa Platería mexicana," unnumbered.

27. Ibid.

28. For a discussion of the impact of intellectuals like de Pauw, Buffon, Robertson, and Raynal on the relationship between Spanish Americans and the Bourbon government, see Brading, *First America*, 422–46. Brading discusses, for example, the work of William Robertson of Scotland, who observed that "in every part of the earth where man exists, the power of climate operates with decisive influence upon his condition and character" (*First America*, 435).

29. Pichardo, *Vida y martirio*, 95.

30. Robles, *Resguardo contra el olvido*, quoted in Pichardo, *Vida y martirio*, 110–11. Robles was a contemporary of Baltasar de Medina, although his Life of Cuevas Dávalos was not published until 1755 (Beristáin de Souza, *Biblioteca hispano-americana septentrional*, 4:240).

31. Unpublished manuscript entitled "Noticia del año y día en que nació el Glorioso Proto Martyr San Felipe de Jesús," quoted in Pichardo, *Vida y martirio*, 107–10.

32. Rodríguez, *El país afortunado;* quoted in Pichardo, *Vida y martirio*, 130.

33. Beristáin de Souza, *Biblioteca hispano-americana septentrional*, 2:424–25, lists the date of Pichardo's birth as 1748, noting that he died on November 11, 1812, at age sixty-four. José Toribio Medina gives the date of birth as 1732. The former date seems more likely, for in a letter of 1812 written to solicit compensation for his exhausting labors on the Texas-Louisiana project, Pichardo refers to himself as a sexagenarian (Hackett, *Pichardo's Treatise*).

34. The Oratorio of San Felipe de Neri, named after the sixteenth-century Italian saint, claimed a sacred tie to the criollo San Felipe de Jesús.

35. José Antonio Pichardo Papers, Génaro García Collection, Nettie Lee Benson Latin American Collection, University of Texas at Austin. For a guide to the Pichardo Papers, see Castañeda and Dabbs, eds., *Guide to the Latin American Manuscripts*.

36. Castañeda, "El Rev. P. Don José Antonio Pichardo," in Pichardo, *Vida y martirio*, v.

37. Pichardo, *Vida y martirio*, 1–7, 26–28.

38. Ibid., 132–35.

39. Granados y Gálvez, *Tardes americanas*, xx. On José de Gálvez, see Tenenbaum, *Encyclopedia*, 3:11–12.

40. Pichardo, *Vida y martirio*, 38–56.

41. The letter from Juan Joseph de la Presilla, along with the eighteen handwritten responses by parish priests of Salamanca are among the Pichardo Papers at the University of Texas.

42. Pichardo, *Vida y martirio*, 43–44. Pichardo identifies the chronicle as one coauthored by Fr. Juan de San Antonio and Fr. Domingo Martínez. The two friars in fact authored separate works, both of which were published between 1738 and 1756 (see Martínez, *Compendio histórico de la apostólica provincia;* and San Antonio, *Chrónicas de la apostólica provincia*).

43. Pichardo, *Vida y martirio*, 46–47.

44. Ibid., 52. Pichardo writes:

> How many months after having married would they have embarked? Without a doubt, after seven or eight full months. During this short time, could they have given birth to a son of legitimate matrimony? If he had been born prior to seven

months, he would have been premature and would not have survived. After seven months [of gestation], he could have lived, but would it have been prudent [for Alonso de las Casas] to have embarked with his wife on such a long voyage so soon after having given birth to her offspring? If she was with child when they embarked, then her son could not have been born in Spain. Nor [would she have given birth] at sea, for since such a voyage would take about two months, it would not have been prudent to embark without some compelling reason, and there was none.

45. Ibid., 58–70.

46. Letter from Pichardo to José Francisco Valdéz, May 13, 1794 (Pichardo Papers, Benson Latin American Collection, University of Texas at Austin).

47. Pichardo refutes Rodríguez's claim in *Vida y martirio,* 106–7.

48. Pichardo Papers, Benson Latin American Collection, University of Texas at Austin.

49. Pichardo, *Vida y martirio,* 136–60, quotation on p. 160. Among the sources cited are chroniclers (Frois, Ribadeneyra, Juan de Torquemada) who knew Felipe personally, the saint's mother, preachers who could have known his parents and siblings (Vaca Salazar, Miguel Sánchez, Jacinto de la Serna), and later preachers and chroniclers from Baltasar de Medina to José Francisco Valdés.

50. Ibid., 161.

51. Ibid., 182.

52. Ibid., 182–88. According to Castañeda (*Vida y martirio,* 182, n. 3), Pichardo quotes the original Latin text of the *Dialogos* in his manuscript. In the 1934 published version of Pichardo's *Vida y martirio,* Castañeda replaced this Latin text with a Spanish translation from Joaquin García Icazbalceta's 1875 edition of the *Dialogos.* For a more recent discussion of Cervantes Salazar's literary product, see Millares Carlo, *Cuatro estudios.*

53. There is a facsimile edition of this devotional work in Quesada Brandi, *San Felipe de Jesús.*

54. Estrada de Gerlero discusses the relationship between the Montes de Oca engravings and the books of hagiography proper in "Los protomártires del Japón," 82–86.

55. Munibe, *Breve resumen,* 29. All page references are to the 1962 facsimile edition in Quesada Brandi, *San Felipe de Jesús.*

56. "Carta," in Munibe, *Breve resumen,* 23.

57. See Munibe, *Breve resumen,* 23–28. There is a facsimile edition of Sartorio's "Devoción para el día cinco" (1812) in Quesada Brandi, *San Felipe de Jesús,* 171–80.

58. Munibe, *Breve resumen,* 40, 46–75, 70.

59. Fernández de Lizardi, *El glorioso protomártir,* 1–2. Emphasis in original.

60. Ibid., 1.

61. Brading, *First America;* and Poole, *Our Lady of Guadalupe.*

62. Munibe, *Breve resumen,* 35–36.

63. Ibid., 37.

64. Poole, *Our Lady of Guadalupe,* 3.

Chapter 8. Conclusion

1. See Reynolds and Capps, *Biographical Process.* The authors discuss religious biography within the context of history of religions, anthropology of religion, and psychology of religion.

2. Geertz, *Islam Observed,* 25–35.

3. Graziano, "Una verdad ficticia," 309–10.

4. Brading, *First America,* 334–37; Lavallé, *Las promesas ambiguas,* 129–41.

5. Kubler, *Shape of Time,* 112, quoted in Brading, *First America,* 4.

6. Brading, *First America,* 5. For a more recent discussion of cultural dependence, see Klor de Alva, "Colonialism and Postcolonialism."

7. Rubial García, *La santidad controvertida,* 13, 52, 53.

8. Anderson, *Imagined Communities,* 62.

9. Rejection of one's indigenous blood and history was not, however, the only option. The early-seventeenth-century case of Garcilaso de la Vega, who claimed descent through his mother's lineage from the Inca nobility, is a familiar one. (Varner, *El Inca.* Also see Tenenbaum, *Encyclopedia of Latin American History,* 3:32–33.) A similar ideology empowered the resistance movement of Túpac Amaru II in 1780. And as I discussed in chapter 6, the Mexico City female convent of Corpus Christi required that each applicant for admission prove direct descent from an Indian cacique and the purity of her Indian blood (Gallagher, "Indian Nuns").

10. See related discussions in Brading, *First America,* 369–71; and Méndez G., "Incas Sí, Indios No."

11. Brading, *First America,* 4.

12. Rubial, *La santidad controvertida,* 299.

13. Ibid., 54.

14. The Constitution of 1857 incorporated most of the Liberal legislation of the previous months, including the Ley Juárez, Ley Lerdo, and Ley Iglesias. The Ley Juárez restricted within civil law the so-called fuero eclesiástico, which had granted special privileges and immunities to Roman Catholic personnel and institutions. The Ley Lerdo attacked the corporate ownership of property; the measure was particularly onerous to indigenous communities and ecclesiastical entities. Finally, the Ley Iglesias sought to regulate the fees traditionally charged by parish priests in exchange for performing the sacraments. Church officials vehemently opposed these measures, but found themselves outvoted by the *moderados* (moderate Liberals) and *puros* (radical Liberals) during the years prior to and following the Constitutional Convention of 1857. Besides such measures, the constitution contained articles aimed at ending the monopoly of the Roman Catholic Church on education. For a discussion of the Reform Laws of 1856–57 and 1859–60, see Hamnett, "Reform Laws," in Werner, *Encyclopedia of Mexico,* 2:1239–41.

Works Cited

Acosta, José de. *Historia natural y moral de las Indias*. 1st ed. Sevilla, 1590.

Agueda de S. Ignacio, María Anna. *Marabillas del divino amor, selladas con el sello de la verdad. Escritas por la V.M.R.M. María Anna Agueda de S. Ignacio . . .* [México?], n.d.

———. *Meditaciones de la sagrada Pasión: de gran provecho para las almas escritas por Mariana Agueda de San Ignacio*. México: Imprenta de la Biblioteca del Lic. D. Joseph Jauregui, 1775.

Aguilera, Francisco de. *Sermón en que se da noticia de la vida admirable, virtudes heroicas, y preciossa muerte de la Venerable Catarina de San Joan* [sic], *que floreció en perfección de vida, y murió con acclamación de santidad en la ciudad de la Puebla de los Angeles a cinco de enero de este año de 1688*. Puebla: Diego Fernández de León, 1688 [1689?].

Aguilera Castro y Sotomayor, José Miguel. *Elogio christiano del B. Sebastián de Aparicio, que en la solemne función con que su madre la Apostólica Provincia del Santo Evangelio de México la tributó el primer culto el convento de Las Llagas de N.S.P.S. Francisco de la Puebla de Los Angeles*. México: Don Felipe de Zúñiga y Ontiveros, 1791.

Ahlgren, Gillian T. W. *Teresa of Avila and the Politics of Sanctity*. Ithaca, N.Y.: Cornell University Press, 1996.

Alcaráz, Miguel. "A la devota, noble, y generosa Platería mexicana." In Baltasar de Medina, *Vida, martyrio, y beatificación del invicto proto-martyr del Japon San Felipe de Jesús,* edited by Miguel Alcaráz, O.F.M. 2d ed. Madrid: Herederos de la Viuda de Juan García Infanzon, 1751.

Altman, Ida. "A Family and Region in the Northern Fringe Lands: The Marqueses de Aguayo of Nuevo León and Coahuila." In *Provinces of Early Mexico: Variants of Spanish American Regional Evolution,* edited by Ida Altman and James Lockhart, 253–72. Los Angeles: UCLA Latin American Center Publications, 1976.

Anaya, José Lucas. *La milagrosa aparición de Nuestra Señora María de Guadalupe de México*. 1st ed. México, D.F.: Universidad Nacional Autónoma de México, 1995.

Anderson, Benedict. *Imagined Communities: Reflections on the Origin and Spread of Nationalism*. 2d ed. London and New York: Verso, 1991.

Ángeles Jiménez, Pedro. "Fray Sebastián de Aparicio: hagiografía e historia, vida e imagen." In *Los pinceles de la historia: el origen del Reino de la Nueva España, 1680–1750,* edited by Jaime Soler Frost, 247–58. México, D.F.: Instituto Nacional de Bellas Artes, 1999.

Arenal, Electa, and Stacey Schlau, eds. *Untold Sisters: Hispanic Nuns in Their Own Works*. Translated by Amanda Powell. Albuquerque: University of New Mexico Press, 1989.

Arrom, José Juan. "Carlos de Sigüenza y Góngora: relectura criolla de los *Infortunios de Alonso Ramírez.*" *Thesaurus* 42 (1987): 23–46.

———. *Certidumbre de América: estudios de letras, folklore y cultura*. 2d ed. Madrid: Editorial Gredos, 1971.

Arrom, Silvia. *The Women of Mexico City, 1790–1857*. Stanford: Stanford University Press, 1985.

Bakewell, Peter. "La maduración del gobierno del Perú en la década de 1560." *Historia Mexicana* 153, no. 1 (July–September 1989): 41–70.

Baron, Samuel H., and Carl Pletsch, eds. *Introspection in Biography: The Biographer's Quest for Self-Awareness*. Hillsdale, N.J.: Analytic Press, 1985.

Barrera Caraza, Estanislao. "Santa Rosa entre los otomíes de El Zapote de Bravo." *La Palabra y el Hombre* (Xalapa, Mexico) 74 (April–June 1990): 207–19.

Bartoli, Daniello, S.J. *Missione al Gran Mogor del P. Ridolfo Acquaviva della Compagnia de Gesù: sua vita, e morte, e d'altri quattro Compagni uccisi in odio della fede Salsete di Goa*. Bologna: Per l'Erede del Benacci, 1672.

Bataillon, Marcel. *Erasme et l'Espagne*. 3d ed. 3 vols. Geneva, 1991.

Bellido, José. *Vida de la V.M.R.M. María Anna Agueda de S. Ignacio, primera priora del religiosíssimo convento de dominicas recoletas de Santa Rosa de la Puebla de los Angeles*. México: Imprenta de la Biblioteca Mexicana, 1758.

Beristáin de Souza, José Mariano. *Biblioteca hispano-americana septentrional*. 5 vols. Mexico: Editorial Fuente Cultural, n.d.

Bibliotheca sanctorum. 13 vols. Roma: Instituto Giovanni XXIII nella Pontificia Università Lateranense, 1970.

Bilinkoff, Jodi. *The Avila of Saint Teresa: Religious Reform in a Sixteenth-Century City*. Ithaca and London: Cornell University Press, 1989.

————. "Confessors, Penitents, and the Construction of Identities." In *Culture and Identity in Early Modern Europe (1500–1800): Essays in Honor of Natalie Zemon Davis*, edited by Barbara B. Diefendorf and Carla Hesse, 83–100. Ann Arbor: University of Michigan Press, 1993.

————. "Francisco Losa and Gregorio López: Spiritual Friendship and Identity Formation on the New Spain Frontier." Paper presented at the conference Saints in the Colonial Americas: Hagiography and the Cult of Saints in the Americas, 1500–1800, University of Toronto, May 2000.

Bonaventure, St. *Bonaventure: Selected Works*. Translated and with an introduction by Ewert Cousins. Classics in Western Spirituality Series. New York: Paulist Press, 1978.

Boureau, Alain. "Franciscan Piety and Voracity: Uses and Stratagems in the Hagiographic Pamphlet." In *The Culture of Print: Power and the Uses of Print in Early Modern Europe*, edited by Roger Chartier, 15–58. Princeton, N.J.: Princeton University Press, 1989.

Boxer, Charles R. *The Christian Century in Japan, 1549–1650*. Berkeley and Los Angeles: University of California Press, 1951.

Boyajian, James C. *Portuguese Trade in Asia under the Habsburgs, 1580–1640*. Baltimore: Johns Hopkins University Press, 1993.

Brading, David. *The First America: The Spanish Monarchy, Creole Patriots, and the Liberal State 1492–1867*. Cambridge: Cambridge University Press, 1991.

————. *Miners and Merchants in Bourbon Mexico, 1763–1810*. Cambridge: Cambridge University Press, 1971.

Bradley, Peter T. *The Lure of Peru: Maritime Intrusion into the South Sea, 1598–1701*. New York: St. Martin's Press, 1989.

————. "Maritime Defense of the Viceroyalty of Peru (1600–1700)." *The Americas* 38, no. 2 (1979): 155–75.

Brennan, Brian. "Athanasius' *Vita Antonii:* A Sociological Interpretation." *Vigiliae Christianae* 39 (1985): 205–27.

Brown, Cynthia. *Poets, Patrons, and Printers: Crisis of Authority in Late Medieval France.* Ithaca, N.Y.: Cornell University Press, 1995.

Brown, Peter. *The Cult of the Saints: Its Rise and Function in Latin Christianity.* Chicago: University of Chicago Press, 1981.

Bruno, Cayetano, S.D.B. "Rosa de Santa María. Muerte y glorificación de la santa limeña, con arreglo a los procesos de su beatificación y canonización." *Investigación y Ensayos* (Buenos Aires) 33 (July–December 1982): 183–214.

Burke, Peter. "How to Be a Counter-Reformation Saint." In *Religion and Society in Early Modern Europe,* edited by Kaspar von Greyerz, 45–55. London: George Allen and Unwin, 1984.

Burkholder, Mark A., and D. S. Chandler. *From Impotence to Authority: The Spanish Crown and the American Audiencias, 1687–1808.* Columbia: University of Missouri Press, 1977.

Burns, Kathryn. *Colonial Habits: Convents and the Spiritual Economy of Cuzco, Peru.* Durham, N.C.: Duke University Press, 1999.

Bynum, Caroline Walker. *Holy Feast, Holy Fast: The Religious Significance of Food to Medieval Women.* Los Angeles: University of California Press, 1987.

Caciola, Nancy. "Through a Glass, Darkly: Recent Work on Sanctity and Society." *Comparative Studies in Society and History* 58, no. 2 (April 1996): 301–9.

Cahill, David. "After the Fall: Constructing Incan Identity in Late Colonial Cuzco." In *Constructing Collective Identities and Shaping Public Spheres: Latin American Paths,* edited by Luis Roniger and Mario Sznajder, 65–99. Brighton, U.K.: Sussex Academic Press, 1998.

Calancha, Antonio de la, O.S.A. *Crónica moralizada del orden de S. Agustín en el Perú.* Barcelona, 1639–53. Reprint, Lima: Universidad Nacional Mayor de San Marcos, 1974–82.

Cañeque, Alejandro. "Theater of Power: Writing and Representing the Auto de Fe in Colonial Mexico." *The Americas* 52:3 (January 1996): 321–43.

Carmona, Joseph [José]. *Panegírico sagrado del B. Sebastián de Aparicio, predicado el día 18 de octubre de 1790.* Puebla: Oficina del Real Seminario Palafoxiano, 1792.

Carrillo y Ancona, Crescencio. *Vigesimatercera carta pastoral sobre el tercer centenario del glorioso protomartir mexicano, San Felipe de Jesús.* Mérida, México: Gamboa Guzman, 1897.

Castañeda, Carlos E., and Jack Autrey Dabbs, eds. *Guide to the Latin American Manuscripts in the University of Texas Library.* Cambridge, Mass.: Harvard University Press, 1939.

Castillo, Pedro del. *La estrella del occidente, la Rosa de Lima. Que de lo regio del lugar se erigió princesa de las flores. Vida y milagros de la Santa Rosa de Santa María.* México: Bartolomé de Gama, 1670.

Castillo Grajeda [Graxeda], José del. *Compendio de la vida y virtudes de la venerable Catarina de San Juan.* 1692. Reprint, México, D.F.: Ediciones Xochitl, 1946.

Castillo y Guevara, María Josefa del. *Obras completas.* Edited by Dario Achury Valenzuela. Bogotá: Talleres Gráficos del Banco de la República, 1968.

Certeau, Michel de. *The Writing of History.* Translated by Tom Conley. New York: Columbia University Press, 1988.

Cervantes Salazar, Francisco. *Tres diálogos latinos que Francisco Cervantes Salazar escribió e imprimió en México en dicho año, y en los cuales hizo una descripción de la ciudad.* 1554. Reprint, edited and translated by D. Joaquin García Icazbalceta, México, 1875.

Chartier, Roger, ed. *The Culture of Print: Power and the Uses of Print in Early Modern Europe.* Princeton, N.J.: Princeton University Press, 1989.

————. "Texts, Printing, Readings." In *The New Cultural History*, edited by Lynn Hunt, 154–75. Berkeley: University of California Press, 1989.

Chevalier, François. "La signification sociale de la fondation de Puebla de Los Angeles." *Revista de Historia de Americas* 23 (June 1947): 105–30.

Chocano Mena, Magdalena. "Colonial Printing and Metropolitan Books: Printed Texts and the Shaping of Scholarly Culture in New Spain, 1539–1700." *Colonial Latin American Historical Review* 6, no. 1 (Winter 1997): 69–90.

————. "Colonial Scholars in the Cultural Establishment of Seventeenth-Century New Spain." Ph.D. diss., State University of New York at Stony Brook. Ann Arbor: University Microfilms, 1995.

Christian, William. *Local Religion in Sixteenth-Century Spain*. Princeton, N.J.: Princeton University Press, 1981.

Cline, Sarah L. *Colonial Culhuacan, 1580–1600*. Albuquerque: University of New Mexico Press, 1986.

Coakley, John Wayland. "Friars as Confidants of Holy Women in Medieval Dominican Hagiography." In *Images of Sainthood in Medieval Europe*, edited by Renate Blumenfeld-Kosinski and Timea Szell, 222–46. Ithaca: Cornell University Press, 1991.

————. "Gender and the Authority of Friars: The Significance of Holy Women for Thirteenth-Century Franciscans and Dominicans." *Church History* 60 (1991): 445–60.

————. "The Representation of Sanctity in Late Medieval Hagiography: Evidence from Lives of Saints of the Dominican Order." Ph.D. diss., Harvard University, 1980.

Compte, Francisco María, O.F.M. *Varones ilustres de la orden seráfica en el Ecuador, desde la fundación de Quito hasta nuestros días*. 2d ed. Quito: Imprenta del Clero, 1885.

Córdoba Salinas [Córdoba y Salinas], Fr. Diego de, O.F.M. *Crónica de la religiosísima provincia de los doce Apóstoles del Perú, de la orden de N.P.S. Francisco*. Lima, 1651. Reprinted as *Crónica franciscana de las provincias del Perú*. Edited by Lino Canedo. Washington, D.C.: Academy of American Franciscan History, 1957.

————. *Teatro de la Santa Iglesia Metropolitana de los Reyes*. Lima: Biblioteca de Historia Peruana, 1958.

Correia Afonso, João, S.J. *Jesuit Letters and Indian History, 1542–1773*. 2d ed. New York: Oxford University Press, 1969.

Cuadriello, Jaime. "La personificación de la Nueva España y la tradición de la iconografía de 'los reinos.'" In *Del libro de emblemas a la ciudad simbólica: actas del III Simposio Internacional de Emblemática Hispánica*, edited by Víctor Mínguez, vol. 2, pp. 123–50. Castelló de la Plana, Spain: Universitat Jaume I, 2000.

Cuevas, Mariano, S.J., *Historia de la iglesia en México*. 3d ed. 5 vols. El Paso, Tex.: Editorial Revista Católica, 1928.

Cummins, Victoria H. "Blessed Connections: Sociological Aspects of Sainthood in Colonial Mexico and Peru." *Colonial Latin American Historical Review* 3, no. 1 (Winter 1994): 3–18.

Curcio-Nagy, Linda A. "Introduction: Spectacle in Mexico." *The Americas* 52, no. 3 (January 1996): 275–81.

————. "Native Icon to City Protectress to Royal Patroness: Ritual, Political Symbolism, and the Virgin of Remedies." *The Americas* 52, no. 3 (January 1996): 367–91.

Curiel, Gustavo. "San Felipe de Jesús: figura y culto (1629–1862)." In *Historia, leyendas y mitos de México: su expresión en el arte*, 73–93. XI Coloquio Internacional de la Historia del Arte. México, D.F.: Universidad Autónoma Nacional de México, 1988.

Cussen, Celia L. "Fray Martín de Porres and the Religious Imagination of Creole Lima." Ph.D. diss., University of Pennsylvania, 1996.

Davis, Natalie Z. *Fiction in the Archives: Pardon Tales and Their Tellers in Sixteenth-Century France*. Stanford: Stanford University Press, 1987.

Daza, Fr. Antonio. *Quarta parte de la chrónica general de nuestro padre San Francisco y su apóstolica orden*. Valladolid: Juan Godines y Diego de Cordova, 1611.

DeStefano, Michael. "Miracles and Monasticism in Mid-Colonial Puebla, 1600–1750: Charismatic Religion in a Conservative Society." Ph.D. diss., University of Florida, 1977.

Donahue, Darcy. "Writing Lives: Nuns and Confessors as Autobiographers in Early Modern Spain." *Journal of Hispanic Philology* 13 (1989): 231–39.

Durand Flórez, Luis, ed. *Colección documental del bicentenario de la revolución emancipadora de Túpac Amaru*. 2 vols. Lima: Talleres Gráficos, 1980.

Duviols, Pierre. *La destrucción de las religiones andinas: conquista y colonia*. Translated by Albor Maruenda. México, D.F.: Universidad Nacional Autónoma de México, 1977.

Elizondo, Virgil. *Mary: Prophetess and Model of Freedom for Responsibility*. San Antonio, Tex.: Mexican American Cultural Center, 1974.

———. *La Morenita: Evangelizer of the Americas*. San Antonio, Tex.: Mexican American Cultural Center, 1980.

Elliott, Dyan. *Spiritual Marriage: Sexual Abstinence in Medieval Wedlock*. Princeton, N.J.: Princeton University Press, 1993.

Elvira, Fr. León, O.P. *Compendio histórico de la vida de Santa Rosa de Lima*. Valladolid: Imprenta de Aparicio, 1828.

Espinosa Pólit, Aurelio S.J. *Santa Mariana de Jesús, hija de la Compañía de Jesús: estudio histórico-ascético de su espiritualidad*. Quito: La Prensa Católica, 1956.

Estrada de Gerlero, Elena Isabel. "Los protomártires del Japón en la hagiografía novohispana." In *Los pinceles de la historia de la patria criolla a la nación mexicana, 1750–1860*, edited by Jaime Soler Frost. México, D.F.: Consejo Nacional para la Cultura y las Artes, 2000.

Farmer, David Hugh. *The Oxford Dictionary of Saints*. 3d ed. New York: Oxford University Press, 1992.

Fernández de Echeverría y Veytia, Mariano. *Historia de la fundación de la ciudad de la Puebla de los Angeles en la Nueva España: su descripción y presente estado*. Edited by Efraín Castro Morales. 2 vols. Puebla: Ediciones Altiplano, 1962.

Fernández de Lizardi, José Joaquin. *El glorioso protomartir San Felipe de Jesús. P.D.J.F. de L. Octavas*. México, 1811.

———. *Memorial de la madre de San Felipe de Jesús. Presentado en cabildo el viernes 26 de enero del año de 1629*. México: J. M. Benavente y Socios, 1821.

Ferrer de Valdecebro, Andrés, O.P. *Historia de la vida de la Ba. Me. Rosa de Santa María de la orden de predicadores*. Madrid: M. Rey Vda. de D. Díaz de la Carrera, 1669.

Florencia, Francisco de, S.J. *Descripción histórica y moral del yermo de San Miguel de las Cuevas en el Reino de la Nueva España . . . Con un breve compendio de la admirable vida del venerable anacoreta fray Bartolomé de Jesús María y algunas noticias del santo fray Juan de San Joseph, su compañero*. Cádiz: Imprenta de la Compañía de Jesús, Cristoval de Requena, 1689.

Flores Araoz, José, Ramón Mujica Pinilla, Luis Eduardo Wuffarden, and Pedro Guibovich Pérez. *Santa Rosa de Lima y su tiempo*. Lima: Banco de Crédito del Perú, 1995.

Florescano, Enrique. *La bandera mexicana: breve historia de su formación y simbolismo*. Colección Popular 551. México, D.F.: Fondo de Cultura Económica, 1998.

Franco, Jean. *Plotting Women: Gender and Representation in Mexico.* New York: Columbia University Press, 1989.

Frois, Fr. Luis. *De rebus iaponicis historia relatio.* 3 vols. Moguntiae [Mainz]: I. Albini, 1599.

Gallagher, Ann Miriam. "The Indian Nuns of Mexico City's Monasterio of Corpus Christi, 1724–1821." In *Latin American Women: Historical Perspectives,* edited by Asunción Lavrin, 150–72. Westport, Conn.: Greenwood Press, 1978.

Gálvez, Antonio. *Sermón que en la bendición solemne de la bandera del primer batallón cívico de la capital del estado de Zacatecas en 5 de febrero, día consagrado a los cultos del inclito protomartir mexicano San Felipe de Jesús.* Guadalajara: Oficina de la Viuda de J. Romero, 1824.

García Ayluardo, Clara, and Manuel Ramos Medina, eds. *Manifestaciones religiosas en el mundo colonial americano.* 2 vols. México, D.F.: Condumex, 1993–94.

García-Rivera, Alex. *St. Martin de Porres: The "Little Stories" and the Semiotics of Culture.* Maryknoll, N.Y.: Orbis Books, 1995.

García Sáiz, María Concepción. *Las castas mexicanas: un género pictórico americano.* [Milan]: Olivetti, 1989.

Garcilaso de la Vega, El Inca. *Royal Commentaries of the Incas and General History of Peru.* 2 vols. Translated with an introduction by Harold V. Livermore. Austin: University of Texas Press, 1966.

Geertz, Clifford. *Islam Observed: Religious Development in Morocco and Indonesia.* New Haven: Yale University Press, 1968.

Genette, Gérard. *Seuils.* Paris: Seuil, 1982.

Getino, Luis, O.P. *Santa Rosa de Lima, patrona de América: su retrato corporal y su talla intelectual según los nuevos documentos.* Madrid: M. Aguilar, 1943.

Glave Testino, Luis Miguel. "Santa Rosa de Lima y sus espinas: la emergencia de mentalidades urbanas de crisis y la sociedad andina (1600–1630)." In *Manifestaciones religiosas en el mundo colonial americano,* edited by Clara García Ayluardo and Manuel Ramos Medina. Vol. 1: *Espiritualidad barroca colonial: santos y demonios en America,* 53–70. México, D.F.: Condumex, 1993.

———. "El virreinato peruano y la llamada 'crisis general' del siglo XVII." Lima: Universidad de Lima, Departamento Académico de Ciencias Humanas, 1986.

Godínez, Miguel [Michael Wadding]. *Práctica de la theología mystica.* Sevilla: Juan Vejarano, 1582.

Gómez, Joseph. *Vida de la venerable madre Antonia de San Jacinto, monja profesa de velo negro, y hija, de el real y religiosíssimo convento de Santa Clara de Jesús de la ciudad de Santiago de Querétaro.* México: Herederos de la Viuda de Bernardo Calderón, 1689.

Gonzalbo Aizpuru, Pilar. "Las devociones marianas en la vieja provincia de la Compañía de Jesús." In *Manifestaciones religiosas en el mundo colonial americano,* edited by Clara García Ayluardo and Manuel Ramos Medina. Vol. 2: *Mujeres, instituciones y culto a María,* 105–15. México, D.F.: Condumex, 1994.

———. *Historia de la educación en la época colonial: la educación de los criollos y la vida urbana.* México, D.F.: El Colegio de México, 1990.

———. *El humanismo y la educación en la Nueva España.* México, D.F.: Secretaría de Educación Pública, 1985.

———. *Las mujeres en la Nueva España: educación y vida cotidiana.* México, D.F.: Colegio de México, 1987.

Granados y Gálvez, José Joaquin. *Tardes americanas: gobierno gentil y católico: breve y particular*

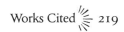

noticia de toda la historia indiana: sucesos, casos notables, y cosas ignoradas, desde la entrada de la gran nación tolteca a esta tierra. 1768, 1778. Reprint, México, D.F.: M. A. Porrúa, 1987.

Graziano, Frank. "Una verdad ficticia: Santa Rosa de Lima y la hagiografía." In *Historia, memoria y ficción,* edited by Moises Lemlij and Luis Millones, 302–11. Lima: Seminario Interdisciplinario de Estudios Andinos, 1996.

Greer, Allan. "Iroquois Virgin: The Story of Catherine Tekakwitha in New France and New Spain." Paper presented at the conference Saints in the Colonial Americas: Hagiography and the Cult of Saints in the Americas, 1500–1800, University of Toronto, May 2000.

Hackett, Charles Wilson. *Pichardo's Treatise on the Limits of Louisiana and Texas.* 2 vols. Austin: University of Texas Press, 1931.

Hampe Martínez, Teodoro. "El proceso de canonización de Santa Rosa: nuevas luces sobre la identidad criolla en el Perú colonial." *Hispania Sacra* 48 (1996): 719–37.

———. *Santidad e identidad criolla: estudio del proceso de canonización de Santa Rosa.* Cusco: Centro de Estudios Regionales Andinos, Bartolomé de las Casas, 1998.

———. "Los testigos de Santa Rosa. Una aproximación social a la identidad criolla en el Perú colonial." *Revista del Archivo General de la Nación* (Lima) 13 (1996): 151–71.

Hansen, Leonardo. *Vida admirable de Santa Rosa de Lima, patrona del nuevo mundo, escrita en latín por el P. Leonardo Hansen [1664], traducido al castellano por el P. Fray Jacinto Parra, religiosos ambos de la orden de predicadores, y reformada por el Zuavo Pontificio Sevilla, Caballero de Pío.* Translated by Fr. Jacinto Parra. Lima: Centro Católico, 1895.

Herrera, Pablo, and Alcides Enriquez. *Apunte cronológico de las obras y trabajos del cabildo o municipalidad de Quito desde 1534 hasta 1714.* Quito: Imprenta Municipal, 1916–25.

Hunt, Lynn. *The Family Romance of the French Revolution.* Berkeley: University of California Press, 1992.

———, ed. *The New Cultural History.* Berkeley: University of California Press, 1989.

Ibsen, Kristine. *Women's Spiritual Autobiography in Colonial Spanish America.* Gainesville: University Press of Florida, 1999.

Imirizaldu, Jesús. *Monjas y beatas embaucadoras.* Madrid: Editora Nacional, 1977.

Isturizaga, Fr. Juan de. *Sermón en la publicación de la beatificación de la Beata Rosa de Santa María, Patrona del Perú. Predicóle en la Santa Iglesia Metropolitana de Lima.* Madrid: Domingo García Morrás, 1670.

Iwasaki Cauti, Fernando. "Fray Martín de Porras: santo, ensalmador y sacamuelas." *Colonial Latin American Review* 3 (1994): 158–84.

———. "Mujeres al borde de la perfección: Rosa de Santa María y las alumbradas de Lima." *Hispanic American Historical Review* 73, no. 4 (1993): 581–613.

———. "Santos y alumbrados: Santa Rosa y el imaginario limeño del siglo XVII." In *Actas del III Congreso Internacional sobre los Dominicos y el Nuevo Mundo, Granada, 10–14 de septiembre de 1990,* 531–76. Madrid: Editorial Deimos, 1991.

———. "Vidas de santos y santas vidas: hagiografías reales e imaginarias en Lima colonial." *Anuario de Estudios Americanos* 51, no. 1 (1994): 47–64.

Jackson, Robert H. "Race/Caste and the Creation and Meaning of Identity in Colonial Spanish America." *Revista de Indias* 55, no. 203 (1995): 149–73.

Jaramillo, María Mercedes, Angela Inés Robledo, and Flor María Rodríguez-Arenas, eds. *¿Y las mujeres? Ensayos sobre literatura colombiana.* Antioquia: Editorial Universidad de Antioquia, 1991.

Jesús María, Félix de. *Vida, virtudes y dones sobrenaturales de la venerable sierva de Jesús, sor María*

de Jesús, religiosa profesa en el v. monasterio de la Inmaculada Concepción de la Puebla de los Ange- les en las Indias Occidentales. Roma: Joseph y Phelipe Rossi, 1756.

Jiménez, Francisco, O.F.M. "Vida de Fr. Martín de Valencia." Edited by Fr. Atanasio López. Archivo Ibero-Americano 26 (1926): 48–83.

Jouanen, José. Historia de la Compañía de Jesús en la antigua provincia de Quito, 1570–1774. Quito: Tipografía de la Prensa Católica, 1941–43.

———. El modelo de las jóvenes cristianas: vida de la Beata Mariana de Jesús, llamada vulgarmente la Azucena de Quito. Quito: Tipografía de la Prensa Católica, 1920.

Kagan, Richard. Lucrecia's Dreams: Politics and Prophecy in Sixteenth-Century Spain. Berkeley: Uni- versity of California Press, 1990.

Kay, Sarah, and Miri Rubin, eds. Framing Medieval Bodies. Manchester: Manchester Universi- ty Press, 1994.

Kemp, Eric W. Canonization and Authority in the Western Church. London: Oxford University Press, 1948.

Keyes, Charles F. "Charisma: From Social Life to Sacred Biography." In Charisma and Sacred Biography. Special edition of Journal of the American Academy of Religious Studies 48, nos. 3–4 (1982): 1–22.

Keyes, Francis Parkinson. The Rose and the Lily. New York: Hawthorn Books, 1961.

Kieckhefer, Richard. "Imitators of Christ: Sainthood in the Christian Tradition." In Sainthood, edited by Richard Kieckhefer and George S. Bond, 1–42. Berkeley and Los Angeles: Uni- versity of California Press, 1988.

———. Unquiet Souls: Fourteenth-Century Saints and Their Religious Milieu. Chicago: University of Chicago Press, 1984.

Kleinberg, Aviad. Prophets in Their Own Country: Living Saints and the Making of Sainthood in the Later Middle Ages. Chicago: University of Chicago Press, 1992.

Klor de Alva, J. Jorge. "Colonialism and Postcolonialism as (Latin) American Mirages." Colo- nial Latin American Review 1 (1992): 3–23.

Kubler, George. The Shape of Time: Remarks on the History of Things. New Haven: Yale Uni- versity Press, 1970.

Lafaye, Jacques. Quetzalcoatl and Guadalupe: The Formation of the Mexican National Conscious- ness, 1531–1813. Translated by Benjamin Keen. Chicago: University of Chicago Press, 1976.

Larrea, Carlos Manuel. Las biografías de Santa Mariana de Jesús. Quito: Corporación de Estu- dios y Publicaciones, 1970.

Lavallé, Bernard. Las promesas ambiguas: ensayos sobre el criollismo colonial en los Andes. Lima: Pon- tificia Universidad Católica del Perú, 1993.

Lavrin, Asunción. "Female Religious." In Cities and Society in Colonial Latin America, edited by Louisa Schell Hoberman and Susan Migden Socolow, 165–95. Albuquerque: University of New Mexico Press, 1986.

———. "Indian Brides of Christ: Creating New Spaces for Indigenous Women in New Spain." Mexican Studies/Estudios Mexicanos 15 (Summer 1999): 225–60.

———. "La normatividad de la vida cotidiana: base de la espiritualidad." In Memoria del Coloquio Internacional Sor Juana Inés de la Cruz y el Pensamiento Novohispano, 203–19. Toluca: Instituto Mexiquense de Cultura, 1995.

———. Sexuality and Marriage in Colonial Latin America. Lincoln: University of Nebraska Press, 1989.

———. "Unlike Sor Juana? The Model Nun in the Religious Literature of Colonial Mex-

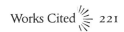

ico." In *Feminist Perspectives on Sor Juana Inés de la Cruz,* edited by Stephanie Merrim, 94–123. Detroit: Wayne State University Press, 1991.

———. "La vida femenina como experiencia religiosa: biografía y hagiografía en Hispanoamérica colonial." *Colonial Latin American Review* 2, nos. 1–2 (1993): 27–51.

———. "Women and Convents: Their Economic and Social Role in Colonial Mexico." In *Liberating Women's History: Theoretical and Critical Essays,* edited by Berenice A. Carroll, 250–77. Urbana: University of Illinois Press, 1976.

Lemus, Diego de. *Vida, virtudes, trabajos, fabores y milagros de la Ven. M. Sor María de Jesús, angelopolitana religiosa del convento de la Limpia Concepción de la ciudad de los Ángeles en la Nueva España y natural de ella.* Lyons: Anisson y Posuel, 1683.

León, Fr. Luis de. *La perfecta casada.* Madrid, 1582. Reprint, 1917.

León, Nicolás. *Catarina de San Juan y la china poblana.* México, D.F.: Vargas Rea, 1946.

Letona, Fr. Bartolomé. "Relación auténtica sumaria de la vida, virtudes y maravillas del V.P. Fr. Sebastián de Aparicio, lego franciscano de la provincia de México que hace su procurador Fray Bartolomé de Letona. Año de 1662, descubierta y publicada por Fr. José Alvarez, O.F.M." *Anales de la Provincia del Santo Evangelio de México* vol. 4, no. 3. México, D.F.: Biblioteca Nacional, 1947.

Leyba, Diego de, O.F.M. *Virtudes y milagros en la vida y muerte del V.P. Fr. Sebastián de Aparicio, religioso lego de la regular observancia de N.S.P.S. Francisco, e hijo de la provincia de Santo Evangelio de México, en la Nueva España, que floreció . . .* Sevilla: Lucas Martin, 1687.

Lezamis, José de. *Dedicatoria y breve relación de la vida y muerte del Illmo. Y Rmo. Señor Dr. D. Francisco de Aguiar y Seixas, arzobispo de México, mi señor.* México: Imprenta de María Benavides, 1699.

Loayza, Pedro de, O.P. *Oraciones que se pronunciaron en el diez y diez y seis de julio del presente año: la una en la iglesia catedral de Lima . . . la otra en el santuario de nuestra patrona Santa Rosa en el ocasión de colocarse en él una de las banderas del ejército derrotado.* Lima: Imprenta de los Huérfanos, 1811.

Loayza, Pedro de, O.P. *Vida de Santa Rosa de Lima.* 1619. Reprint, Lima: Iberia, S.A., 1965.

Lockhart, James. *The Nahuas after the Conquest: A Social and Cultural History of the Indians of Central Mexico, Sixteenth through Eighteenth Centuries.* Stanford: Stanford University Press, 1992.

Lockhart, James, and Stuart B. Schwartz. *Early Latin America: A History of Colonial Spanish America and Brazil.* Cambridge: Cambridge University Press, 1983.

Lohmann Villena, Guillermo. "De Santa Rosa, su padre y su hermano." *El Comercio* (Lima), January 18, 1995.

López, Kimberle S. "Identity and Alterity in the Emergence of a Creole Discourse: Sigüenza y Góngora's *Infortunios de Alonso Ramírez.*" *Colonial Latin American Review* 5, no. 2 (December 1996): 253–76.

López Beltrán, Clara. "La buena vecindad: las mujeres de élite en la sociedad colonial del siglo XVII." *Colonial Latin American Review* 5, no. 2 (December 1996): 219–36.

Lorea, Fr. Antonio de. *Santa Rosa, religiosa de la tercera orden de S. Domingo, patrona universal del nuevo mundo, milagro de la naturaleza y portentosa efecto de la gracia . . .* Madrid: Viuda de Juan García Infanzon, 1726.

Loreto López, Rosalva. "Familial Religiosity and Images in the Home: Eighteenth-Century Puebla de los Angeles, Mexico." *Journal of Family History* 22, no. 1 (January 1997): 26–49.

———. "La fiesta de la Concepción y las identidades colectivas." In *Manifestaciones religiosas en el mundo colonial americano,* edited by Clara García Ayluardo and Manuel Ramos Medina. Vol. 2: *Mujeres, instituciones y culto a María*, 87–104. México, D.F.: Condumex, 1994.

Losa, Francisco. *La vida que hizo el siervo de Dios Gregorio López, en algunos lugares de esta Nueva España*... México: Juan Ruiz, 1613.

Lynch, John. *Bourbon Spain, 1700–1808*. Oxford: Basil Blackwell, 1989.

Macklin, June, and Luise Margolies. "Saints, Near-Saints and Society." *Journal of Latin American Lore* 14, no. 1 (Summer 1988): 5–16.

———. "Two Faces of Sainthood: The Pious and the Popular." *Journal of Latin American Lore* 14, no. 1 (Summer 1988): 67–92.

Martínez, Domingo. *Compendio histórico de la apostólica provincia de San Gregorio de Filipinas, de religiosos menores descalzos de N.P. San Francisco*. Madrid: Fernández, 1756.

Martínez de Adame, José. *Sermón de San Felipe de Jesús, predicado el dia 5 de febrero del ano de 1781*. México: Zúñiga y Ontiveros, 1781.

Mateos Herrera, Ignacio. *Tierno recuerdo, dulcíssima memoria de el glorioso campeón de Christo, el proto-martyr americano San Felipe de Jesús: novena devota que las señoras religiosas capuchinas ofrecen a su patria*. México: Imprenta de Joseph de Jauregui, 1774.

Mathes, W. Michael. "Humanism in Sixteenth- and Seventeenth-Century Libraries of New Spain." *Catholic Historical Review* 82, no. 3 (July 1996): 412–35.

Maza, Francisco de la. *Arquitectura de los coros de monjas*. México, D.F.: Imprenta Universitaria, 1956.

———. *Catarina de San Juan: princesa de la india y visionaria de Puebla*. 2d ed. México, D.F.: Consejo Nacional para la Cultura y las Artes, 1990.

Maza, Sarah. "Stories in History: Cultural Narratives in Recent Works in European History." *American Historical Review* 101, no. 5 (December 1996): 1493–1515.

McBrien, Richard E., ed. *The HarperCollins Encyclopedia of Catholicism*. New York: Harper-Collins, 1995.

McCaa, Robert. "Calidad, Class, and Marriage in Colonial Mexico: The Case of Parral, 1788–1790." *Hispanic American Historical Review* 64, no. 3 (1984): 477–501.

Medina, Fray Baltasar de. *Chrónica de la santa prouincia de San Diego de México, de religiosos descalços de N.S.P.S. Francisco en la Nueva España. Vidas de ilustres, y venerables varones*... México: J. de Ribera, 1682.

———. *Vida, martyrio, y beatificación del invicto proto-martyr del Japón San Felipe de Jesús, patrón de México, su patria, imperial corte de Nueva España en el nuevo mundo*. México: Juan de Ribera, 1683.

———. *Vida, martyrio, y beatificación del invicto proto-martyr del Japón San Felipe de Jesús*. Edited by Miguel Alcaráz, O.F.M. 2d ed. Madrid: Herederos de la Viuda de Juan García Infanzon, 1751.

———. *Vida, martyrio, y beatificación*. Abbreviated facsimile of 1683 edition in *San Felipe de Jesús, 1572–97*, edited by Manuel Quesada Brandi. México, D.F.: Manuel Porrúa, 1962.

Meléndez, Juan. *Tesoros verdaderos de las indias*. 4 vols. Roma: Imprenta de Angel Tinassio, 1681.

Melville, Elinor G. K. *A Plague of Sheep: Environmental Consequences of the Conquest of Mexico*. New York: Cambridge University Press, 1994.

Méndez G., Cecilia. "Incas Sí, Indios No: Notes on Peruvian Creole Nationalism and Its Contemporary Crisis." *Journal of Latin American Studies* 28 (1996): 197–225.

Merrim, Stephanie, ed. *Feminist Perspectives on Sor Juana Inés de la Cruz*. Detroit: Wayne State University Press, 1991.

Mier Noriega y Guerra, José Servando Teresa de. *The Memoirs of Fray Servando Teresa de Mier*.

Translated by Helen Lane. Edited and with an introduction by Susan Rotker. New York: Oxford University Press, 1998.

Millares Carlo, Agustín. *Cuatro estudios biobibliográficos mexicanos*. México, D.F.: Fondo de Cultura Económica, 1986.

Millones, Luis. *Una partecita del cielo: la vida de Santa Rosa de Lima narrada por don Gonzalo de la Maza a quien ella llamaba padre*. Lima: Editorial Horizonte, 1993.

Mills, Kenneth. *An Evil Lost to View?: An Investigation of Post-Evangelisation Andean Religion in Mid-Colonial Peru*. Liverpool, U.K.: University of Liverpool, Institute of Latin American Studies, 1994.

———. *Idolatry and Its Enemies: Colonial Andean Religion and Extirpation, 1640–1750*. Princeton, N.J.: Princeton University Press, 1997.

Moncayo de Monge, Germania. *Mariana de Jesús, Señora de Indias*. Quito: La Prensa Católica, 1950.

Montes de Oca, José María. *Vida de San Felipe de Jesús: protomártir de Japón y patrón de su patria México*. México: Calle del Bautisterio de S. Catalina, 1801. Facsimile in *San Felipe de Jesús, 1572–97*, edited by Manuel Quesada Brandi. México, D.F.: Manuel Porrúa, 1962.

Morales, Francisco, O.F.M. *Ethnic and Social Background of the Franciscan Friars in Seventeenth-Century Mexico*. Washington, D.C.: Academy of American Franciscan History, 1973.

Morán de Butrón, Jacinto, S.J. *La Azucena de Quito que brotó en el florido campo de la iglesia en las Indias . . .* México: Herederos de la Viuda de Miguel de Rivera, 1732.

———. *Vida de la B. Mariana de Jesús de Paredes y Flores, conocida vulgarmente bajo el nombre de la Azucena de Quito*. Madrid: Imprenta de la Viuda de Palacios e Hijos, 1854.

———. *Vida de Santa Mariana de Jesús*. Edited by Aurelio Espinosa Pólit, S.J. Quito: Imprenta Municipal, 1955.

Motolinía [Toribio de Benavente]. *Memoriales, ó libro de las cosas de la Nueva España y de los naturales de ella*. Edited by Edmundo O'Gorman. México, D.F.: Universidad Nacional Autónoma de México, 1971.

Mugaburu, Josephe, and Francisco Mugaburu. *Chronicle of Colonial Lima: The Diary of Josephe and Francisco Mugaburu, 1640–97*. Translated and edited by Robert Ryal Miller. Norman: Oklahoma University Press, 1975.

Munibe, José María. *Breve resumen de la vida y martyrio del Beato Felipe de Jesús*. México: Oficina Madrileña de la Calle Sto. Domingo y Esquina de Tacuba, 1802. Facsimile in *San Felipe de Jesús, 1572–97*, edited by Manuel Quesada Brandi. México, D.F.: Manuel Porrúa, 1962.

Muriel, Josefina. *Conventos de monjas en la Nueva España*. 2d ed. México, D.F.: Editorial Jus, 1995.

———. *Las indias caciques de Corpus Christi*. México, D.F.: Universidad Autónoma Nacional de México, 1963.

Myers, Kathleen A. "The Mystic Triad in Colonial Mystic Nuns' Discourse: Divine Author, Visionary Scribe, and Clerical Mediator." *Colonial Latin American Historical Review* 5, no. 4 (Fall 1997): 479–524.

———, ed. "Testimony for Canonization or Proof of Blasphemy? The New Spanish Inquisition and the Hagiographic Biography of Catarina de San Juan." In *Women in the Inquisition: Spain and the New World*, edited by Mary E. Giles, 270–95. Baltimore: Johns Hopkins University Press, 1999.

———. *Word from New Spain: The Spiritual Autobiography of Madre María de San José (1656–1719)*. Hispanic Studies Textual Research and Criticism, vol. 4. Liverpool, U.K.: Liverpool University Press, 1993.

Myers, Kathleen A., and Amanda Powell. *A Wild Country out in the Garden: The Spiritual Journals of a Colonial Mexican Nun.* Bloomington: Indiana University Press, 1999.

Nava y Saavedra, Jerónima. *Autobiografía de una monja venerable.* Edited by Angela Inés Robledo. Cali, Colombia: Ediciones Universidad del Valle, 1994.

Neill, Stephen. *A History of Christianity in India: The Beginnings to 1707.* Cambridge: Cambridge University Press, 1984.

————. *A History of Christian Missions.* 2d ed. New York: Penguin Books, 1986.

New Catholic Encyclopedia. 18 vols. New York: McGraw-Hill, 1967–88.

Núñez de Miranda, Antonio, S.J. "Carta y discurso preocupativo, de algunas dificultades, que pueden resaltar luego a la primera vista de esta historia." In Alonso Ramos, *Primera parte de los prodigios de la omnipotencia y milagros de la gracia en la vida de la V. sierva de Dios Catarina de San Juan, natural del Gran Mogor difunta en la imperial ciudad de los Angeles en la Nueva España, por el padre Alonso Ramos, profeso de la Compañía de Jesús.* Puebla: Imprenta Plantiniana de Diego Fernández de León, 1689.

Ocaranza, Fernando. *La beatificación del venerable Sebastián de Aparicio.* México, D.F.: n.p., 1934.

O'Gorman, Edmundo. *Destierro de sombras: luz en el origen de la imagen y culto de Nuestra Señora de Guadalupe del Tepeyac.* México, D.F.: Universidad Nacional Autónoma de México, 1986.

Oviedo y Herrera, Luis Antonio. *Vida de la esclarecida virgen Santa Rosa de Santa María, natural de Lima y patrona de el Peru, poema heroyco.* México: Imprenta Real del Superior Gobierno de los Herederos de la Viuda de Miguel de Rivera Calderón, 1729.

Padden, Robert C. "The Ordenanza del Patronazgo of 1574: An Interpretive Essay." In *The Church in Colonial Latin America,* edited by John F. Schwaller, 27–47. Wilmington, Del.: Scholarly Resource Books, 2000.

Páez, J. Roberto. "El biógrafo de la Azucena de Quito, Jacinto Morán de Butrón, S.J." *Boletín de la Academia Nacional de Historia* (Quito) 25, no. 66 (1945): 183–200.

Pagden, Anthony. "Identity Formation in Spanish America." In *Colonial Identity in the Atlantic World, 1500–1800,* edited by Anthony Pagden and Nicholas Canny. Princeton, N.J.: Princeton University Press, 1987.

Palou, Francisco, O.F.M. *Relación histórica de la vida y apostólicas tareas del venerable padre fray Junípero Serra.* 1787. Reprint edited and translated by Maynard J. Geiger, O.F.M.; Washington, D.C.: Academy of American Franciscan History, 1955.

Pardo, Francisco. *Vida y virtudes heroycas de la madre María de Jesús, religiosa profesa en el convento de la Limpia Concepción de la Virgen María, Nuestra Señora en la ciudad de los Ángeles.* México: Viuda de Bernardo Calderón, 1676. Reprint, México, D.F.: Condumex Archive.

Pauw, Corneille de. *Recherches philosophiques sur les Américains.* Berlin, 1768; London, 1791.

Paz, Octavio. *Sor Juana; or, The Traps of Faith.* Translated by Margaret Sayers Peden. Cambridge, Mass.: Belknap Press, 1988.

Pérez Pimentel, Rodolfo. *Diccionario biográfico del Ecuador.* 16 vols. Guayaquil, Ecuador: Universidad de Guayaquil, 1987–97.

Perry, Mary Elizabeth. "Beatas and the Inquisition in Early Modern Seville." In *Inquisition and Society in Early Modern Europe,* edited and translated by Stephen Haliczer, 147–68. London and Sydney: Croom Helmm, 1987.

————. "Magdalens and Jezebels in Counter-Reformation Spain." In *Culture and Control in Counter-Reformation Spain,* edited by Anne J. Cruz and Mary Elizabeth Perry, 124–44. Minneapolis: University of Minnesota Press, 1992.

Phelan, John Leddy. *Kingdom of Quito in the Seventeenth Century: Bureaucratic Politics in the Spanish Empire.* Madison: University of Wisconsin Press, 1967.

Pichardo, José Antonio. *Vida y martirio del protomártir mexicano San Felipe de Jesús de las Casas, religioso del hábito y orden de San Francisco de Manila.* Edited by Carlos E. Castañeda. [ca. 1800]. Guadalajara, México: Loreto y Dieguez, 1934.

Polvorosa López, Tomás. "La canonización de Santa Rosa de Lima a través del *Bullarium Ordinis FF. Praedicatorum.*" In *Actas del I Congreso Internacional sobre los Dominicos y el Nuevo Mundo,* 603–639. Madrid: Editorial DEIMOS, 1987.

Ponce de León, José Eugenio. *La abeja de Michoacán, la venerable señora doña Josepha Antonia de N. Señora de la Salud.* México: Imprenta Doña M. de Rivera, 1752.

———. *La azuzena entre espinas representada en la vida, y virtudes de la V. madre Luysa de Santa Catharina, definidora en su convento de religiosas dominicas de Santa Catharina de Sena de la ciudad de Valladolid provincia de Michoacán.* México: Imprenta del Colegio Real y Más Antiguo de San Ildefonso, 1756.

Poole, Stafford. *Our Lady of Guadalupe: The Origins and Sources of a Mexican National Symbol, 1531–1797.* Tucson: University of Arizona Press, 1995.

———. *Pedro Moya de Contreras: Catholic Reform and Royal Power in New Spain, 1571–1591.* Berkeley and Los Angeles: University of California Press, 1987.

Powell, Philip Wayne. *Soldiers, Indians and Silver: North America's First Frontier War.* Tempe: Center for Latin American Studies, Arizona State University, 1975.

Quesada Brandi, Manuel, ed. *San Felipe de Jesús, 1572–97.* México, D.F.: Manuel Porrúa, 1962.

Quintela, Agustín. *La sencillez hermanada con la sabiduría. Oración panegírica que el día 27 de febrero de 1791, en que la M.I. y Real Congregación del Apóstol Santiago de Señores Gallegos celebró la beatificación del B. Sebastian de Aparicio. . .* México: Felipe de Zúñiga y Ontiveros, 1791.

Ragon, Pierre. "Libros de devoción y culto a los santos en el México colonial (siglos XVII a XVIII)." In *Actas del XI Congreso Internacional de AHILA (Liverpool, 17–22 de septiembre de 1996),* edited by John R. Fisher, vol. 4, pp. 210–25. Liverpool: Instituto de Estudios Latinoamericanos, 1997.

———. "Sebastián de Aparicio: Un santo mediterráneo en el altiplano mexicano." In *Estudios de Historia Novohispana* 23 (2000): 17–45.

Ramos, Alonso, S.J. *Primera parte de los prodigios de la omnipotencia y milagros de la gracia en la vida de la V. sierva de Dios Catarina de San Juan, natural del Gran Mogor difunta en la imperial ciudad de los Angeles en la Nueva España, por el padre Alonso Ramos, profeso de la Compañía de Jesús.* Puebla: Imprenta Plantiniana de Diego Fernández de León, 1689.

———. *Segunda parte de los prodigios de la omnipotencia y milagros de la gracia en la vida de la V. sierva de Dios Catarina de San Juan, natural del Gran Mogor difunta en la imperial ciudad de los Angeles en la Nueva España, por el padre Alonso Ramos, profeso de la Compañía de Jesús.* México: Imprenta de Diego Fernández de León, 1690.

Ramos Medina, Manuel. *Imagen de santidad en un mundo profano.* México, D.F.: Universidad Iberoamericana, 1990.

———. "Isabel de la Encarnación, monja posesa del siglo XVII." In *Manifestaciones religiosas en el mundo colonial americano,* vol. 1: *Espiritualidad barroca colonial: santos y demonios en América,* edited by Clara García Ayluardo and Manuel Ramos Medina, 41–52. México D.F.: Condumex, 1993.

———. *Místicas y descalzas: Fundaciones femeninas carmelitas en la Nueva España.* Chimalistac, México, D.F.: Centro de Estudios de Historia de México Condumex, 1997.

Raymond of Capua. *The Life of St. Catherine of Siena.* Translated by George Lamb. London: Harvill Press, 1960.

Remon, Alonso, O.M. *Historia general de la orden de Nuestra Señora de la Merced, Redención de Cautivos.* Madrid: L. Sánchez, 1618–33.

Reynolds, Frank E., and Donald Capps. *The Biographical Process: Studies in the History and Psychology of Religion.* The Hague and Paris: Mouton, 1976.

Ribadeneyra, Marcello de. *Historia de las islas del archipelago, y reynos de la gran China, Tartaria, Cuchinchina, Malaca, Sian, Camboxa y Iappon.* Barcelona: Gabriel Graells y Giraldo Dotil, 1601.

Ricard, Robert. *The Spiritual Conquest of Mexico: An Essay on the Apostolate and the Evangelizing Methods of the Mendicant Orders in New Spain, 1523–1572.* Translated by Lesley Byrd Simpson. Berkeley and Los Angeles: University of California Press, 1966.

Río, Alfonso Mariano del. *Separación y singularidad entre los veinte y seis prothomártires del Japón de San Felipe de Jesús, indiano, patricio, y patrón de México.* México: Francisco de Rivera Calderón, 1715.

Rivera, Diego de. *Breve relación de la plausible prompa, y cordial recocijo, con que se celebró la dedicación de el templo del inclyto martyr San Felipe de Jesús, titular de las religiosas Capuchinas, en la muy noble, y leal ciudad de México.* México, 1673.

Riviere, Edouard. *San Felipe de Jesús, patrón de México. Novela histórica y religiosa dedicada a las señoritas devotas de este santo, proto-martir del Japón.* México: Delanoe Hermanos, 1853.

Robles, Antonio de. *Resguardo contra el olvido, en el breve compendio de la vida admirable, y virtudes heroycas del illmo. Sr. Dr. D. Alonso de Cuevas Dávalos.* México: Herederos de la Viuda de Don Joseph Bernardo de Hogal, 1757.

Rodriguez, Jeanette. *Our Lady of Guadalupe: Faith and Empowerment among Mexican-American Women.* Austin: University of Texas Press, 1994.

Rodríguez, José Manuel. *El país afortunado. Oración panegyrica que en la anual solemnidad con que celebra la nobilíssima ciudad de México la maravillosa aparición de Nuestra Señora de Guadalupe.* México: Felipe Zúñiga y Ontiveros, 1768.

———. *Vida prodigiosa del siervo de Dios fray Sebastián de Aparicio, religioso lego de la regular observancia de N.S.P.S. Francisco, e hijo de la Provincia del Santo Evangelio de México.* México: Phelipe de Zúñiga y Ontiveros, 1769.

Rodríguez Cruz, Agueda María. "Juan de Lorenzana, universitario salmantino y catedrático de la universidad de San Marcos de Lima." In *Actas del II Congreso Internacional Sobre los Dominicos y el Nuevo Mundo,* edited by José Barrado, O.P. Salamanca: Editorial San Esteban, 1990.

Rodríguez Valencia, Vicente. *Santo Toribio de Mogrovejo, organizador y apóstol de Sur-América.* Madrid: Consejo Superior de Investigaciones Científicas, Instituto Santo Toribio de Mogrovejo, 1956–57.

Rojas, Alonso de, S.J. *Sermón que predicó el muy Rdo. P. Alonso de Rojas, catedrático que fue de teología y hoy prefecto de los estudios de la Compañía de Jesús en Quito. A las honras de Mariana de Jesús, virgen ilustre en virtudes y santidad. Sacado a luz por el doctor Tomás Martín de la Peña, capellán mayor del convento real de la Limpia Concepción de la Virgen Santísima de Quito.* Lima: Pedro de Cabrera, 1646. Reprinted in José Jouanen, *El modelo de las jóvenes cristianas. Vida de la Beata Mariana de Jesús, llamada vulgarmente la Azucena de Quito,* 310–23. Quito: Tipografía de la Prensa Católica, 1920.

Romero de Valle, Emilia. *El indio santo del Perú: rasgos biográficos del Venerable Siervo de Dios Nicolás de Dios Ayllón.* [Lima]: Comité Ejecutivo Nacional, 1958.

Romero y Quevedo, Francisco. "Sentir." In Baltasar de Medina, *Vida, martyrio, y beatificación del invicto proto-martyr del Japón San Felipe de Jesús, patrón de México, su patria, imperial corte de Nueva España en el nuevo mundo*. México: Juan de Ribera, 1683.

Roniger, Luis, and Mario Sznajder, eds. *Constructing Collective Identities and Shaping Public Spheres: Latin American Paths*. Brighton, U.K.: Sussex Academic Press, 1998.

Rubial García, Antonio. *La hermana pobreza: el franciscanismo de la edad media a la evangelización novohispana*. México, D.F.: Facultad de Filosofía y Letras, UNAM, 1996.

———. "Mariofanías extravagantes: las visiones de Catarina de San Juan." In *Revista de la Universidad Autónoma de México* (August 1992): 15–17.

———. *La santidad controvertida: hagiografía y conciencia criolla alrededor de los venerables no canonizados de Nueva España*. México, D.F.: Fondo de Cultura Económica, 1999.

———. "Los santos milagreros y malogrados de la Nueva España." In *Manifestaciones religiosas en el mundo colonial americano*, edited by Clara García Ayluardo and Manuel Ramos Medina, vol. 1, pp. 71–105. México, D.F.: Condumex, 1993.

Salinas y Córdoba, Fr. Buenaventura de, O.F.M. *Memorial de las historias del nuevo mundo Piru: méritos, y excelencias de la ciudad de los reyes, Lima, cabeca de sus ricos estendidos reynos, y el estado presente en que se hallan*. 1630. Reprint, Lima: Universidad Nacional Mayor de San Marcos, 1957.

Salmerón, Pedro. *Vida de la venerable madre Isabel de la Encarnación, carmelita descalça, natural de la ciudad de los Angeles*. México: Francisco Rodríguez Lupercio, 1675.

Sampson Vera Tudela, Elisa. *Colonial Angels: Narratives of Gender and Spirituality in Mexico, 1580–1750*. Austin: University of Texas Press, 2000.

San Antonio, Juan Francisco de. *Chrónicas de la apostólica provincia de S. Gregorio de Religiosos Descalzos de N.S.P.S. Francisco en las Islas Philipinas, China, Japón, etc.* Manila: Impreso por J. del Sotillo, 1738–44.

Sánchez Ortega, María Helena. "Woman as Source of 'Evil' in Counter-Reformation Spain." In *Culture and Control in Counter-Reformation Spain*, edited by Anne J. Cruz and Mary Elizabeth Perry, 196–215. Minneapolis: University of Minnesota Press, 1992.

Sánchez Parejo, Bartolomé. *Vida y milagros del glorioso confesor de Cristo, el padre fray Sebastián de Aparicio, fraile lego de la orden de San Francisco de la regular observancia, por Bartolomé Sánchez Parejo*. Introduction and notes by Fr. Fidel de Jesús Chauvet. Mexico: Editorial Fray Junípero Serra, 1965.

Sarabia Viejo, María Justina. "La Concepción y Corpus Christi: raza y vida conventual femenina en México, siglo XVIII." In *Manifestaciones religiosas en el mundo colonial americano*, edited by Clara García Ayluardo and Manuel Ramos Medina, vol. 2, pp. 15–27. México, D.F.: Condumex, 1993–94.

Sartorio, José. "Devoción para el día cinco." México: Imprenta de la Doña María Fernández de Jauregui, 1812. Facsimile in *San Felipe de Jesús, 1572–97*, edited by Manuel Quesada Brandi. México, D.F.: Manuel Porrúa, 1962.

Schroeder, H. J., O.P., ed. and trans. *Canons and Decrees of the Council of Trent*. St. Louis and London: B. Herder, 1941.

Schwaller, John Frederick. *The Church and Clergy in Sixteenth-Century Mexico*. Albuquerque: University of New Mexico Press, 1987.

———. "The Ordenanza del Patronazgo in New Spain, 1574–1600." In *The Church in Colonial Latin America*, edited by John F. Schwaller, 49–69. Wilmington, Del.: Scholarly Resources Books, 2000.

Seed, Patricia. "Social Dimensions of Race: Mexico City, 1753." *Hispanic American Historical Review* 64, no. 4 (1982): 569–606.

———. *To Love, Honor, and Obey in Colonial Mexico: Conflicts over Marriage Choice, 1574–1821.* Stanford: Stanford University Press, 1988.

Shiels, W. Eugene. *King and Church: The Rise and Fall of the Patronato Real.* Chicago: Loyola University Press, 1961.

Sicardo, José. *Christiandad del Japón.* Madrid: F. Sanz, 1698.

———. *Interrogatoria de la vida y virtudes del venerable hermano fray Bartolomé de Jesús María, natural de Xalapa.* México: Imprenta de Juan de Ribera, 1683. Biblioteca Nacional de México, Colección Lafragua, no. 1389.

Simons, Walter. "Reading a Saint's Body: Rapture and Bodily Movement in the *Vitae* of Thirteenth-Century Beguines." In *Framing Medieval Bodies,* edited by Sarah Kay and Miri Rubin, 10–23. Manchester: Manchester University Press, 1994.

Smith, Carol A. "Race-Class-Gender Ideology in Guatemala: Modern and Anti-Modern Forms." *Comparative Studies in Society and History* 37, no. 4 (October 1995): 723–49.

Soons, Alan. "Alonso Ramírez in an Enchanted and a Disenchanted World." *Bulletin of Hispanic Studies* 53 (1976): 201–5.

Spalding, Karen. *Huarochirí: An Andean Society under Inca and Spanish Rule.* Stanford: Stanford University Press, 1984.

Stern, Steve J. *Peru's Indian Peoples and the Challenge of Spanish Conquest: Huamanga to 1640.* Madison: University of Wisconsin Press, 1982.

Stone, Lawrence. *The Past and the Present.* Boston and London: Routledge and Kegan Paul, 1981.

Suárez, Ursula. *Relación autobiográfica.* Edited by Mario Ferreccio Podestá. Concepción, Chile: Academia Chilena de la Historia, 1984.

Szeminski, Jan. "Why Kill the Spaniard? New Perspectives on Andean Insurrectionary Ideology in the Eighteenth Century." In *Resistance, Rebellion, and Consciousness in the Andean Peasant World: Eighteenth to Twentieth Centuries,* edited by Steve Stern, 166–92. Madison: University of Wisconsin Press, 1987.

Taylor, William B. *Magistrates of the Sacred: Priests and Parishioners in Eighteenth-Century Mexico.* Stanford: Stanford University Press, 1996.

———. "The Virgin of Guadalupe in New Spain: An Inquiry into the Social History of Marian Devotion." *American Ethnologist* 14, no. 1 (Feb. 1987): 9–33.

Tenenbaum, Barbara A., ed. *Encyclopedia of Latin American History and Culture.* 5 vols. New York: Charles Scribner's Sons, 1996.

Teresa of Ávila, St. *The Life of Teresa de Jesús: The Autobiography of Teresa of Ávila.* Translated and edited by E. Allison Peers. New York: Doubleday, 1991.

Torquemada, Juan de, O.F.M. *Monarquía indiana.* 3 vols. 1615. Facsimile of 1723 edition. México, D.F.: Editorial Porrúa, 1969.

———. *Vida y milagros del sancto confesor de Christo Fr. Sebastián de Aparicio.* México: Santiago Tlatelolco, 1602. Reprint, Valladolid, Spain, 1615.

Twinam, Ann. "Honor, Sexuality, and Illegitimacy in Colonial Spanish America." In *Sexuality and Marriage in Colonial Latin America,* edited by Asunción Lavrin, 118–55. Lincoln: University of Nebraska Press, 1989.

Urtassum, Juan de. *La gracia triunfante en la vida de Catharina Tegakovita, india iroquesa, y en las de otras, Assi de su nación, como de esta Nueva-España.* México: Joseph Bernardo de Hogal, 1724.

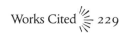

Reprint, edited by Michael W. Mathes; Madrid: Ediciones José Porrúa Turanzas, 1994.

Valdés, Joseph Francisco. *Novena consagrada al culto del gloriosísimo protomartyr del Japón, el señor San Felipe de Jesús, dirigida a implorar su protección y patrocinio.* México: Imprenta de Doña María Fernández de Jauregui, 1804.

———. *Sermón, que en la festividad del glorioso martyr mexicano San Felipe de Jesús, celebrada en la santa iglesia catedral de esta corte de México el día 5 de febrero de 1782.* México: Felipe de Zúñiga y Ontiveros, 1782.

Vallarta, Luz del Carmen. "Voces sin sonido: José Eugenio Ponce de León y su modelo de mujer religiosa." *Relaciones* (Zamora, México) 45 (1990): 33–61.

Van Duesen, Nancy E. "Instituciones religiosas y seglares para mujeres en el siglo XVII en Lima." In *Manifestaciones religiosas en el mundo colonial americano,* edited by Clara García Ayluardo and Manuel Ramos Medina, vol. 2, pp. 65–86. México, D.F.: Condumex, 1993–94.

Van Oss, Adriaan C. *Catholic Colonialism: A Parish History of Guatemala, 1524–1821.* Cambridge Latin American Studies Series no. 57. Cambridge: Cambridge University Press, 1986.

Vargas, José María. *Historia de la iglesia en el Ecuador durante el patronato español.* Quito: Editorial Santo Domingo, 1962.

Vargas Lugo, Elisa. "Proceso iconológico del culto a Santa Rosa de Lima." In *Actes du XLII Congres International des Américanistes,* 69–86. Paris: Société de Américanistes, Musée de l'Homme, 1976.

Vargas Ugarte, Rubén, S.J. *Vida de Santa Rosa de Lima.* 3d ed. Buenos Aires: Imprenta López, 1961.

———. *Vida del siervo de Dios Nicolás Ayllón, o por otro nombre, Nicolás de Dios, natural de Chiclayo.* Buenos Aires: Imprenta López, 1960.

Varner, John Grier. *El Inca: The Life and Times of Garcilaso de la Vega.* Austin: University of Texas Press, 1968.

Vauchez, André. *Les laïcs au Moyen âge: pratiques et expériences religieuses.* Paris: Cerf, 1987.

———. *La sainteté en occident aux dernieres siècles du Moyen âge, d'après les procès de canonisation et les documents hagiographiques.* Roma: École Française de Roma, 1981.

Viforcos Marinas, María Isabel. "Los recogimientos: de centros de integración social a cárceles privadas; Santa Marta de Quito." *Anuario de Estudios Americanos* 50, no. 2 (1993): 59–92.

Villanueva, A. P. *Vida del protomártir mexicano San Felipe de Jesús, natural y patrón de México, dispuesta por A. P. Villanueva, con motivo del quincuagésimo aniversario de su canonización por S.S. Pio IX, de feliz memoria.* México, D.F.: Antigua Imprenta de Murguia, 1912. Biblioteca Nacional, México, D.F.

Weber, Alison. "Saint Teresa, Demonologist." In *Culture and Control in Counter-Reformation Spain,* edited by Anne J. Cruz and Mary Elizabeth Perry, 171–95. Minneapolis: University of Minnesota Press, 1992.

———. *Teresa de Avila and the Rhetoric of Femininity.* Princeton: Princeton University Press, 1990.

Weckmann, Luis. *The Medieval Heritage of Mexico.* Translated by Frances M. López-Morillas. New York: Fordham University Press, 1992.

Weinstein, Donald, and Rudolph M. Bell, eds. *Saints and Society: The Two Worlds of Western Christendom, 1000–1700.* Chicago: University of Chicago Press, 1982.

Werner, Michael S. *Encyclopedia of Mexico: History, Society and Culture.* 2 vols. Chicago: Fitzroy Dearborn, 1997.

Williams, Michael A. "The *Life of Antony* and the Domestication of Charismatic Wisdom."

In *Charisma and Sacred Biography*, edited by Michael A. Williams, 23–45. Special edition of *Journal of the American Academy of Religious Studies* 48, nos. 3–4 (1982).

Woodward, Kenneth L. *Making Saints: How the Catholic Church Determines Who Becomes a Saint, Who Doesn't, and Why*. New York: Simon and Schuster, 1990.

Ximénez, Mateo. *Colección de estampas que representan los principales pasos, hechos y prodigios del beato Frai Sebastián de Aparizio*. Roma: Pedro Bombelli, 1789.

———. *Compendio della vita del Beato Sebastiano d'Apparizio, laico professo dell ordine de Minori osservanti del padre S. Francesco della provincia del Santo Evangelio nel Messico*. Roma: Stamperia Salomoni, 1789.

Zavaleta, Joaquina María de. *Copia de la carta, que la M.R.M. Joaquina María de Zavaleta, abbadesa del monasterio de San Phelipe de Jesús y pobres capuchinas de esta imperial ciudad de México, escribe a las M. RR. MM. preladas de los demás monasterios, dándoles noticia de las heroycas virtudes, y dichosa muerte de la M.F.M. Augustina Nicolasa María de los Dolores Muñoz y Sandoval, abbadesa, que fue, tercera vez del referido monasterio*. México: Imprenta Nueva de la Biblioteca Mexicana, 1755.

Zevallos Ortega, Oscar Noé. *Rosa de Lima: compromiso y contemplación*. Lima: CEP, 1988.

Index

Mota y Escobar (bishop), 127
Motolinía, Toribio de, 49, 183n. 11
Moya de Contreras, Pedro (bishop), 21
Mugaburu, Josephe, 80–81, 88–89
Mughal dynasty, 17, 120–123
Mujica Pinilla, Ramón, 96
Munibe, José María (hagiographer), 162–169
Myers, Kathleen, 201n. 3, 205n. 61, 206n. 86
Mystical marriage to Christ: Rosa de Santa María's, 36–37, 78–79
Mystical transport, 124, 134–135

Nagasaki. See Japan
Name change: from Isabel to Rosa, 70–71, 108; from Mariana to Lily, 108–109; from Mirrha to Catarina, 122, 126
Narrative: narrative strategies as focal point, 12–13, 181n. 39; revival of, 5
Nettie Lee Benson Collection, 154–155
Niños de Tlaxcala, 183n. 11
Non cultu: impact on hagiographic texts, 32, 43–44, 187n. 12; papal decrees of, 29–30
Nopal cactus as New World product, 162. See also Iconography
Novena, defined, 182n. 3
Núñez de Miranda, Antonio, 135
Núñez de Roxas, Miguel, 92, 195n. 70
Nuns as hagiographic subjects, 21–22. See also Convents

Official saint/popular saint idea, 31–33
O'Gorman, Edmundo, 189n. 28
Oliva, María de (mother of Rosa), 70
Oliva, Mariana de (witness), 81
Oratorio de San Felipe de Neri, 149
Origins. See Criollo consciousness
Orozco y Jiménez, Francisco (patron), 155
Oviedo y Herrera, Luis Antonio, 67–97, 173, 200n. 45

Paganism. See Idolatry
Pagden, Anthony, 6, 9
Palafox y Mendoza, Juan de (bishop), 21, 141, 180n. 14, 183n. 10, 185n. 33, 203n. 41
Palma, Ricardo, 195n. 78
Palou, Francisco (hagiographer), 23
Paratext, defined, 30

Pardo, Francisco (hagiographer), 183n. 12, 187n. 13
Paredes, Jerónima de, 102, 110, 197n. 7
Paredes y Flores, Jerónimo Zenel, 102
Paredes y Flores, Mariana. See Mariana de Jesús
Paschal Baylon, St., 44
Patria chica, 99–118, 174; defined, 16
Patronage: hagiographic text as solicitation of, 26–28, 61–65, 168
Pauw, Corneille de, 151
Pedro Claver, St., 21, 190n. 58
Peninsular, defined, 6
Perpetual chastity: Aparicio's practice of, 52–54; Catalina's vow and practice of, 128–131, 139–141; Mariana's vow of, 102, 109; Rosa's vow of, 70–72
Petronila de la Concepción (India), 141
Phelan, John Leddy, 74
Philip II, 50, 94
Philippines, 16, 67, 126, 130–131, 145–148
Pichardo, José (hagiographer), 154–169
Pichincha (volcano), 111
Piracy: and Catarina's kidnapping, 125–126; Catarina's protection of Spanish ships from, 205n. 60; and Morán's lost manuscript, 116; as threat to Lima, 14, 83–84, 88–97. See also Portuguese; Protestant threat
Pius VI, 63
Pius IX, 176
Platería de México, 151, 155
Ponce de León, José Eugenio (hagiographer), 23
Poole, Stafford, 4
"Popular Saint." See Official saint/popular saint idea
Porras, Isabel de (holy woman), 93
Portuguese: Jesuits in India, 122–126; role in Manila trade and kidnapping, 125–126, 130
Presilla, Juan Joseph de la, 159, 209n. 41
Printing press: absence of, in Quito, 114–116; high cost of, and publication strategies, 28, 35, 114–117; Saint's Life and the hispanization of, 20–21
Proceso apostólico, 41–42, 82, 105–107, 191n. 4; defined, 30

About the Author

Ronald J. Morgan is assistant professor of history at Biola University in La Mirada, California. He holds a Ph.D. in Latin American history from the University of California at Santa Barbara (1998). Professor Morgan's primary research interests lie in the religious and cultural history of early modern Roman Catholicism, particularly in Spanish and Portuguese America. His previous publications include a chapter on Jesuit confessional practices among African converts in Katherine Lualdi and Anne Thayer, eds., *Penitence in the Age of Reformations.*